Regionalism in the Age of Globalism
Volume 1: Concepts of Regionalism

Regionalism in the Age of Globalism
Volume 1: Concepts of Regionalism

Edited by
Lothar Hönnighausen, Marc Frey,
James Peacock, and Niklaus Steiner

Center for the Study of Upper Midwestern Cultures
University of Wisconsin–Madison

Center for the Study of Upper Midwestern Cultures
901 University Bay Dr.
Madison, WI 53705

Printed in the United States of America

Regionalism in the Age of Globalism, Volume 1: Concepts of
Regionalism / edited by Lothar Hönnighausen, Marc Frey, James Peacock,
and Niklaus Steiner
ISBN 0-924119-12-8

To the memory of Jürgen Heideking

Acknowledgments

We gratefully acknowledge the German-American Academic Council and the Ministry of Education and Research (Federal Republic of Germany) for their generous support of this publication.

Contents

Contributors

Marc Frey received his Ph.D. and his *Habilitation* in modern history from the University of Cologne. He currently teaches at the University of Münster. His research focuses on the history of twentieth-century international relations, American foreign relations, and on the international history of Southeast Asia. Among his more recent publications are *History of the Vietnam War* (7th edn., 2004), *Decolonization and Transformation: The United States and the Dissolution of the European Empires in Southeast Asia* (2005), and an edited volume titled *The Transformation of Southeast Asia: International Perspectives on Decolonization* (2003).

Gerald Friesen teaches at the University of Manitoba and has been a visiting professor at McGill, Yale, and the Free University of Berlin. He has written and edited a number of works, including *Rural Life* (2004), *Citizens and Nation: An Essay on History, Communication and Canada* (2000), *The West* (1999), *River Road* (1996), and *The Canadian Prairies: A History* (1984). He edited the fifteen-volume series, *Manitoba Studies in Native History*.

Thaddeus C. Guldbrandsen is Research Assistant Professor of Anthropology and Director of the Center for the Study of Community at Strawbery Banke (NH) Museum. He earned his Ph.D. in anthropology from the University of North Carolina at Chapel Hill in 2001. He has published on urban planning and governance, social inequality, local politics, environmental activism, educational anthropology, and anthropological theory and methods. He is coauthor of the forthcoming book, *If This is Democracy ... Public Interests and Private Politics in a Neoliberal Age*. He is currently completing a book-length manuscript entitled, *Bull City Futures: Transformations of Political Action, Inequality, and Public Space*. In addition to his work with the Center for the Study of Community, he is collaborating with Nina Glick Schiller on a study of contemporary migration and people's transnational relationships in Manchester, New Hampshire, and Halle, Germany.

Kornelia Hahn is an assistant professor of sociology at the University of Lüneburg (Germany). Her research interests include theory of modern and postmodern societies, sociology of intimate relationships, and media communication. Among her more recent publications are two edited volumes: *Öffentlichkeit und Offenbarung: Eine interdisziplinäre Mediendiskussion* (2002) and *Körperrepräsentationen: Die Ordnung des Sozialen und der Körper* (2002).

Steven Hoelscher is a cultural geographer with research interests in the connections between identity, region, and cultural memory. His books include *Heritage on Stage* and *Textures of Place*, and he is also the author of articles in *American Quarterly, Annals of the Association of American Geographers, The Journal of Historical Geography, Ecumene*, and *The Geographical Review*. He lives in Austin, Texas, where he is Associate Professor of American Studies and Geography at the University of Texas.

Lothar Hönnighausen is Professor Emeritus of British and North American Literature at the University of Bonn. He is editor of the series *Transatlantic Perspectives*. Among his recent books are *Faulkner: Masks and Metaphors* (1997), *William Faulkner: German Responses* (ed. 1997), *Regional Images and Regional Realities* (ed. 2000), and *Space—Place—Environment* (coedited with Julia Apitzsch and Wibke Reger, 2004).

Robert Ostergren is Professor of Geography at the University of Wisconsin–Madison. He specializes in the cultural and historical geography of Europe and North America, and in particular on issues pertaining to region, place, and identity. He is best known for his articles and books on nineteenth-century European trans-Atlantic migration and settlement in North America.

James L. Peacock is Kenan Professor of Anthropology, Professor of Comparative Literature, and Director of the University Center for International Studies at the University of North Carolina at Chapel Hill. His fieldwork includes studies of proletarian culture in Surabaja, Indonesia (see *Rites of Modernization*, University of Chicago Press), of Muslim fundamentalism in Southeast Asia (see *Muslim Puritans*, University of California Press), and of Primitive Baptists in Appalachia (see *Pilgrims of Paradox*, Smithsonian). He is also the author of *The Anthropological Lens* (Cambridge University Press, revision in press).

Celeste Ray is Associate Professor of Anthropology at the University of the South. Her books include *Highland Heritage: Scottish Americans in the American South* (2001), *Southern Heritage on Display: Public Ritual and Ethnic Diversity within Southern Regionalism* (2003), *Signifying Serpents and Mardi Gras Runners: Representing Identity in Selected Souths* (2003).

Michaela Röll completed her doctoral dissertation on space and identity in novels of John Irving and Margaret Atwood at the University of Bonn in 2002 (http://hss.ulb.uni-bonn.de/diss_online/phil_fak/2002/roell_michaela/index.htm). She has published essays and reviewed articles on William Shakespeare and is currently a literary agent with the firm Eggers & Landwehr in Berlin.

Caroline Rosenthal is Assistant Professor of North American Literature at the University of Constance where she teaches Canadian and American literature from the seventeenth century to the present. She has published articles in the fields of contemporary Canadian literature, gender theory, and on literature and ideology. Her books include *Schwellentexte der Weltliteratur* (ed. 2002) and *Narrative Deconstructions of Gender* (2003).

Joseph Salmons is Professor of German at the University of Wisconsin–Madison. He edits *Diachronica: International Journal for Historical Linguistics* and co-directs the Center for the Study of Upper Midwestern Cultures. In addition to research on language change and phonology, he is currently co-authoring the *Cambridge History of the Germanic Languages.*

Klaus P. Schneider studied English, Russian, and education in Marburg, Edinburgh, and Moscow. He received his Ph.D. and his *Habilitation* from the University of Marburg. He taught at the Universities of Marburg, Hamburg, and Rostock, at University College Dublin and in Bonn, where since 1998 he holds a chair in Applied English Linguistics. His areas of specialization are pragmatics, discourse analysis, sociolinguistics, dialectology, psycholinguistics and translation studies. Current research interests include variational pragmatics, verbal (im)politeness, political rhetoric in the USA, and language use in dementia. Recent book publications: *Diminutives in English* (2003), *Variational Pragmatics: The Case of English in Ireland* (2005, coedited with Anne Barron).

Niklaus Steiner is Associate Director of the University Center for International Studies at the University of North Carolina at Chapel Hill. His research interests include refugees, nationalism, and national identity, and he has published a number of articles on these topics. His books include *Arguing About Asylum: The Complexity of Refugee Debates in Europe* (2000, St. Martin's) and the edited volume (with Mark Gibney and Gil Loescher) *The Problems of Protection: UNHCR, Refugees, and Human Rights* (2003, Routledge).

Andrea Witt has recently completed her Ph.D. thesis on "Models of Cross-Border Cooperation. A Comparison between the German-Polish and the U.S.-Mexican Border" at the Humboldt University Berlin. In 2000/2001 she was an American Political Science Association (APSA) Congressional Fellow with Senator Bob Graham from Florida. She also was a reporter and newspaper editor at the German-Polish border and currently works for the German Marshall Fund of the United States (GMF).

Introduction: Concepts of Regionalism

Lothar Hönnighausen

T his volume and the conferences on which it is based are part of an
ongoing inquiry concerning the place of region in the world. Why
region? Are not region and regionalism concerns of the past rather
than of the present or future? Has not globalism erased all boundaries, all
identities based on place? Region may have mattered to some provincials,
and regionalism may be of historical interest to some scholars, but do these
concerns not express more of the Zeitgeist of the nineteenth or early twentieth
centuries than of the twenty-first?

Why, then, has the European Union created the Committee of the Regions?
Why is the world rife with conflict based on particularistic, territorial identities;
secession of regions from nations; and genocide based on "cleansing" a region
of one or another group? And why are new nations created from regions?
In addition to new nations, why are other kinds of groupings — religious,
political, linguistic, cultural, or economic — emerging on regional bases? In
fact, globalism may pave the way for regionalism by breaking down national
boundaries, thus promoting subnational or crossnational identities, including
regional ones. Samuel Huntington may not be correct in all particulars, but
surely he has a point in arguing that peoples have moved, since the end of the
Cold War, from coalitions based on national identity to coalitions based on
shared cultural values, which are, among other things, regionally grounded,
both within and between nations.

Considerations such as these have stimulated an inquiry perceived of by
two programs, the North America Program at the Universität Bonn, Germany,
and the University Center for International Studies at the University of North
Carolina, Chapel Hill, U.S.A. Supported by a grant from the German-American
Academic Council and the Ministry of Education and Research of the Federal
Republic of Germany we were guided by the following plan: An international
team of scholars from relevant disciplines in both North America and Europe
was to address the question of region and its place in the world in two steps. The
first step, reflected in a conference held at Chapel Hill, explored questions and
concepts. The second step, guiding a conference held in Bonn, dug deeper into
these questions through empirical scholarship. The outcome of the research
project on *Regionalism in the Age of Globalism* is the two volumes *Concepts
of Regionalism* and *Forms of Regionalism*.

What, then, are the key questions and issues framed by the chapters in this first volume? Robert Ostergren's overview helpfully frames many of the points. Surveying geographers' approaches to region, he traces an evolution from classic and essentialist approaches to the current constructivist phase —from region "is" to region "is constructed." He classifies three perspectives on region: regions as instituted, as objectively denoted, or as naively perceived. These correspond, one might say, to the governmental, academic, and lived experiences of region.

Marc Frey and Gerald Friesen approach the topic historically. Frey emphasizes the constructivist character of region, both on the subnational and the subglobal level: By drawing on concepts from political scientists, Frey suggests categories with which region and degrees of "regionness" can be analyzed. These categories help to measure compression and the intensification of processes leading to the production of regions over time. Friesen's history of the meaning of region in Canada illustrates many of the issues broached above. Current conceptions of region in Canada involve physical environment and local histories in addition to the federal state and economic concerns. In earlier times, regions were clearly important, however by the twentieth century debates over the relevance and significance of region had made the concept ambiguous. Some scholars saw regions as dependent on physical and economic factors; others viewed them as purely imaginative constructs. The current vision reflects debates about the conceptualization of place, the relation of region to nation, and the understanding of time.

Andrea Witt's disciplinary focus is political science, which converges with Ostergren's "instituted" idea of region. She considers the implications of regional definitions for decision making at levels from subnational to multinational. She compares the European Union to cross-border cooperation of the United States and Mexico. Thaddeus Guldbrandsen and Celeste Ray usefully reflect current thinking about region in anthropology, which is not so sharply focused on region or place as such but more broadly on questions of how cultural identities generally are constructed and how their meanings are best construed. Guldbrandsen calls for a dynamic approach influenced by sociology and urban and regional planning. Ray uses her research on Scottish Americans in the American South to show how two regional identities merge in interesting ways. Pointing to the French Annales as a model for historical study of region, she inquires why regional identities persist even when circumstances and culture change.

Steven Hoelscher, like Ostergren, notes a transition from naturalistic, essentialist notions of region to an emphasis on regions as socially constructed. Hoelscher traces this shift across disciplines, including geography, anthropology, and history. He wants to avoid replacing "natural reductionism" with "social reductionism" and seeks balance and synergy between the two perspectives. He also reminds us that construction of regions happens within networks of power. The concept of "landscape" provides an example, as a place, an artifact, that provides an illusion of stability and permanence. The debate about the Confederate battle flag illustrates another aspect of construction of region as process and conflict.

Kornelia Hahn treats the interplay of regional and global aspects, referring to sociologist Roland Robertson's term "glocalization." She proposes a combination of micro- and macroanalysis to study "local interactions or symbolic tokens that refer to global conditions." Hahn draws us strongly into confronting our subject phenomenologically and ethnographically, accosting the human experience in its localized immediacy while at the same time recognizing relations to the wider forces of the world: in a word, finding relations between life world and system, to use the terms of Habermas.

Linguistic and literary studies show how regional identities are expressed quite sharply and subtly, in ways accessible through close reading of texts and documentation of language use. Joseph Salmons argues that changes in the structure of regions account for language shift. Linguistics, Salmons asserts, has overlooked the importance of region, and sociolinguists' and dialectologists' work cannot explain why people stop speaking a minority language and begin to speak only the majority language. Focusing on the shift from German to English by immigrant groups in Wisconsin, Salmons follows Warren, arguing that "horizontally structured communities will typically maintain a minority language, while verticalization will lead to shift to the majority language."

Michaela Röll notes that a search for "home" has become a major theme in postmodern narratives, as a counterpoint to mobility and displacement. She shows how regions have become "sites of various re-inscriptions of memory," referring to works by Jane Urquhart, Margaret Atwood, and Annie Proulx. She concludes by highlighting literary criticism's contribution to the study of regions, arguing that social sciences "quantify" regions, while literature "monitors quality."

The volume concludes with two companion pieces, in which Klaus P. Schneider and Lothar Hönnighausen present methodological overviews on "Regions and Regionalism in Linguistics: A Brief Survey of Concepts and

Methods" and "Defining Regionalism in North American Studies." Schneider traces the history of the linguistic study of regionalism from dialect geography, with its emphasis on linguistic atlases and the regional distribution of linguistic variants, to the era of urban dialectology in the 1960s when sociolinguists like William Labov shifted interest away from the distribution of linguistic features in geographical space and toward the covariation of linguistic and social markers such as social class, ethnicity, and gender. After this radical shift of paradigm in variationalism, Labov rediscovered regions in the 1990s, initiating a new atlas project combining elements of dialect geography and urban dialectology. In the latest development, perceptual dialectologists no longer investigate language but rather language users, examining stereotypical perceptions of and prejudices about dialects and dialect speakers. The reason for linguists' continued interest in regionalism is that, contrary to popular (and learned) belief that had assumed that regional speech differences were gradually vanishing due to the impact of job mobility and the mass media, regional dialects are not only surviving, but are actually diverging — owing, it is suggested, to the fact that regional speech constitutes an important part of regional identity.

While regions and regionalism are unproblematic, commonly used terms in disciplines such as geography, marketing, or planning and development, students of linguistics, as well as Americanists, have had their difficulties with them. This is in large part a consequence of the limited and limiting use of *regions* and *regionalism* in literary histories where the terms tend to be confined to specific periods and schools. Reopening the debate within the wider context of American studies as interdisciplinary and comparative cultural studies, Lothar Hönnighausen sees the tradition of a conscious, i.e. "constructed *regionalism*," emerging with the painters of the Hudson River School and with Washington Irving's stylized rendering of the Dutch ethnoregional heritage, enduring in the "local color school" of the nineteenth century and in the regionalism of the 1930s and 1940s, and reaching a surprising climax in a peculiar postmodern regionalism of our time. As distinctive features of this new regionalism of the 1990s, Hönnighausen cites the ironic rewriting of regional history, a new sense of the hybridity of the ethnoregional heritage, and a peculiar predilection for parody and pastiche.

Where, then, have we gotten in this opening exploration of region? Certainly the discussions refute any notion that region is dead, either as a phenomenon in the world or as a topic of analysis. On the contrary, region, like other vehicles of identity and existence, proves a dynamic and vibrant focus for history, for contemporary processes, and for interdisciplinary study, many facets of which are explored in this volume.

1

Concepts of Region: A Geographical Perspective

Robert Ostergren

Geographers have long concerned themselves with issues of region. Indeed, one might well contend that conceptions of region, place, and identity are the essence of geography as an academic discipline, and that geographers have been actively engaged in the study of region, per se, for longer than anyone else.[1] Geographers, of course, have no monopoly on the subject. They share their interest in the study of region with practitioners from a wide range of disciplines, as is amply demonstrated by the many interests represented in this volume. Geographic conceptions of region, nonetheless, are both useful to our general understanding of the subject and critical as a theoretical foundation to a cross-disciplinary project such as ours.

Accordingly, my purpose here is to provide a few geographical perspectives on the subject. I first offer some basic definitions and then outline the manner in which geographical thinking on regions and regionalism has evolved from its "classic phase" of the late nineteenth and early twentieth centuries to the "constructivist phase" to which most geographers would currently subscribe. I conclude by briefly calling attention to the rise of new regions and regional identities in a Europe that is today becoming increasingly fluid with respect to territorial organization and by suggesting that these transformations represent an interesting field for the study of the human creation and use of regions.

Definitions of Region

Because the idea of region is so central to our discussion, it seems appropriate to begin with an examination of what regions are. Most simply, a region may be defined as a bounded segment of earth space. At the same time regions are understood to be human constructions that may manifest themselves in both real and imaginary ways. They are also thought to exist at

---

1.   The use of region as a geographic conception and descriptive tool may be traced back to the ancients and in particular to the Greek geographer and historian Strabo, who perhaps went farthest in practicing and articulating an art of regional description.

all scales (although there is always some debate about whether there is a scale distinction between place and region) and to be fundamental to the way our world is subdivided spatially, even in an age when globalizing revolutions in communication and transportation technologies might appear to be rendering human organizations of space and attachments to place less relevant.

We can and should distinguish between different kinds of regions. It is clear that not everyone has the same thing in mind when they speak of regions. Geographers have traditionally recognized at least three ways to characterize regions: as *instituted*, as *objectively denoted*, and as *naively perceived*.[2]

Instituted regions are perhaps the type most familiar to everyone. We encounter them everywhere, in the past as well as the present. Authorities within some organization, such as national, state, or local governments; religious denominations; or business corporations, typically create them. They do so for the purpose of isolating people, activities, or things in space in order to administer or control them more easily and efficiently. As geographer Robert Sack has persuasively demonstrated, the institution of regions is a basic tendency of human territoriality, often motivated by the need to accomplish quite specific objectives.[3] Such regions may even be created expressly for the very manipulative purposes of dividing, prioritizing, or denying certain activities or uses of space. Whether their purposes are benign or manipulative, once instituted, these regions are recognized as existing entities and normally have boundaries that are clearly delimited, on paper if not always on the ground, and are usually agreed on by everyone. Indeed, elaborate efforts may be undertaken, as in the case of state formation, to construct a sense of respectful recognition, allegiance, or citizenship among those who fall within the boundaries of such spatial units. Systems of instituted regions also exist. They are often hierarchical; that is, they may nest within each other as, for example, federal, state, county, and local administrative units in the United States, or archdiocese, diocese, and parish in the Roman Catholic Church.

Objectively denoted regions are something very different. They are most commonly created by scholars or analysts, sometimes by planners or promoters, in order to reduce the complexity of the real world so that it can better be understood. The process of creating denoted regions is analogous

---

2. The elements of this scheme are typical of what one might find in many traditional regional geography texts. See also Robert C. Ostergren and John G. Rice, *The Europeans: A Geography of People, Culture and Environment* (New York: Guilford Press, 2004).

3. Robert D. Sack, *Human Territoriality: Its Theory and History* (Cambridge: Cambridge University Press, 1986). See also Robert D. Sack, *Homo Geographicus: A Framework for Action, Awareness, and Moral Concern* (Baltimore: Johns Hopkins University Press, 1997).

to the process of classification common to nearly all scholarly disciplines. Historians construct eras, periods of time during which events fit together in some meaningful way; students of literature group writers into genres based on similarities in their approach to the human condition; biologists classify the organisms of the plant and animal worlds on either the distribution of taxa or the basis of similarities in the form and function of their parts. All are creating classes within which there is a degree of similarity or cohesiveness among the things they are studying.

Objectively denoted regions are of two kinds: formal and functional. *Formal regions*, also known as uniform regions, are homogenous or uniform with respect to certain selected phenomena. Such a region may be defined, for example, by the dominance of Lutherans within its boundaries. The precise extent of such a region is determined by how great a dominance of Lutherans is required in order to be included. The region is thus the product of the mind of the scholar who conceives it. It is entirely an intellectual concept and has no existence independent of the person who creates it. *Functional regions*, sometimes called nodal, are also denoted on the basis of homogeneity, but in this case the emphasis is on the idea that all places within the region are tied to some central or nodal place by the movement of people, ideas and things. In other words all places within the region experience more spatial interaction with the same central place or node than they do with any other. The most common example is the trade area or hinterland of a town as determined by such things as shopping trips or newspaper circulation. Here again the creation of the region is entirely dependent on the analytical criteria developed to measure interaction by some person or group of persons.

Objectively denoted regions generally have no independent existence, although in the case of both formal and functional regions, a general public recognition or acceptance may eventually occur through a process of popularization. In this way we do have popular, but often imprecise understandings in America of objectively denoted regions such as the "Corn Belt," the "Bible Belt," or the "Sun Belt." In some cases functional regions may eventually become institutionalized as a matter of public or economic policy.

This leads us to the last of our regional types: *naively perceived regions*. In contrast to instituted regions and objectively denoted regions, which are the purposeful creations of authorities or spatial analysts of some kind, naively perceived regions are created informally. They come into existence through popular recognition and without official sanction. Place identity is critical here. Recognition of the identity of a region may come from people living either within the region or outside it. At the most intimate scale naively perceived regions are closely associated with the notion of community and arise as the result of a closely knit group of people identifying in their own minds a territory that belongs to them rather than to others, and that somehow reflects a collective sense of belonging or lived experience—in other words a "sense of place." Unlike the other regional types there is much more subjectivity involved in the identification of regions of this type. The perception of region may be only passively articulated, and the region's extent and boundaries may be only generally, rather than precisely, understood or known.

These three definitions of region are, of course, not mutually exclusive. They can appear or evolve in concert. Naively perceived or historically created regions may in fact become institutionalized over time, for example as nation states, or at least that might be the stated ideal. Conversely, institutionalized states and regions may dissolve through processes of regional transformation arising out of changes in institutional practices or from the demands of newly emerging social or cultural forces. Objectively denoted regions, as we have seen, have the potential to become perceived as real over time and take on an independent life of their own or may become institutionalized in the pursuit of developmental policies or marketing strategies.

There are many examples of how these categories may overlap. Europe, for instance, is a continental-scale region that may be simultaneously defined as instituted, objectively denoted, and naively perceived—instituted in the sense that today's Europe has become increasingly synonymous with the integrative powers and agenda of the European Union; denoted in the sense that it is conventionally, but still rather loosely defined and understood in terms of a set of common cultural, political, and economic traits that distinguish it from other parts of the world; and naively perceived in that its people may, at least at some level, have a developed awareness of a European identity. The American South is another example of a region that might arguably be defined in all three ways. The essential point remains: Regions differ in who creates them, why they are created, and how they function, and these differences may change over time.

Changing Geographic Perspectives on the Region

All academic disciplines are noted for their periodic shifts in approach and emphasis. The study of regions and regionalism in geography is no exception, having passed through several phases over the decades since the beginning of its modern development at the end of the nineteenth century.[4]

Early work took what might be described as an essentialist outlook. In the so-called classical period of regional geography, regions were seen as very real entities—things that could be objectively denoted and delimited rather precisely on a map. They were in essence objects that could be used to subdivide the world or that, conversely, could be combined together to form larger entities. To identify and study them geographers employed a chorological approach, which emphasized the use of descriptive narratives or spatial analyses that were often strongly set in the natural environment and predicated on the identification of formal or homogenous regions. In this the geographer was an objective observer, decentered from the phenomenon to be studied.

Thus an important preoccupation among French geographers, who did much of the pioneering work at this time,[5] was the study of the many small homogenous regions of France, with particular attention to how they might be understood, through the notions of *pays* and *genre de vie*, as an ecological equilibrium of natural conditions and human activity.[6] In fact, the physical basis for such regions—climate, soils, vegetation, and landforms—was often afforded such strong emphasis as to make it appear to be the deterministic factor in regional definition; a practice that did much to fuel a long standing and at times vitriolic debate in geography over how much emphasis should appropriately be given to natural and cultural factors in defining and describing regions. The classical regional geographers have often been vilified for the environmentally deterministic flavor of their work, but there is an element of unfairness in the charge, which overlooks the fact that they were also attentive to the power of social groups to mold the character or "personality" of the

---

4.   A number of useful historical sketches of the regional approach in geography exist. A recent and particularly useful example is Paul Claval, "The Development of Regional Studies," in *An Introduction to Regional Geography*, trans. Ian Thompson (Oxford: Blackwell, 1998): 9–27. See also section (IV) on Region, Place, and Locality in *Human Geography: An Essential Anthology*, ed. John Agnew, David N. Livingstone, and Alisdair Rogers (Oxford: Blackwell, 1996), 365–512; or the relevant sections of R. J. Johnston et al., eds., *The Dictionary of Human Geography*, 4th ed. (Oxford: Blackwell, 2000).

5.   The leading exponents of regional perspectives at this time were the French geographer, Paul Vidal de la Blache, and the German, Alfred Hettner.

6.   The classic English language work on early French geography and its focus on the regional community is Anne Buttimer, *Society and Milieu in the French Geographic Tradition* (Washington, DC: The Association of American Geographers, 1971).

regions they inhabited, and that a holistic understanding of region was their ultimate goal.[7]

Many of the classical regional geographers were especially interested in identifying what they would describe as the "personality" of individual regions within a larger national setting. Paul Vidal de la Blache, for example, took pains in his *Tableau de la géographie de la France* to portray the harmonious character of France in terms of the combination and integration of the distinctive regional parts into a national whole.[8] Scandinavian geographers and ethnologists had a similar fascination with the individual characters and collective role of small cultural regions, known as *bygder*.[9] In America Carl O. Sauer wrote about the assemblage of constituent parts that made up the "personality of Mexico."[10]

In all of these examples the role of a historically perceived identity or regional consciousness was an important leitmotif. Distinctive regional identities and ways of life were perceived at the time as sadly disappearing before the onrushing forces of modernity and ideological nationalism. The study of regions and regional cultures was thus, for some, a means of drawing attention to what was happening or, at the very least, of documenting distinctive regional identities, landscapes, and symbols before they were lost altogether. The identification of regional identities could also be used for nationalist geopolitical purposes, as in the case of Vidal de la Blache's *France de l'Est*, which was written during World War I to demonstrate that Alsace-Lorraine, ceded from France to Germany in 1871 after the Franco-Prussian War, was in fact a distinctive *pays* that exhibited far stronger natural and cultural ties to France than to Germany.[11]

---

7.   Nigel Thrift, "Taking Aim at the Heart of the Region," in *Human Geography: Society, Space and Social Science*, ed. Derek Gregory, Ron Martin and Graham Smith (Minneapolis: University of Minnesota Press, 1994), 203. See also Kevin Archer, "Regions as Social Organisms: The Lamarckian Characteristics of Vidal de la Blache's Regional Geography," *Annals of the Association of American Geographers* 83 (1993): 498–514.

8.   Paul Vidal de La Blache, *Tableau de la géographie de la France* (Paris: Hachette, 1903). See also the discussion in Paul Claval, "From Michelet to Braudel: Personality, Identity, and Organization of France," in *Geography and National Identity*, ed. David Hooson (Oxford: Blackwell, 1992), 39–57.

9.   See, for example, Gerd Enquist, "Bygd som geografisk term," *Svensk Geografisk Årsbok* 17 (1941): 7–21.

10.   Carl O. Sauer, "The Personality of Mexico," in *Land and Life: A Selection from the Writings of Carl Ortwin Sauer*, ed. John Leighly (Berkeley: University of California Press, 1969), 104–117.

11.   Derek Gregory, *Geographical Imaginations* (Cambridge: Blackwell, 1994), 42–45.

Classical regional geography went on to produce shelf after shelf of descriptive regional monographs to celebrate the distinctive character of individual regions and the differentiation of phenomena over space, and at least well into the 1950s this kind of regional geography was able to claim a special place as a centerpiece of geographical scholarship. In American geography its importance was justified and institutionalized in Richard Hartshorne's retrospective statement of the field, *The Nature of Geography*, which identified the study of regions as the principal means of achieving the overarching synthetic and integrative goals of a discipline devoted to understanding the differentiation of phenomena in space.[12] Partly as a consequence of the debate over environmental determinism, regional geography also invented modifications in approach designed to better balance and integrate the treatment of natural and social forces, as well as a range of specific techniques in regional description. Historical regional geography, for example, attempted to depict the development of regions by constructing snapshots of regional landscapes at selected intervals.

The middle decades of the last century meanwhile saw the emergence of a second approach to region, also essentialist but with very different emphases. By the 1930s regions began to be seen not so much as distinctive parts of a national whole to be studied in themselves, but as objectively denoted functional units essential to the operation and comprehension of a modern and highly integrated society and economy. The realism and naturalism that characterized the essentialist approach of the early part of the century were to be replaced by midcentury with an abiding faith in instrumentalism.[13]

For many geographers, who by the 1950s and 1960s were striving as the times demanded to become more meticulous and scientific, the study of regions largely became a spatially descriptive and analytical tool for meeting the needs of administrative and economic planning, locational analyses, or demonstrating the "laws" of spatial behavior. Regions were transformed

---

12. Richard Hartshorne, *The Nature of Geography: A Critical Survey of Current Thought in the Light of the Past* (Lancaster, PA: The Association of American Geographers, 1939). See also Derwent Whittlesey, "The Regional Concept and the Regional Method," in *American Geography: Inventory and Prospect*, ed. Preston E. James and Clarence F. Jones (Syracuse: Syracuse University Press, 1954), 19–69.

13. The sequence of terms—"realism, naturalism, instrumentalism, and constructivism (yet to come)"—is a useful way of characterizing changing perspectives on region in geography. These terms are used effectively in Peter Aronsson, "The Desire for Regions: The Production of Space in Sweden's History and Historiography," Institut für Europäische Regionalforschungen, Siegen, *Interregiones* 4 (1995): 49–99.

conceptually into receptacles for data collection, and were often functionally defined by geographers, and others, on the basis of scientific measurements of such phenomena as commuting distances, market areas, central place services, industrial production indices, or tax bases.[14] Regions also became an essential instrument, especially from the 1960s on, in national development policies. They were often instituted, most commonly in European national administrative structures, as the primary basis for evaluating and leveling out national differences in the distribution of jobs and incomes. The move toward spatial analyses in geography led to a break with traditional regional studies, which were viewed as idiographic and merely descriptive, and the gradual disappearance of the regional monograph.

Beginning in the 1970s and early 1980s, geography as a discipline began to diversify its perspectives and distance itself from the intense preoccupation with the positivist spatial analytical tradition that held sway over the discipline through much of the 1950s and 1960s. Accompanying this was a renewal of interest in issues of region and place. The renewal took different forms, and with the exception of a nostalgic plea to revitalize the lost art of descriptive regional writing,[15] these new initiatives bore only passing resemblance to the "classical" past. By the end of the 1970s it was clear that the essentialism of the past could no longer be taken for granted. Conceptions of region were becoming more varied and more sensitive to issues of human structure, agency, and perception. There was a growing interest in focusing on the subjectiveness of place and place experience and seeing regions as situated in tangled webs of social relations.

At issue was how to reconceptualize places and regions, and what to study within and between them. One strand arose out of efforts to develop a radical Marxist geography that attempted to explore the uneven development of capitalism through the study of region or "locality" as a setting for economic production or to examine how the formation and transformation of individual regions was conditioned by emergent social structures and historic layers of investment across regions, often associated with a changing spatial division of labor.[16] A second development stemmed from the rise of a humanistic

14. The most often cited prescriptive statement of this development is Étienne Juillard, "La région: essai de définition," *Annales de géographie* 71 (1962): 483–499.

15. John Fraser Hart, "The Highest Form of the Geographer's Art," *Annals of the Association of American Geographers* 72 (1982): 1–29.

16. For an example of a Marxist study of regional transformation see Derek Gregory, *Regional Transformation and Industrial Revolution: A Geography of the Yorkshire Woolen Industry*

geography emphasizing a subjective concept of place that blended a sense of living in the world with a "sense of place" that came with living in a specific place or region.[17] A third influence was the attempt to create a geographically contextual theory of human action, most often referred to as "time-geography," in which region or place mediates between human agency and social structure and thus becomes critical to the production of society.[18]

What seems to have emerged in the end is an approach to the study of regions and regionalism that is antiessentialist and constructivist. Geographers, like everyone else, have been much affected over the past decade or two by developments in social theory,[19] often self-consciously so. Most geographical studies of region and regionalism today are built around a consensus that regions are social constructs and are driven to examine the complexities and vagaries of both the social production and use of region.

The current conceptual view, which is at times referred to as the "new regional geography," seems to incorporate a number of assumptions.[20] Among them is the idea that there is a persistence of regional diversity in our world, and that despite the ever-present standardizing and deterritorializing forces of globalization, the world is not necessarily becoming more homogenous. Differences persist and are continuously being formed and transformed in place-specific contexts. A second assumption is that regions should be seen as structures, constituted by a dialectic of social, political, and economic interactions between individuals, groups, and institutions. Regions are viewed in this way as both outcomes and mediums of social interaction. A third

---

(Minneapolis: University of Minnesota Press, 1982); see also Doreen B. Massey, *Spatial Divisions of Labour: Social Structures and the Geography of Production* (London: Macmillan, 1984).

17. Yi-Fu Tuan, "Space and Place: Humanistic Perspective," *Progress in Geography* 6 (1974): 233–246.

18. The ideas and techniques of time-geography were developed at Lund University in Sweden by Torsten Hägerstrand and his associates. A useful statement of its application to the study of regions may be found in Allan Pred, "The Choreography of Existence: Comments on Hägerstrand's Time-Geography and Its Usefulness," *Economic Geography* 53 (1977): 207–221.

19. See the review of time-geography and its relationship to social structuration theory in Anthony Giddens, "Time, Space and Regionalization," in *Social Relations and Spatial Structures*, ed. Derek Gregory and John Urry (London: Macmillan, 1990), 265–295.

20. The assumptions listed here are drawn from the discussion in Anne Gilbert, "The New Regional Geography in English- and French-speaking Countries," *Progress in Human Geography* 12 (1988): 213–218.

assumption is that these structures are always in a state of evolution, their boundaries always malleable. Regional formation is therefore a process in which the region is constantly reimagined and reconstructed. The geographic study of region demands, accordingly, that the historical dynamics of this process receive careful attention; that geographers understand regions through a kind of geohistorical synthesis of texts and symbolic images, informed by an appreciation of relevant systems of social and political practice.

Nothing is more important in all of this than the question of place identity, and much effort is expended on issues of identity and representation, particularly on the relationship between social politics and power and geographical meanings of identity and representation. A very good example of this is the work of the Finnish geographer, Aansi Paasi, who is interested in the analysis of "signification," the interplay of political and cultural processes with the social and symbolic construction of regional communities using metaphors and images derived from such things as landscape, heritage, and cultural artifacts.[21] Also of importance in this respect has been the study of rhetoric and language.[22] The contribution of the new regional geography, according to Alexander Murphy, is that it offers us ". . . a view of regions as constantly changing and socially significant historical and geographic formations, whose inhabitants interpret and respond to events and processes in particular ways as a consequence of the unique social and physical contexts in which they are situated."[23]

At the same time it is important to point out that the current and decidedly sociological shift in the geographic study of region carries some potential pitfalls. There are some who worry that the emphasis on social construction and social production carries with it a danger of reductionism that leaves our understanding of regions ignorant of the role of other important aspects of place that may lie outside the realm of social interaction, such as relationships with the natural environment or realities that derive simply as a matter of spatial location. Equally worrisome is the tendency to collapse culture and moral

---

21. Aansi Paasi, "The Institutionalization of Regions: A Theoretical Framework for Understanding the Emergence of Regions and the Constitution of Regional Identity," *Fennia* 164 (1986): 105–146.

22. See, for example, Alan Pred, *Lost Words and Lost Worlds: Modernity and Language of Everyday Life in Late Nineteenth-century Stockholm* (Cambridge: Cambridge University Press, 1990).

23. Alexander B. Murphy, "Regions as Social Constructs: The Gap between Theory and Practice," *Progress in Human Geography* 15 (1991): 25.

agency into the social.[24] And finally, as we increasingly engage in complex geohistorical synthetic treatments or analyses of regions and places, largely through the construction of narratives, we have come to recognize very real potential problems in representation and bias that must be responsibly engaged.[25] The latter is an issue that, interestingly enough, bears some resemblance to the age-old idiographic versus nomothetic debate that once estranged classical regional geographers from their more scientifically minded critics.

Europe's New Regionalism

Just as it was in the time of classical regional geography, Europe has once again become one of the world's most interesting arenas for the study of regions and regionalism. This is largely due to a set of transformations taking place in the regional geography of the continent, which raise important issues about the character, societal significance, and future role of regions. Two seemingly contradictory trends appear to be in the making. The nation state, which has been the dominant force in the organization of European space for more than two centuries, seems to be in the process of surrendering some of its sovereignty to regional units both above and below it. That this is happening has become generally accepted over the last decade or so. Indeed, it has become rather commonplace to say that the territorial structure of Europe is being inexorably stretched in two directions.

In the first instance worldwide processes of globalization and ongoing efforts within Europe to achieve an ever greater degree of integration and cooperation among nations have combined to greatly enhance the role of supranational structures and identities. The most obvious and salient example is the European Union, which today commands considerable supranational influence over the lives of the citizens of twenty-five member countries as well as over those of a fairly large number of applicant nations that are in the process of reshaping their economies and societies to meet the norms of membership.

At the same time a great deal of attention has been paid to the creation or the re-emergence of regions and regional movements, both within and across national boundaries. This new regional assertiveness comes in different forms. It may feature the revival of some kind of long-suppressed, historical regional identity (a ghost of the past), or it may involve the formation of an entirely new

24. J. Nicholas Entrikin, "Place and Region 2," *Progress in Human Geography* 20 (1996): 215–221.

25. Andrew Sayer, "The 'New' Regional Geography and Problems of Narrative," *Environment and Planning D: Society and Space* 7 (1989): 253–276.

regional assemblage (often a modernistic mélange of technology, economy, and culture). Interestingly, the European Union has itself encouraged this trend by promoting the idea of a "Europe of the regions" and facilitating the devolution of administrative powers to the regions through its policies of subsidiarity.

The net result, some would say, has been a gradual "hollowing out" of the sovereign nation-state system in favor of these new, less state-centered forms of political, economic, and cultural space. The nation state is, of course, in no danger of disappearing anytime soon, and whether it is even unduly threatened by current developments is a matter of debate, but it does appear to be increasingly forced to share some measure of its former powers and prestige with new structures from above and below.[26]

What is of specific interest is in the latter of these two phenomena—the emergence of a new European regionalism that lies either beneath or between the territories of the state—and in particular how individual instances have been socially constructed or produced. A very broad-based and rather popularized review of the general process is the 1994 book, *The New Superregions of Europe*, whose journalist author, Darrel Delamaide, argues for a new understanding of the territorial organization of the continent, based not on the familiar nation states but on the emergence of a whole new set of regions that reflect historical patterns of trade and conquest, ethnic and linguistic heritage, and current trends in business investment and economic development.[27] Delamaide presents these new superregions as expressions of the way in which Europe "really works," and as the most relevant terrain for economic and social interaction.

---

26. There is a growing literature on the pace and variety of regional transformations in contemporary Europe and their relationship to the future of the nation state. See, for example, David H Kaplan and Jouni Häkli. eds., *Boundaries and Place: European Borderlands in Geopolitical* Context (Lanham, Md: Rowan and Littlefield, 2002); Special issue on "The geopolitics of cross-border cooperation in the 'European Union'," *Space and Polity* 6:2 (2002); Christer Jönsson, Sven Tägil, and Gunnar Törnqvist, *Organizing European Space* (London: Sage, 2000); Michael Emerson, *Redrawing the Map of Europe* (London: Macmillan, 1998); Patrick Le Galès and Christian Lequesne, eds., *Regions in Europe* (London: Routledge, 1998); Liam O'Dowd and Thomas M. Wilson, "Frontiers of Sovereignty in the New Europe," in *Borders, Nations and States: Frontiers of Sovereignty in the New Europe*, ed. Liam O'Dowd and Thomas M. Wilson (Aldershot: Avebury, 1996), 1–18; M. Peterson, "Forces of Dynamism or Regression? The New Regionalism in Europe," in *Borders, Regions and Ethnicity in Central Europe* György Éger and Joseph Langer (Klagenfurt: Norea, 1966), 31–48; Christopher Harvie, *The Rise of Regional Europe* (London: Routledge, 1994); Alexander Murphy, "Emerging Regional Linkages within the European Community: Challenging the Dominance of the State," *Tijdschrift voor Economische en Sociale Geografie* 84 (1993): 103–118.

27. Darrel Delamaide, *The New Superregions of Europe* (New York: Dutton, 1994).

The rise of such regional claims is something that is found all across Europe. Of particular interest is the recent outpouring of cross-border regional promotional efforts, in which historic or sometimes entirely new regions are portrayed, through imaginative representations of heritage, landscape, and culture, as places of unique cultural identity and economic opportunity in an increasingly fluid European cultural and economic landscape. We often hear today, for example, of a new Baltic identity suddenly made possible by the break-up of the Soviet Union and potentially centered on a greater Copenhagen (or Ørestad) urban agglomeration. Another example is an emergent "Mediterranean Arc" of city regions that claim to offer a unique and highly attractive blend of history, environment, and high-tech prosperity. We also hear of various examples of "Regio" cross-border experiments at regional integration and cooperation, such as Regio Basiliensis, Regio Genevensis, and Regio Haut-Rhin.

I want to suggest that today's cross-border regional movements are potentially fertile ground for the study of how we as humans actively attempt to create and delimit regions, imbuing them with a legitimizing common history and logic and with unique symbols and purpose; however imaginative such contrivances may be. They also present an opportunity to see how such creations may or may not become generally accepted or institutionalized over time, or how they may or may not take on meaning.[28]

The circumstances are inherently interesting. A general relaxation or fluidization of the political map of Europe has opened the possibility, while ongoing processes of globalization and economic restructuring have given subnational units, whether within or between countries, incentive to develop independent regional identities and attempt to capture their fair share of investment capital. Moreover, the richness of the past, which in most parts of Europe provides a wealth of potential links between history and geography, may be selectively mobilized to add a natural or cultural legitimacy to the project (old or submerged identities) that makes it more than an just an exercise in attracting economic investment. In other words the invention of cross-border regions has often come to involve a unique combination of conceptions of place, cultural identity, and economic advantage, as well as an interesting array of institutionalizing and dissenting actors and voices.

---

28. One empirical example and theoretical approach may be found in Aansi Paasi, *Territories, Boundaries, and Consciousness: The Changing Geographies of the Finnish-Russian Border* (Chichester: Wiley, 1996). See also, Jouni Häkli, "Cross-Border Regionalization in the 'New Europe': Theoretical Reflection with Two Illustrative Examples," *Geopolitics* 3 (1998): 83–103.

Europe's cross-border regional projects have already been the subject of much study and comment, but they continue to be promising areas of study for many now have a history of up to ten years or more. They have been around long enough to identify the various texts and images employed to imagine or portray these regional formations and understand the mélange of actors and intertwined networks of social, political, and cultural factors and motivations that lie behind the process of regional invention. An important question to ask about these many new regional claims is how real they are. Most regions are only weakly institutionalized at best. So what do they represent? Are they areas of cultural, economic, and political significance that really matter to the everyday experience of the people who live in them and have a substantive role to play politically and economically with respect to the established hierarchy of European spatial units, or are they nothing more than a convenient invention for political and business elites who hope to profit by selling place and region in a globalizing marketplace? If the latter is the case, they may be viewed as superficial constructions of limited lasting value. In the former case we are witnessing a significant remaking of the European territorial landscape.

2

Concepts of Region in International History

Marc Frey

In a recent introduction to regionalism in Europe Christopher Harvie comments on the fragmentation of research on region and regionalism by comparing it to "a badly organised dinner party," at which the guests—the various disciplines—"somehow contrive to speak not *to* but *alongside* one another."[1] By and large, this observation seems valid. Specialization within academic disciplines, terminological differences, and an overall increase in the number of publications tend to discourage cross-disciplinary discourses. This understandable but deplorable pheonomenon stands in contrast to widespread calls for interdisciplinary research and integrative approaches. Indeed, cross-disciplinary fertilization has proven to be of enormous value. For instance, the "linguistic" turn and the use of anthropological methods and theories in historical research have had a significant impact on the historical discipline as a whole. The study of human behavior and actions, of perceptions, emotions, and belief systems has not only led to the development of the so-called "new cultural history."[2] It has also deeply influenced other subdisciplines of history such as "international history," where the focus has shifted somewhat from an analysis of interests of states, organizations, bureaucracies, or companies to a deeper appreciation of the underlying ideas that motivate human behavior and actions.[3]

This essay does not attempt to offer a comprehensive approach to the study of "region" and "regionalism."[4] More modestly, by outlining what "region" and

1.　Christopher Harvie, *The Rise of Regional Europe* (New York: Routledge, 1994), x.

2.　Jürgen Heideking and Vera Nünning, *Einführung in die amerikanische Geschichte* (München: C. H. Beck, 1998), 148–156.

3.　See, for example, John Lewis Gaddis, *We Now Know. Rethinking Cold War History* (Oxford: Clarendon Press, 1997).

4.　On interdiscplinary approaches to the study of regions and regionalism, see Celia Applegate, "A Europe of Regions: Reflections on the Historiography of Sub-National Places in Modern Times," *American Historical Review* 104 (1999): 1156–1182; Georg Bossong et al., eds., *Westeuropäische Regionen und ihre Identität. Beiträge aus interdisciplinärer Sicht* (Mannheim: Palatium Verlag, 1994); Lothar Hönnighausen et al., eds., Regional Images and Regional Realities (Tübingen: Stauffenburg, 2000).

"regionalism" mean for international history, it tries to provide "contact zones," argumentative spaces that open up possibilities for further interdisciplinary research.[5] The essay addresses the following questions: What do "region" and/ or "regionalism" mean in the context of international history? In which ways are the concepts of "region" and "regionalism" important for the discipline? What kind of approaches and theories of "region" and "regionalism" exist, and to what extent could they be used for interdisciplinary research?[6]

I

Time and space are essential categories of historical inquiry, and, indeed, of human experience. As such, regions as spaces of human experience have played an important role in international history. Historians of international relations employ concepts of regions in three ways: (1) region as a subsystem of a larger political, economic, or cultural entity; (2) region as an alignment or conglomerate of nation states; and (3) regions as "global" or macro-regions.[7]

Region as a subsystem is an analytical category that has been closely related to the study of empires and hegemony or, within the context of the so-called Westphalian system of early modern and modern times, to the nation state. Region is defined in opposition to or as a function of the nation state:

---

5.   I borrow the term from Mary Louise Pratt, *Imperial Eyes: Travel Writing and Transculturation* (New York: Routledge, 1992), 4.

6.   International history is a well-established subdivision of history. It has developed alongside and in opposition to diplomatic history, which deals with foreign relations and the interaction of states. International history is a response to the critique on diplomatic history by a number of historical disciplines—gender history, social history, cultural and intellectual history—as being too traditional, too focused on "dead white males," and too concerned with elites. To put it succinctly, while traditional diplomatic history analyzed what one clerk in the State Department or Foreign Office said to another, international history in the past twenty years has widened the scope of enquiry and introduced new approaches that originated in other disciplines like political science, anthropology, sociology, and cultural history. The new international history claims to transcend the limitations of one culture and nation. It deals with the study of international economic systems, cultures and cultural interaction, ideologies, ethnic relations, migrations, and conflicts and cooperation between nations and peoples. See Alexander DeConde, "Essay and Reflection: On the Nature of International History," *International History Review* 10 (1988): 282–301; Wilfried Loth and Jürgen Osterhammel, eds., *Internationale Geschichte* (München: Oldenbourg, 2000); Paul W. Schroeder, "History and International Relations Theory: Not Use or Abuse, but Fit or Misfit," *International Security* 22 (1997): 64–74.

7.   Tom Nierop, "Macro-Regions and the Global Institutional Network, 1950–1980," *Political Science Quarterly* 8 (1989): 43–65.

Regions are territories larger than the local, but smaller than the nation state.[8] Common to this concept of the region is its pragmatic character. Depending on the research object, regions can be provinces, states, or *Bundesländer*, or they may be units that at some point in time acquired distinctive political, religious, cultural, or economic features that make them distinctive, such as the American South, the Palatine, Brittany, or Atjeh. Endogenous and exogenous factors bear on the definition of a territory as region: "Otherness" has to be recognized by individuals living within and outside a given spatial entity.

On the second level of enquiry regions are perceived as "a group of countries with a more or less explicitly shared political objective."[9] The emphasis here is on functional and developmental aspects. Prominent fields of analysis have been integrationist projects in different parts of the world such as the European integration process (from European Economic Community to the European Union), the Association of Southeast Asian Nations (ASEAN), the Mekong River Region, the North American Free Trade Area (NAFTA), and security pacts that are regionally defined organizations such as the North Atlantic Treaty Organization (NATO).[10]

Macroregions, the third level of analysis, applies to different global centers of power and culture. They are perceived as heterogenous but distinct entities with shared characteristics such as a common religion comparable forms of administration and government, economic systems, the degree of technical development, etc. Employed mainly by historians of world history and by scholars of geopolitics, macroregions as epistemological tools are important for understanding different developments of societies and cultures at given periods of time. For instance, a comparative study of the factors which facilitated,

8.   Rolf Lindner, ed., *Die Wiederkehr des Regionalen. Über neue Formen kultureller Identität* (Frankfurt/a.M. and New York: Peter Lang, 1994); Gerhard Brunn, ed., *Region und Regionsbildung in Europa. Konzeptionen der Forschung und empirische Befunde* (Baden-Baden: Nomos, 1996); Paul Taylor, *The European Union in the 1990s* (Oxford: Oxford University Press, 1996), 90–96; Patrick Le Galès and Christian Lequesne, eds., *Regions in Europe* (London and New York: Routledge, 1996); Thomas Ellwein and Jürgen Mittelstraß, eds., *Regionen, Regionalismus, Regionalentwicklung* (Oldenburg: Isensee Verlag, 1996).

9.   Björn Hettne, "Globalization and the New Regionalism: The Second Great Transformation," in *Globalism and the New Regionalism*, ed. Björn Hettne, András Inotai and Osvaldo Sunkel (London: Routledge, 1999), 1.

10.   Bijit Bora and Christopher Findley, eds., *Regional Integration and the Asia-Pacific* (Melbourne: Oxford University Press, 1996); Andrew Gamble and Anthony Payne, eds., *Regionalism and World Order* (New York: St. Martin's Press, 1996); Tom Nierop, *Systems and Regions in Global Politics: An Empirical Study of Diplomacy, International Organization, and Trade, 1950–1991* (Chichester: Wiley, 1994); Joseph S. Nye, ed., *International Regionalism: Readings* (Boston: Little, Brown and Company, 1968).

fuelled or retarded ocean-bound discoveries and expansions is central to an understanding of the formation of the modern world system, of imperialism and colonialism, or of capitalism and communism. Another example would be Samuel Huntington's cultural interpretation of contemporary global politics.[11]

II

A number of factors have contributed to a general questioning of regional definitions based on geography and/or politics, and it is sufficient here to name but a few: the rise of postmodernism, the linguistic turn, the end of the Cold War, and the changing character of the international system. Moreover, globalization challenges traditional state sovereignties, national norms, values, and institutions; contributes to the worldwide spread of information, knowledge, technology, and capital; and promotes the proliferation of cultural artifacts.[12] Some critics have pointed out that regions and regionalism have been treated as merely political-administrative units. By referring to economic entities such as the Sterling Bloc of the British Empire and the Commonwealth, critics have argued that groups of highly heterogenous nations, constituting economic units or regions of shared currency regulations or tariffs, need not necessarily base their distinctiveness as a region on geography. Another example could be the group of nations producing "dollar bananas." Here, too, critics argue that neither the political nor the geographical dimension would sufficiently explain what a region actually is.

The introduction, or rather reintroduction, of "culture" in its various forms in scholarly discourses—culture as artistic expression, as identity, as business culture, and so forth—has dramatically altered our understanding of region and regionalism. Unfortunately, "culture" is as complex a phenomenon as "region," and definitions of culture are as heterogenous as those of "region." For practical purposes "culture" is defined here as a shared set of values, traditions, customs, beliefs, and behavior.[13] Three examples of the usefulness

11.   Paul Kennedy, *The Rise and Fall of the Great Powers: Economic Change and Military Conflict from 1500 to 2000* (London: Unwin Hyman, 1988); David Landes, *The Wealth and Poverty of Nations: Why Some Are So Rich and Some So Poor* (New York: W. W. Norton & Co., 1998); Lawrence E. Harrison and Samuel P. Huntington, eds., *Culture Matters: How Values Shape Human Progress* (New York: Basic Books, 2000); Samuel Huntington, *The Clash of Civilizations* (New York: Simon & Schuster, 1996).
12.   Thomas L. Friedman, *The Lexus and the Olive Tree* (New York: Farrar, Straus & Giroux, 1999).

of "cultural" categories in the study of "region" and "regionness" illustrate this point.

Two thousand years before Foucault, Derrida, and others shattered the realist paradigm by arguing that meaning is never static but relational, a young, ambitious Roman, Julius Caesar, wrote one of the most famous sentences in the history of western civilization: "Gallia est omnes divisa in partes tres" (The whole of Gaul is divided into three parts), and he continued to define the three regions by observing: "They are different in language, tradition, and law."[14] Obviously, the notion of the nation state and the relation of region to nation did not play a role in Caesar's definition. He was concerned with culture, and he defined culture by perceiving differences in modes of social organization, expression, and customs.

A second, much more familiar example is "Europe." What is Europe? Is Europe a region based on a shared culture—the classical heritage, Christianity, common roots of language, the division of state and church, the rule of law, social pluralism, representative administration, individualism, a belief in being different from "others"—or is it an entity of like-minded nation states eager to create a security, political, cultural, and economic regional grouping?[15]

Harvard politicial scientist Samuel Huntington provides a third example. In his famous book *The Clash of Civilizations* he distinguishes certain regions of the globe by highlighting (and constructing) their cultural differences, mainly by referring to unique historical developments and different religions. In contrast to much of the current scholarly debate Huntington perceives regions as culturally homogenous areas, both from an endogenous and from an exogenous perspective: Members of one cultural region define themselves as belonging to a specific region, and they view other areas as distinctly different.

Whether these examples actually provide plausible and all-encompassing interpretations of regions is not the point here. Rather, the important issue is that the three examples have one thing in common: Areas and territories are *perceived* as being different from one another. Therefore, regions in international history are increasingly regarded as *constructs*. As Max Weber put it: Nations and, *inter alia*, regions constitute themselves through "geglaubte Gemeinsamkeit"

---

13.   This definition follows Akira Iriye, "Culture and Power: International Relations and Intercultural Relations," *Diplomatic History* 10 (Spring 1979): 115–128.

14.   Julius Caesar, *Bellum Gallicum* (Münster 1992), 43.

15.   Wilfried Loth, "Regionale, nationale und europäische Identität. Überlegungen zum Wandel europäischer Staatlichkeit," in *Internationale Geschichte*, 357–369.

or what Benedict Anderson came to call "imagined communities."[16] To apply Anderson's valuable concept of the formation of nation states as "imagined communities" to the study of region and regionalism means to investigate the processes that provide for shared identities ultimately leading to the creation of regions (the evolution of networks of communication, infrastructure, shared knowledge, common perceptions of reality, and so forth).

III

To acknowledge the constructed character of regions is important because it leads to the question of contextuality. Comparable to concepts of nation and ethnicity, regions possess subjective qualities, particularly with respect to "identity," that is, the shared belief of a community in the distinctiveness of its habitat.[17] However, to leave the matter here would be unsatisfactory and would disregard the factors responsible for the formation of regions and of distinct regional identities. Historians have identified a number of factors contributing to the formation of regions. Historically, they have evolved around centers of power and/or culture (towns, cities, or concentrations of rural communities), or they have emerged as a consequence of the devolution of political or administrative power. There is some indication to assume that while geography, religion, language, ethnicity, and the economy play important roles in the formation of regions, the administrative-political realm seems to be dominant.

Geography can play a role in the formation of regions. Physical barriers, climate, and ecological characteristics are preconditions for the ways human societies have developed over time. A territory shielded by rivers or mountains may enjoy a relatively high degree of security, thus facilitating the long-term evolution of homogenous societies. Conversely, territories geographically open to aggression from outside might be better suited to the development of fragmented units and the evolution of culturally hybrid communities, which in turn develop distinct regional traits. Climate and geographic conditions may also foster specific economies with distinct regional specifications or modes of production. Numerous examples from the subnational level on all continents

---

16.   Max Weber, *Wirtschaft und Gesellschaft*, vol. 1, 5th ed. (Tübingen: Mohr, 1976), 237; Max Weber, *Economy and Society: An Outline of Interpretive Sociology*, vol. 1 (Berkeley, CA: University of California Press, 1978), 388; Benedict Anderson, *Imagined Communities*, rev. ed. (London: Verso, 1991).

17.   Joachim Kuropka, "Thesen zur regionalen Identität," in *Region und Regionalismus,* ed. Volker Hagen (Cloppenburg: Verlag Druckerei Runge, 1994), 11–34.

support this thesis.[18] However, with regard to macroregions natural factors have only a limited explanatory capacity. It may be argued that Europe's geographic openness, its diversity of climate, the existence of numerous navigable rivers, and similar factors prevented the development of a single power center that could impose its conceptions on large spaces, thereby retarding competition between subcenters (or regions) and ultimately preventing progress (as was the case with China under the Ming dynasty).[19] However, a macroregion like Southeast Asia does not possess any unifying geographical traits except perhaps its climate.[20]

Economic developments have always been powerful reasons for the evolution of regions. Specialized economies, whether agricultural, industrial, or service-oriented, create complex systems of interaction among individuals, interest groups, centers of production, and markets. They attract immigration and increase connectedness. The necessary infrastructure for further economic development reduces length of travel within a certain territory. Thus, the annihilation of space and time in the interest of capital accumulation has a strong homogenizing effect. This observation applies equally to subsystems or regions, the development of the nation state, and the evolution of "global" regions. Consider, for example, the formation of an integrated national market in the early nineteenth-century United States as one explanation for the development of the nation state.[21] Or look at the European integration process, where economic considerations have played a very significant role.[22] With regard to subcenters, examples are equally abundant, whether one looks at fifteenth-century Flanders as the major economic center of Northern Europe or at the seventeenth-century Thai kingdom of Ayutthaya.

18.   Immanuel Wallerstein, *The Modern World System*, vol. 1, *Capitalist Agriculture and the Origins of the European World-Economy in the ixteenth Century* (New York and London: Academic Press, 1974).

19.   Fernand Braudel, *The Mediterranean and the Mediterranean World in the Age of Philip II*, vol. 2 (London: Collins, 1972), 661ff.; C. O. Hucker, *China's Imperial Past* (Palo Alto, CA: Stanford University Press, 1981), 303ff.; E. L. Jones, *The European Miracle: Environments, Economies and Geopolitics in the History of Europe and Asia* (Cambridge: Cambridge University Press, 1981).

20.   Michael J. G. Parnwell, "Naturraum und Geographie," in *Südostasien-Handbuch*, ed. Bernhard Dahm and Roderich Ptak, (Munich: Beck, 1999), 23–33.

21.   Paul Nolte, "Der Markt und seine Kultur—ein neues Paradigma der amerikanischen Geschichte?" *Historische Zeitschrift* 264 (1997): 329–360.

22.   John Gillingham, *Coal, Steel and the Rebirth of Europe, 1945–55: The German and French from Ruhr Conflict to Economic Community* (Cambridge: Cambridge University Press, 1991).

As important as economic considerations are, I suggest that political and strategic developments are the main driving forces for the evolution of regions. In particular, administrative acts, the drawing and redrawing of boundaries, the imposition of religious practices from the top of social hierarchies down to society at large, the organization of communities, the ways in which economies can flourish or are restrained, the judicial system, and so forth all depend to a large degree on political or strategic choices. One example of a region within a nation and one pertaining to a macroregion may illustrate this hypothesis.

The American South, widely regarded as the most distinct region (or section) of the United States, acquired its peculiar character in no small measure from the institution of slavery. While perceived economic necessities played an important role in the defense of slavery, political considerations and acts were ultimately responsible for the prolongation of a system of forced migration and bonded labor. At various points, most notably during the constitution-making process, political decisions were made that impacted on and reinforced a specific regional culture—in this case the conviction that white men and women had the right to "own" black men, women and children as their "property." Typical (and stereotyped) expressions of Southern culture like the insistence on states' rights may not have been so resilient or may have been completely different if not for the conscious decision of politicians to uphold slavery.

The other example refers to the macroregion called Southeast Asia. The term, originally introduced by the German geopolitician Karl Haushofer, first came into vogue with the Allied decision during World War II to establish a "Southeast Asia Command."[23] Although non-European outsiders traditionally perceived "Southeast Asia" as a distinct region (the Chinese and Japanese called it Nanyang and Nan'yo, respectively, meaning "South Seas," and in Sanskrit the region was termed Suvarnabhumi, meaning "land of gold"), there was almost no regional awareness on the part of the people living in the territories stretching from Burma and Vietnam to the outer islands of Indonesia. However, once the strategic decision to assign various utterly different territories to a functional region was made, a process began, which, under the influence of endogenous and exogenous factors (decolonization and nation-building, conflict resolution, capitalism), led to the establishment of ASEAN in 1967. Since then, institutionalized cooperation among the member countries (I deliberately avoid the term "nation states.") has contributed to the development of a regional identity.[24]

---

23.   Bernhard Dahm and Roderich Ptak, "Vorwort," *Südostasien-Handbuch*, 9–13.

Political and strategic decisions are of fundamental importance for the creation of regions. However, a given spatial unit has to be recognized and rerecognized by insiders and outsiders. Inhabitants of a territory want to identify in order to feel "at home" in a given region, and outsiders need to perceive the distinctive character of a region in order to recognize it as such. Thus, regions have to be actively promoted. This promotion, undertaken by a supply of identificatory features, can be termed regionalization. These features can be economic, political, social, or cultural. They foster identity. Identification is created through a process by which individuals avoid behavior that they assume to be in contrast to the value system and culture they live in, since such behavior would be negatively sanctioned.[25] Regions are not only constructs created by empirically recognizable decisions and developments, they are re-created in the minds of their inhabitants and by individuals perceiving a region from the outside. Collective images, mental maps, and belief systems are transmittors of identity, and they reinforce identification.[26]

IV

Situated between the local and the global, regions can be entities that are either smaller or larger than the nation state. They can take cultural, economic, political, and social forms. Regions can overlap, and one frequently finds regions within subregions. Likewise, the identification of people with a region or with regions within a region can take on a great variety of forms. Concepts of regions are fluid and in constant change. In this connection scholars of international history have been interested in two aspects of the study of regions and macroregions in particular: the comparison between different regions and the relative degree of cohesiveness and the level of integration within regions. By and large, however, they have refrained from developing models or typologies by which to measure cohesiveness and integration. From a historian's point of view this is understandable, since historical inquiry is usually interested in the particular, in the uniqueness of the object of study.

24.   Amitav Acharya, *The Quest for Identity: International Relations of Southeast Asia* (Oxford: Oxford University Press, 2000); C. M. Turnbull, "Regionalism and Nationalism" in *The Cambridge History of Southeast Asia*, vol. 4, *From World War II to the Present*, ed. Nicholas Tarling (Cambridge: Cambridge University Press, 1999), 257–318.

25.   Fredrik Barth, ed., *Ethnic Groups and Boundarie: The Social Organization of Culture Difference* (London: Allen & Unwin, 1969), 18.

26.   Jan Assmann, *Das kulturelle Gedächtnis: Schrift, Erinnerung und politische Identität in frühen Hochkulturen* (Munich: C. H. Beck, 1997); Erik H. Erikson, *Identität und Lebenszyklus* (Frankfurt a.M.: Suhrkamp, 1971), 17 ff.

However, a more structural approach seems promising if we want to study the historical roots of some of the major developments of our time: globalization; the dichotomy between a developing homogeneous global popular culture and the resilience and/or evolution of multiple local/regional cultures; the impact of regional associations of nation states on the distribution of power and influence in different parts of the world; and the dynamics of interaction between regions and the global capitalist system. The following typology with special emphasis on macroregions is suggested as one means of analysis for the degree of cohesiveness and integration of regions.[27]

On the first level a region assumes identifiable geographical forms. It need not be, but can be delimited by physical barriers, climate, or ecology. Regions in this sense are usually perceived in terms of physical geography. One example would be the six regions of the United States as put forward by Howard Odum in 1936 and still widely used for statistical purposes (Northeast, Southeast, Mid-States, Northwest, Southwest, Pacific West).[28] Other examples would be the "Indian subcontinent" or "Europe from the Atlantic to the Ural." On a second level a region is perceived as a social system characterized by multiple relations between individuals and communities in a given space. A low level of integration occurs via trade links, infrastructure, and diffuse common cultural traditions. An awareness of the latter, however, does not lead to organized or institutionalized cooperation among the constituent members of a region. Military conflicts are frequent, due in part to the fact that there is no hegemon able to dictate the terms of conflict resolution. Examples would be Europe from circa 1300 onward or the above mentioned Nanyang.[29] The third level of "regionness" concerns phenomena such as organized and institutionalized cooperation in the fields of culture, economy, politics, or strategy. These formal regions, characterized and held together by regimes, are a phenomenon of the post-World War II period.[30] Here, the region is defined according to the membership. Examples would be the Southeast Asian Treaty Organization (SEATO, 1954–1974), NATO, the EEC/EC (until the treaty of

27. The following typology follows in part Hettne, "Globalization and the New Regionalism," in *Globalism and the New Regionalism*, 10ff.

28. Howard W. Odum, *American Regionalism* (Gloucester, MA: P. Smith, 1966).

29. David Kaiser, *Politics and War: European Conflict from Philip II to Hitler*, enlarged ed. (Cambridge, MA: Harvard University Press, 2000); David Joel Steinberg, ed., *In Search of Southeast Asia: A Modern History*, rev. ed. (London: Allen & Unwin, 1987).

30. Beate Kohler-Koch, "Zur Empirie und Theorie internationaler Regime," in *Regime in den internationalen Beziehungen* ed. Beate Kohler-Koch (Baden-Baden: Nomos, 1989), 17–89.

Maastricht in 1992), NAFTA, and ASEAN. On a fourth level of "regionness," still very much in the making, one can observe the emergence of a regional civil society and the establishment of institutions with independent actor capability. Multidimensional cooperation and interaction takes place, and the convergence of values, facilitated by a reconstruction of once-diffuse common cultural traditions, is actively promoted by the regional institutions, the participating member states, and decisive segments of the regional population. With the exception of the European Union, formal regions have not reached this level, and it is doubtful whether ASEAN or NAFTA will move in the direction of closer integration in the foreseeable future. In contrast the European Central Bank and the European Court of Justice are examples for independent regional institutions with actor capability. In the European Union, shared sovereignties between national and regional institutions in many aspects of economic organization and political decision-making are already a reality, and it is more than likely that the identification of the peoples within the European Union with Europe as a region will increase. Unifying factors are institutionalized bonds, an increasingly like-minded political behavior, trade, increasing closeness through infrastructure and communication, and a gradual leveling of socioeconomic disparaties. A simultaneous process will be the development of regions within the macroregion and the spread of multilingualism (with the probable exception of the British Isles) as expressions of national and regional cultures. To what extent concepts of regions will then still possess analytical qualities remains to be seen.

V

Max Weber's and Benedict Anderson's concept of the "imagined community" offers ample opportunity for interdisciplinary research. Moreover, the dimensions of regionness—geographical unit, social system, organized cooperation, civil society, acting subject—can be applied not only to international history, but to a wide range of disciplines dealing with concepts of region and regionness. The evolution and development of a civil society seems particularly suited for interdisciplinary research. While, for example, economists study regional trade and business networks, anthropologists look at questions of regional identity formation, and literary scholars explore the way in which cultural agents reproduce notions of "regionness." On the other hand, scholars of international history can greatly profit from the findings of other disciplines. The still prevalent preoccupation with political regions and political regionalization, important as they are, confuses the complexity of "region" and tends to disregard factors responsible for the production of regions. In an age of globalization, where nation states and politics are forced to transfer part of their influence and power to nonstate actors, multilateral organizations, or even supranational institutions, a fresh look on the importance of regions in history seems necessary. Only then can we truly overcome the still powerful attraction of the nation-state paradigm, and only then can we really value the realization that for most of human history, people organized and identified themselves not on national, but on local and regional levels.

3

Memory, Heritage, and Tradition in the Construction of Regional Identity: A View from Geography

Steven Hoelscher

As recently as 1980, it was possible for the French sociologist Pierre Bourdieu to chastise geographers and other social scientists for their tendency to naturalize the concept of region. His article, "Identity and Representation: Elements for a Critical Reflection on the Idea of Region," is foundational in its advocacy of two overlapping themes that have become a baseline in current geographic research: the social "construction" or "production" of place and region, and the social uses of geographic identity and representation. Geographers and their colleagues across academe, according to Bourdieu, tended to make the process of regional formation appear natural and uncompromised by political and economic forces. "Even the 'landscapes' or 'native soil' so dear to geographers," Bourdieu argued, "are in fact inheritances, in other words, historical products of social determinants." Put somewhat differently, regional classifications result less from "natural continuity" than "a social act."[1]

Twenty years later, Bourdieu's perspective has taken firm root: the notion that place and region are socially constructed or produced appears to be a truism among contemporary human geographers. Anne Godlweska and Neil Smith are hardly alone in suggesting that "among the most powerful agendas in human geography today is the sustained commitment to understanding the social construction of geographic space and movement: how do specific societies produce equally specific geographies and, consequently, how do these geographies help shape social change?"[2] This latter point is especially

---

1.   Pierre Bourdieu, "Identity and Representation: Elements for a Critical Reflection on the Idea of Region," in *Language and Symbolic Power*, ed. John B. Thompson, trans. Gino Raymond and Matthew Adamson (Cambridge: Polity, 1991), 287, 221. This essay was originally published in 1980.

2.   Anne Godlweska and Neil Smith, eds., *Geography and Empire* (Oxford: Blackwell, 1994), 3. See also the useful essays by J. Nicholas Entrikin, "Place, Region, and Modernity," in *The Power of Place: Bringing Together the Geographical and Sociological Imaginations*,

revealing, for it suggests that geographical space (whether one speaks of place or region) and society are mutually constitutive. In a sense, then, I would argue that geographers today have not only taken Bourdieu's social constructivist viewpoint to heart, but have tried to go one step further: if regions cannot be considered apart from social relations, then surely those very relations depend equally on region.[3]

Geographers, of course, are not the sole proprietors of this perspective—call it "constructionist" for lack of a better term—and indeed one hears echoes of it everywhere. In his perceptive discussion of the invention of New England, the historian Stephen Nissenbaum has written that "a region, much like class, is something that gets *generated* in the process of distinguishing itself from something else." Katherine Morrissey, an American Studies scholar of the Western United States, argues that "regions are *constructed* entities, ways of organizing people and place." And the sociologist John Shelton Reed describes how a regional group—in this case, American Southerners—"*enlist* the identification of its members," and how education and media exposure raise the "consciousness" of Southerners. Even the American region seemingly most "natural" is, in fact, constructed.[4] One could present dozens of similar examples, all of which would reinforce my central point: that both within and outside the discipline of geography, a social construction perspective has been an inevitable consequence of the encounter between regional studies and social theory.

In what follows, I offer one approach for the geographical study of regional identity formation. After briefly reviewing a sampling of recent approaches to the study of region in geography, I then argue that a viewpoint that takes

---

ed. John Agnew and James S. Duncan (Boston: Unwin Hyman, 1989), 30–43; and J. Nicholas Entrikin, "Place and Region," *Progress in Human Geography* 18, no. 2 (1994): 227–233.

3.   Edward Soja, "The Spatiality of Social Life: Toward a Transformative Retheorisation," in *Social Relations and Spatial Structures*, ed. Derek Gregory and John Urry (New York: St. Martin's Press, 1985), 90–127; Henri Lefebvre, *The Production of Space*, trans. Donald Nicholson-Smith (Oxford: Blackwell, 1991). Following Nicholas Entrikin, my argument concerning region applies also to the concept of place: "place and region both refer to areal contexts, but may be distinguished in terms of spatial scale." J. Nicholas Entrikin, *The Betweenness of Place: Towards a Geography of Modernity* (Baltimore: Johns Hopkins University Press, 1990), 1, 137 note 1.

4.   Stephen Nissenbaum, "New England as Region and Nation," in *All Over the Map: Rethinking American Regions*, ed. Edward Ayers et al. (Baltimore: Johns Hopkins University Press, 1996), 46; Katherine Morrissey, *Mental Territories: Mapping the Inland Empire* (Ithaca, NY: Cornell University Press, 1997), 8; and John Shelton Reed, *One South: An Ethnic Approach to Regional Culture* (Baton Rouge: Louisiana State University Press, 1982), 16. Emphasis added.

into account the role of ideas and consciousness is vital to understanding just how regions are constructed. Most immediately, I am interested in the role of tradition, cultural memory, and heritage in the construction of regional identity. These keywords—intuitive as they may appear—require some explanation. I will then suggest that only an interdisciplinary perspective allows us to examine them in a meaningful way. The methodological tools that I offer derive from anthropology and geography, respectively: cultural performance and landscape.

A New Regional Geography and the Study of Identity

Recent approaches to the study of region in geography—collectively sometimes called "the new regional geography"—strive, above all, to develop a sophisticated understanding of regional formation.[5] This perspective (actually, set of perspectives) is distinguished from the discipline's chorological tradition by its move away from studying places themselves (with its predictable inventory of climate, landforms, natural resources, population base, and economic sectors) and toward a theorization of region as a social and cultural category.[6] From time to time, there have been calls for a rekindling of the so-called geographer's art—regional synthesis—but such appeals have attracted

---

5.   Mary Beth Pudup, "Arguments within Regional Geography," *Progress in Human Geography* 12 (1988): 369–390; Anne Gilbert, "The New Regional Geography in English- and French-speaking Countries," *Progress in Human Geography* 12 (1988): 208–228; Andrew Sayer, "The New Regional Geography and Problems of Narrative," *Environment and Planning D: Society and Space* 7 (1989): 253–276; Nigel Thrift, "For a New Regional Geography 2," *Progress in Human Geography* 15 (1991): 456–465; and John Allen, Doreen Massey, and John Cochrane, *Rethinking the Region* (London: Routledge, 1998).

6.   The chorological approach within geography is most clearly identified with the work of Richard Hartshorne and the regional studies that he inspired. For the landmark articulation of his regional approach, see Richard Hartshorne, *The Nature of Geography* (Lancaster, PA: Association of American Geographers, 1939). Inexplicably, Hartshorne maintained a distance from the key leaders of America's interwar regionalist movement, best exemplified (in its social science wing) by Howard W. Odum and Harry Estill Moore's *American Regionalism: A Cultural-Historical Approach to National Integration* (New York: H. Holt, 1938). For more on geography's isolation during this critical period, see Timothy Oakes, "Place and the Politics of Modernity," *Annals of the Association of American Geographers* 87 (1997): 509–531. The importance and influence of Hartshorne's regional approach is explored in the essays in J. Nicholas Entrikin and Stanley D. Brunn, eds., *Reflections on Richard Hartshorne's* The Nature of Geography (Washington, DC: Association of American Geographers, 1990). See especially Neil Smith, "Geography as Museum: Private History and Conservative Idealism in *The Nature of Geography*," 89–120; and John Agnew, "Sameness and Difference: Hartshorne's *The Nature of Geography* and Geography as Areal Variation," 121–140.

few followers.[7] Instead, and as a direct outcome of the turn toward cultural studies and social theory, issues of regional *identity* have assumed central importance. Here, geography sits squarely in the current interdisciplinary heart of regionalism. "Scholars of American regions," the historian Charles Reagan Wilson has argued, "focus above all now on the issue of cultural identity, examined within the framework of constructed cultures."[8]

This new work is further distinguished from earlier studies of regional identity pioneered by the French geographer, Paul Vidal de la Blache. For Vidal, the regions, or *pays*, of France owed their identity (or "personality") to the local cultures that impressed themselves on the local landscapes. His celebrated *Tableau de la géographie de la France* presented a detailed and highly sophisticated "portrait" of the individual regions of pre-Revolutionary France, a portrait that assumed an intimacy between culture, landscape, and region.[9] Today, such intimate connections are problematized. John Allen, Doreen Massey, and John Cochrane capture the discipline's contemporary decontructionist ethos in their *Rethinking the Region* when they note that " . . . there are always multiple ways of seeing a place; there is no complete 'portrait of a region.'" Furthermore they argue that regions "are not 'out there'

---

7.   John Fraser Hart, "The Highest Form of the Geographer's Art," *Annals of the Association of American Geographers* 72 (1982): 1–29. See also John H. Paterson, "Writing Regional Geography," in *Progress in Geography*, ed. C. Board (London: Edward Arnold, 1974), 1–26.

8.   Charles Reagan Wilson, "American Regionalism in a Postmodern World," *Amerikastudien / American Studies* 42 (1997): 145–158, quote on p. 154. See also Charles Reagan Wilson, "Introduction," in *The New Regionalism*, ed. Charles Reagan Wilson (Jackson: University Press of Mississippi, 1998), ix–xxiii; and Charles Reagan Wilson, "The Invention of Southern Tradition: The Writing and Ritualization of Southern History, 1880–1940," in *Rewriting the South: History and Fiction*, ed. Lothar Hönnighausen and V. Lerda (Tübingen: Francke, 1993), 3–21. It should be noted that in addition to the focus on identity, at least two other concerns within a "new" regional geography have emerged. The first is an emphasis on regions as local responses to capitalist processes; and the second is a focus on the region as a medium for social interaction, playing "a basic role with the production and reproduction of social relations" (Gilbert, "The New Regional Geography"). It is clear that, while the specific focus may vary, there is much overlap between notions of identity, local responses to capitalism, and social interaction.

9.   Paul Vidal de la Blache, *Tableau de la géographie de la France* (Paris: Hachette, 1903). See also Anne Buttimer, *Society and Milieu in the French Geographic Tradition*, monograph series vol. 6 (Chicago: Association of American Geographers, 1971); Kevin Archer, "Regions as Social Organisms: The Lamarckian Characteristics of Vidal de la Blache's Regional Geography," *Annals of the Association of American Geographers* 83 (1993): 498–514; and Nigel Thrift, "Taking Aim at the Heart of the Region," in *Human Geography: Society, Space, and Social Science*, ed. Derek Gregory, Ron Martin, and Graham Smith (Minneapolis: University of Minnesota Press, 1994), 200–231.

waiting to be discovered; they are our (and others') constructions."[10] Regions, no less than other categories like nation, race, gender, and class, have been destabilized: any search for an underlying, unchanging, and intrinsic "identity" is thus rendered suspect. What Massey writes elsewhere of place holds for region: "There are indeed multiple meanings of places, held by different social groups, and the question of which identity is dominant will be the result of social negotiation and conflict."[11]

If questions of constructed identity, then, have assumed a central role in the geographical study of regions, the methods, tools, and scales of investigation vary widely. Political geographers, like Alexander Murphy and John Agnew, have examined regional identity as a factor in national politics. Murphy's study of the "social construction of space" in Belgium by Flemish and Walloon groups revealed that territorial boundaries are often employed to reinforce cultural difference. In the process of dividing national space into mutually exclusive enclaves, the two linguistic groups rearticulate their identities. This is quite different from Northern Italy—Agnew's case study. There, political regionalism has not been based on administrative boundaries; rather, social boundaries have sufficed to maintain cultural identity.[12]

Historical geographers, too, have made important uses of the regional concept in their studies of cultural identity. Robert Ostergren has examined the nineteenth-century formation of regional identity in the Dalarna region of Sweden, and how that regional identity survived the trans-Atlantic migration to North America. Making use of demographic, economic, and environmental data, Ostergren demonstrates that the emigrants from a region of Upper Dalarna (Rättvik) transplanted a strong sense of communal identity to a very different American Midwest. Mike Crang has also looked at nineteenth-century regional identity formation in Dalarna, but from a very different perspective. His study investigates the role of one cultural institution—the Open Air Museum—in promoting ideas of national belonging and local identification simultaneously. Crang's critical reading offers many insights into how regional identity interacts

10.   Allen, Massey, and Cochrane, *Rethinking the Region*, 2.

11.   Doreen Massey, "The Political Place of Locality Studies," in *Space, Place, and Gender* (Minneapolis: University of Minnesota Press, 1994), 125–145.

12.   Alexander B. Murphy, "Linguistic Regionalism and the Social Construction of Space in Belgium," *International Journal of the Sociology of Language* 104, no. 1 (1993): 49–64; and John Agnew, "The Rhetoric of Regionalism: The Northern League in Italian Politics, 1983–1994," *Transactions, Institute of British Geographers* NS 20 (1995): 156–172.

with national identity, suggesting that these relationships "are more complex than either simply changing scale or a hierarchical set of affiliations."[13]

The interaction between scales of identity is a leitmotiv for much recent work in cultural geography as well, demonstrated clearly in Catherine Brace's study of regional identity construction in England. As she interrogates a wide array of local writing that invokes the Cotswolds region as an ideal version of England, Brace finds that a powerful myth of regionalism has long informed a discourse of national unity. An interesting comparison with Brace's work is Benjamin Forest's study of the territorial strategy employed by a group of gay men in West Hollywood, California. By declaring and underpinning their identity with the creation of a new local government jurisdiction in which they would have a major stake, West Hollywood became a concrete, regional referent for a more abstract identity: gayness.[14]

A diversity of approaches, methodologies, and case studies, in short, makes the current geographical study of regional identity almost as far-ranging as the concept itself. As the above examples suggest, within current geographical literature the gap between narratives about specific regions and theoretical discussions of place and region seems to be narrowing. Interpretations of specific places and regions are ever more indebted to social theory, and geographical theorists are finding a stronger anchor in case studies of actual regions.

Nevertheless, it is worth remembering, with Alexander Murphy, the importance of problematizing the concept of region in studies of social construction. As Murphy puts it, " . . . [I]f we ask how a region is being transformed or is evolving without probing the genesis and significance of the spatial compartments that we are examining, we are, at least at one level, treating spatial units as untransmutable givens."[15] Murphy's suggestion—and it is one that seems to have been adopted by many geographers recently—is to directly confront questions of *meaning*. As social constructions, regions

---

13. Robert Ostergren, *A Community Transplanted: The Trans-Atlantic Experience of a Swedish Immigrant Settlement in the Upper Middle West, 1835–1915* (Madison: University of Wisconsin Press, 1988); and Mike Crang, "Nation, Region, and Homeland: History and Tradition in Dalarna, Sweden," *Ecumene* 6 (1999): 447–470.

14. Catherine Brace, "Finding England Everywhere: Regional Identity and the Construction of National Identity, 1890–1940," *Ecumene* 6 (1999): 90–109; Benjamin Forrest, "West Hollywood as Symbol: The Significance of Place in the Construction of a Gay Identity," *Environment and Planning D: Society and Space* 13 (1995): 133–157.

15. Alexander B. Murphy, "Regions as Social Constructs: The Gap Between Theory and Practice," *Progress in Human Geography* 15 (1991): 22–35.

are by their very nature ideological. It follows that no explanation of their individuality, character, or power to shape social relations can be complete without explicit consideration of the types of ideas that are developed and sustained in the process of regional identity formation.[16]

Thus, the geographical study of regions and regionalism falls short of its potential if we remain content merely to say that regions are social constructions—as important as that observation remains. Rather, I argue that the crucial role of ideas and consciousness must be embedded in the study of regional identity construction. In order to avoid replacing a long-renounced natural reductionism with a social reductionism, care must be taken to present the full range of factors that enable groups to produce regional space and identity. This requires a social theory in which regional settings are not treated as abstractions or as a priori spatial givens, but instead are seen as the results of social processes that reflect and shape—and in turn, are shaped by—particular ideas about how the world is organized.

The avenue of theory I am suggesting follows closely the relational framework proposed by Robert Sack in which the realms of meaning and social relations overlap and comingle. Identity construction—of both self and place/region—hinges on both political-economic structures and on human agency.[17] As Karen Till, Paul Adams, and I have argued elsewhere, a critical humanist geography can contribute much to thinking about regions as lived-space and contested place. By attending closely to the role of meaning and interpretation in social processes and to large-scale structural constraints, this framework for regional analysis more directly connects the insights of the "new" regional geography with cultural studies.[18] Thus, the first order of business when one speaks of the "construction" of regional identity is to ask: for whom is it constructed, by whom, and for what purposes?

These questions are best answered by examining the *process* of regional identity construction. And three concepts in particular are of special importance

---

16. Murphy, "Regions as Social Constructs," 32. This view is developed further in J. Nicholas Entrikin, "Place and Region 2," *Progress in Human Geography* 20 (1996): 215–221.

17. Robert Sack, *Homo Geographicus* (Baltimore: Johns Hopkins University Press, 1997). See also Michael Keith and Stephen Pile, eds., *Place and the Politics of Identity* (London: Routledge, 1993). It should be noted that Sack includes "nature" as part of his three-part framework. While I acknowledge the importance of this element, for the purposes of this chapter I am confining my focus to both meaning and social relations.

18. Paul Adams, Steven Hoelscher, and Karen Till, "Place in Context: Rethinking Humanist Geographies," in *Textures of Place*, ed. Paul Adams, Steven Hoelscher, and Karen Till (Minneapolis: University of Minnesota Press, 2001), 1–36.

in determining how individuals and societies interact to construct regional identities. All three are linked to various understandings of history and each suggest that competing views of a regional identity are interpreted, negotiated, and contested through the prism of the past. Indeed, an appreciation of the pull of memory is central to my argument: by remembering a regional past, we create a regional identity. Having a firmer notion of what constitutes memory, heritage, and tradition will help build a theory of regional identity construction that is mindful of both powerful social forces that mold space and of the rich human experiences on it. Geographers, with their longstanding interest in place and region, making are well positioned to add to this interdisciplinary discussion.

Keywords for Regional Identity Construction

Tradition

Despite a lengthy Western history that sees tradition as the stable transmission of inherited cultural traits, recent research is unanimous in regarding tradition as a process that involves persistent creation and re-creation. Traditions, Michael Kammen writes, are "born, nurtured, and grow." Particularly fertile grounds for the "invention of tradition" are times of rapid social transformation when old patterns and social formations break down under the uncertainty and chaos of threatening change. More important than the search for "real" versus "invented" traditions—a circular and irresolvable path—is the consideration of the instrumental nature of traditions: the uses to which they are put and the services in which they are mobilized. Tradition is not simply "the surviving past," but a powerful social force that can serve a wide array of purposes. The most notable use, Hobsbawm famously argued, occurs when a group, class, or nation-state deploys tradition in its search for historical legitimacy.[19]

Although most research into the invention of tradition has been focused at the national scale, it is clear that regional studies can benefit from the same type of analysis. After all, if regions, no less than nations, may be considered

---

19. Michael Kammen, *Mystic Chords of Memory: The Transformation of Tradition in American Culture* (New York: Alfred A. Knopf, 1991), 7; and Eric Hobsbawm, "Mass-Producing Tradition: Europe, 1870–1914," in *The Invention of Tradition*, ed. Eric Hobsbawm and Terence Ranger (New York: Cambridge University Press, 1983), 263–308. See also Raymond Williams, *Marxism and Literature* (New York: Oxford University Press, 1977), 115–116; and Richard and Jocelyn Linnekin Handler, "Tradition, Genuine or Spurious," *Journal of American Folklore* 97 (1984): 273–290.

"imagined communities," then the same tools of analysis, questions of power and authority, and philosophical underpinnings should apply. Chris Wilson, in *The Myth of Santa Fe*, argues precisely that. Wilson shows with exceptional insight how key elements of the city's regional-historical legacy—arts and architectural revivals, public ceremony, romantic literature, and historic preservation—are in fact modern creations. The myth of Santa Fe, like invented traditions at other scales, provides a unifying vision of the wider region, its people, and their history; and this regionally invented tradition, despite its rhetoric of social tolerance and its unifying image, obscures longstanding cultural, racial, and class frictions.[20]

Cultural Memory

Even such a "post-traditional" society as modern America has a need for tradition, for its guardians frequently call upon it to generate cultural memory, my second keyword. This is no easy task, since tradition, under conditions of late modernity, offers multivocal readings and is frequently contested. In his *Remaking America*, John Bodnar demonstrates that different people have contrasting views about what constitutes shared tradition and memory. Cultural memory—the body of beliefs and ideas about the past that help a society or group make sense of its past, present, and future—is focused inevitably on concerns of the present. Those who sustain a cultural memory often mobilize it for partisan purposes, commercialize it for the sake of tourism, or invoke it as a way to resist change. Cultural memory, no less than the traditions that conjure memory, is the product of a selective reading of the past.[21]

---

20.   Chris Wilson, *The Myth of Santa Fe: Creating a Modern Regional Tradition* (Albuquerque: University of New Mexico Press, 1997).

21.   Anthony Giddens, "Living in a Post-Traditional Society," in *Reflexive Modernization: Politics, Tradition, and Aesthetics in the Modern Social Order*, ed. Ulrich Beck, Anthony Giddens, and Scott Lash (Stanford: Stanford University Press, 1994), 56–91; and John Bodnar, *Remaking America: Public Memory, Commemoration, and Patriotism in the Twentieth Century* (Princeton: Princeton University Press, 1992). In using the term "cultural memory," instead of the more common term "collective memory," I am following Marita Sturken, who argues that it captures better the sense of self-consciousness that pervades group remembering. Marita Sturken, *Tangled Memories: The Vietnam War, the AIDS Epidemic, and the Politics of Remembering* (Berkeley: University of California Press, 1997), 3. See also Maurice Halbwachs, *The Social Frameworks of Memory* (Chicago: University of Chicago Press, 1992); Barbie Zelizer, "Reading the Past Against the Grain: The Shape of Memory Studies," *Critical Studies in Mass Communication* 12 (1995): 214–239; and John Gillis, "Memory and Identity: The History of a Relationship," in *Commemorations: The Politics of National Identity*, ed. John Gillis (Princeton: Princeton University Press, 1994), 3–24.

It should be clear that what counts as a region's cultural memory is tied inextricably to power. Few sites provide a more dramatic regional example than the Alamo in San Antonio, Texas. Well-known to all Texas school children as their state's birthplace, the Alamo deteriorated badly throughout the nineteenth century. Only in 1905—nearly seventy years after the famous 1836 battle—did a women's patriotic organization, dedicated to promoting the cultural memory of the Republic of Texas, eventually take control of the Alamo's "preservation." Critically, that organization, the Daughters of the Republic of Texas (D.R.T.), was divided into two factions with different conceptions of how the memory of the "Shrine to Texas Liberty" should be presented. On one side was Adina De Zavala, a Latina Texan (*Tejana*) who wished to restore the Alamo to its original condition as a Spanish mission; on the other was Clara Driscoll, an Anglo Texan who aimed to alter the site to emphasize the heroics of Anglo martyrs. In the end, the Anglo preservation plan prevailed. More was at stake than simply the aesthetics of what has become Texas's most important tourist destination, however: "Remembering the Alamo" meant keeping alive the highly selective memory of "Texas heroes" and "Mexican tyrants," a lesson that served to "keep Mexicans 'in line.'" Only by attending to the thoughts and actions of key individuals like De Zavala and Driscoll and by recognizing that the efforts to restore the Alamo coincided with industrialization and new class divisions in South Texas can we disclose the mechanisms that construct regional identities.[22]

Heritage

No better conceptual framework exists to examine the selectivity inherent in cultural memory than that of "heritage," my third and most highly charged keyword. Here, I am drawing on David Lowenthal's provocative discussion of heritage as distinct from history, whose divergent goals and praxes should be clarified. Even for the most politically-engaged historian (and historically-minded geographers), objectivity remains a holy, if unreachable, grail—"that noble dream" as Peter Novick puts it. For, while we may recognize an infinite number of narratives for any history, it is also true that most historians do not believe that all stories about the past are equally good. Bias, of course,

22. Richard Flores, *Remembering the Alamo: Memory, Modernity, and the Master Symbol* (Austin: University of Texas Press, 2002). See also Miguel De Oliver, "Historical Preservation and Identity: The Alamo and the Production of a Consumer Landscape," *Antipode* 28 (1996): 1–23; and Kenneth E. Foote, "The Land-Shape of Memory and Tradition," in *Shadowed Ground: America's Landscapes of Violence and Tragedy* (Austin: University of Texas Press, 1997), 215–236.

inevitably works its way into any history or historical geography; this cannot be avoided for the simple reason that self-interest infuses history as it does all human endeavors.[23]

Heritage, on the other hand, is *premised* on bias and misinformation. "Prejudiced pride in the past is not a sorry consequence of heritage," Lowenthal writes, "it is its essential purpose." As Renan famously relayed to French nationalists more than a century ago: "Getting its history wrong is crucial for the creation of a nation." Heritage thus parts from history not by being biased, but in its attitude toward bias. While history, however imperfectly, seeks to reduce bias, heritage sustains and bolsters it. Equally important are the questions: for whom and why do we construct these divergent paths to the past? Heritage, by its very nature, is exclusive and "normally cherished not as common but private property." Indeed, awarding possession to some while excluding others gives heritage its primary function. Heritage, therefore, is a faith, and like all faiths it originates in the deeply rooted human need to give meaning to temporary chaos, to secure group boundaries, and to provide that symbolic sense of continuity and certainty that is lacking in the real world.[24]

While Lowenthal demonstrates how heritage is deeply antithetical to history, he also takes pains to show their inseparability. Indeed, there is so much traffic across the borders of history and heritage (and, for that matter, between tradition and cultural memory) that it might be more fruitful to think of the concepts as entangled rather than oppositional. As John Gillis puts it, heritage and history are "twins, separated at birth." With its practice of telling what "actually happened" and of knowing the past on its own terms, modern history has had the effect of distancing the past from the present. History became "a foreign country" and often an alienating subject for people to study. No wonder, then, that in times of tension so many people have turned to heritage—the process by which the past is domesticated, made familiar, and translated into contemporary language.[25]

---

23. David Lowenthal, *Possessed by the Past: The Heritage Crusade and the Spoils of History* (New York: The Free Press, 1996); Peter Novick, *That Noble Dream: The "Objectivity Question" and the American Historical Profession* (Cambridge: Cambridge University Press, 1998); and William Cronon, "A Place for Stories: Nature, History, and Narrative," *The Journal of American History* 78 (1992): 1347–1376. See also Pierre Nora, "Between Memory and History: *Les Lieux de Mémoire*," *Representations* 26, no. 1 (1989): 7–25.

24. Nora, "Between Memory and History," 122, 130, 227.

25. John Gillis, "Heritage and History: Twins Separated at Birth," *Reviews in American History* 25 (1997): 375–378. See also David Lowenthal, *The Past is a Foreign County* (Cambridge: Cambridge University Press, 1985); Steven Hoelscher, *Heritage on Stage*

Regional Heritage Today: An Example from the American South

That regional tradition, memory, and heritage remain inherently contentious and inevitably divisive may be seen in the on-going South Carolina Confederate flag controversy. The Confederate battle flag has been flying over the seat of the state government since 1962, when the decision to resurrect represented a clear gesture of hostility and resistance by the all-white legislature to the ongoing Civil Rights struggle. Nearly forty years later, South Carolina remained the only state that still flew the Confederate battle emblem not incorporated into a state flag. Although there had been periodic calls for its removal, on the first day of the new millennium the NAACP's organized boycott of South Carolina's tourism industry brought immediate attention to the issue. Seventeen days later—on Martin Luther King Day—nearly fifty thousand people rallied against the flying of the Confederate flag over the statehouse, chanting, "Your heritage is my slavery."[26]

The protesters' chants were well phrased. As Eric Foner put it, among its defenders, "the Confederate flag represents not slavery but local identity, a way of life and respect for 'heritage.'"[27] In this context, regional "heritage" has become a racially charged codeword for a white, conservative backlash against perceived threats to their own supremacy. Underscoring this point, one week before the King Day rally, the right-wing South Carolina Southern Heritage Coalition organized an event designed to "begin the reversal of the ethnic cleansing process being waged against our proud heritage by the forces of political correctness." The pro-flag rally, dubbed "Heritage Celebration 2000," featured period-costumed men, women, and children re-enacting various roles of the Civil War past.[28] Not surprisingly, the national media caught on to the

(Madison: University of Wisconsin Press, 1998); and Brian Graham, G. J. Ashworth, and J. E. Turnbridge, *A Geography of Heritage* (London: Arnold, 2000).

26.   Bob Herbert, "Of Flags and Slurs," *The New York Times*, 20 January 2000; John White and Sheila Douglas, *Economic Sanctions against South Carolina Now in Effect: NAACP Begins New Century with Economic Sanctions over Confederate Flag in South Carolina* (NAACP, 2000 [cited 7 February 2000]), available from www.naacp.org; David Walsh, *50,000 Protest Confederate Flag in South Carolina: Political Issues in the Fight for Democratic Rights* (World Socialist Web Site, 2000 [cited 11 February 2000]), available from www.wsws. org. A useful overview of the controversy may be found in Gerald R. Webster and Jonathan I. Leib, "Whose South Is It Anyway? Race and the Confederate Flag Battle in South Carolina," *Political Geography* 20 (2001): 271–299.

27.   Eric Foner, "Rebel Yell," *The Nation*, 14 February 2000.

28.   Anonymous, *Heritage Celebration 2000: Why We Must Fight* (South Carolina Heritage Coalition, 2000 [cited 11 February 2000]).

Confederate flag spectacle, drawing in all the major presidential contenders. Political cartoonists from the nation's leading newspapers had a field day lampooning the idea of Southern regional heritage.[29]

In the wake of the hullabaloo, and in response to the economic pressure that cost the state an estimated $100 million in tourist revenues, the South Carolina General Assembly voted to take down the Confederate flag from the capitol dome. At noon on July 1, 2000, South Carolina became the last state to remove the controversial symbol of regional heritage from atop its seat of government. "Today, we bring this debate to an honorable end. Today, the descendants of slaves and the descendants of Confederate soldiers join together in the spirit of mutual respect," Governor Jim Hodges said just before he signed the bill into law. "Today, the debate over the Confederate flag above the Capitol passes into South Carolina history."[30]

Unfortunately, regional heritage is not so easily quelled nor so easily dismissed to the realm of history—especially when its symbol is an element of the landscape, in view for all to see. In order to capture the support of the flag's backers, the law called for a smaller version of it to be flown atop a thirty-foot pole in front of the Capitol, beside a slightly taller monument to the "Lost Cause" of the Confederacy. Even supporters of the regional "heritage" movement to protect the flag recognized that this solution would not appease its opponents. As Republican Senator David Thomas noted, the "compromise" location is arguably a more prominent spot than atop the dome: "If you're going to achieve some balance with this thing, you've got to get it out of people's faces."[31] The NAACP, insulted by the South Carolina decision,

---

29.   Cynthia Tucker, "Bush League: George W. Wimps Out on S.C. Confederate Flag," *Atlanta Journal and Constitution*, 2 February 2000; David Chen, "Matters of Race: Bradley Attacks G.O.P. Over the Confederate Flag," *New York Times*, 9 February 2000; Marc Lacy, "Clinton Enters Confederate Flag Debate," *New York Times*, 30 March 2000; Terry M. Neal, "McCain Reverses Flag Stance; Senator Says He Broke Vow of Honesty in S.C. Race," *Washington Post*, 19 April 2000.

30.   Gov. Hodges quoted in "S.C. Law to Lower Flag July 1," *Washington Post*, 24 May 2000. Although the boycott may have cost the state much in terms of tourist revenues, some entrepreneurs have profited handsomely from the controversy. In the six months following the NCAAP boycott of South Carolina, the CF Flag Company has noted an increase of forty-two percent in sales of Rebel flags. According to sales manager David Krieger, the company refuses to make Nazi flags or Klan flags, offering instead the Confederate flag. Kent Faulk, "Sales of Confederate Flags Still Flying High amid Controversy: South Carolina Debate Has Increased Demand," *New Orleans Times-Picayune*, 21 May 2000.

31.   Sen. Thomas quoted in Tom Baxter, "On Politics: Flag Flap Can't Be Folded Up, Put Away," *Atlanta Journal and Constitution*, 25 May 2000. See also David Firestone, "South Carolina Votes to Remove Confederate Flag From Dome," *New York Times*, 19 May 2000;

determined to expand its boycott of the state, calling on the motion picture industry, professional athletes, and labor organizations to join in until the flag is permanently removed from the Statehouse grounds.[32]

The South Carolina controversy is an especially relevant example because it calls direct attention to several important facets of regional identity construction. These include: the strategic use of the selective memory and tradition for social and political purposes; the multiple and conflictual definitions of what constitutes a regional identity; and the role of landscape and performance in helping construct a meaningful (if contested) interpretation of a region's past. As a visible and prominent element on the public landscape, the Confederate flag crystallizes the conflicting sentiments on what it means to be black, white, Southern, and American today and in the past. And as a way to commemorate the past, donning Civil War garb and re-enacting moments of history make cultural memory palpable and seemingly lifelike. In short, it is through such displays of memory that a regional past is reworked into communicable form.

Displays of Regional Memory: Performance and Landscape

Memory, heritage, and tradition—the foundational elements for the construction of a regional identity—are produced through objects, images, events, and representations. These are the displays of memory. Since the original experiences of memory are irretrievable, we can only grasp them through their remains. Moreover, those displays—images, stories, objects— are not passive containers, but are active vehicles in producing, sharing, and giving meaning to cultural memory.[33] This is especially true when the past being recalled stretches beyond the lifetime and experience of the individual to encompass the region. "The past is not simply there in memory," Andreas

---

and Marlon Manuel, "S.C. Statehouse Drops Confederate Flag," *Duluth News Tribune*, 1 July 2000. For an excellent introduction to the myth of the lost cause, especially as it pertains to the kind of monument building found on the Capitol grounds of Columbia, South Carolina, see Gaines M. Foster, *Ghosts of the Confederacy: Defeat, the Lost Cause, and the Emergence of the New South* (New York: Oxford University Press, 1987).

32.   Anonymous, *NAACP to Continue South Carolina Economic Sanctions* (NAACP, 16 May 2000 [cited 5 June 2000]), available from www.naacp.org/SCEconomic2.html.

33.   In writing about the display of memory, I am indebted to Barbara Kirshenblatt-Gimblett's *Destination Culture: Tourism, Museums, and Heritage* (Berkeley: University of California Press, 1998). As Kirshenblatt-Gimblett writes, " . . . display not only shows and speaks, it also *does*. Display is an interface and thereby transforms what is shown into heritage" (pp. 6–7, emphasis in original). Such a conceptualization is quite similar to what Marita Sturken calls "technologies of memory. Cf. Sturken, *Tangled Memories*, 9–12.

Huyssen notes, "but it must be *articulated* to become memory."[34] Although the range of memory displays is vast and can encompass everything from public art, memorials, television images, photographs, pageants, and yellow ribbons, it strikes me that two articulations are of unusual importance: cultural performances and landscapes.

A Civil War re-enactment, like a festival or pageant, is an excellent example of a *cultural performance*. I am referring to those non-ordinary, framed public events that require participation by a sizable group. They are reflexive instruments of cultural expression in which a group creates its identity by telling a story about itself. As Paul Connerton puts it, performance is the chief way that societies remember. Marked by a higher than usual degree of self-consciousness or reflexivity, performance genres play an essential (and often essentializing) role in the mediation and creation of social communities, including those organized around regional bonds. They provide an intricate counterpoint to the unconscious practices of everyday life as they are "stylistically marked expressions of otherness" and identity. And, importantly, cultural performances invest individuals and social groups with the rhetorical tools necessary to make strategic use of those divisions for their own political ends. Celebration, Frank Manning suggests, "not only represents, but also promotes, dynamic political processes, including the realignment of forces and interests within the body politic." As a chief display of memory, cultural performances are excellent "symbol-vehicles" for the articulation of a regional identity.[35]

---

34. Andreas Huyssen, *Twilight Memories* (New York: Routledge, 1995), 2–3.

35. I develop these ideas further in the context of southern memory in "Making Place, Making Race: Performances of Whiteness in the Jim Crow South," *Annals of the Association of American Geographers* 93, no. 3 (September 2003): 657–686. For general background, see: Paul Connerton, *How Societies Remember* (Cambridge: Cambridge University Press, 1989); Frank Manning, ed., *The Celebration of Society: Perspectives on Contemporary Cultural Performance* (Bowling Green, OH: Bowling Green University Popular Press, 1983); Richard Bauman, "Performance," in *Folklore, Cultural Performances, and Popular Entertainments: A Communications-Centered Handbook*, ed. Richard Bauman (New York: Oxford University Press, 1994), 41–49; Deborah Kapchan, "Performance," *Journal of American Folklore* 108 (1995): 479–508; Regina Bendix, "National Sentiment and the Enactment and Discourse of Swiss Political Ritual," *American Ethnologist* 14 (1992): 768–790; Don Handelman, *Models and Mirrors: Towards an Anthropology of Public Events* (New York: Cambridge University Press, 1990); and Alessandro Falassi, ed., *Time Out of Time: Essays on the Festival* (Albuquerque: University of New Mexico Press, 1987). An excellent journalistic treatment of Civil War re-enactments and performances is found in Tony Horowitz, *Confederates in the Attic: Dispatches from the Unfinished Civil War* (New York: Random House, 1998).

That the study of cultural performance can add much to a geographical
interpretation of region is illustrated nicely in Susan Smith's ethnographic
analysis of Borderlands festivals in Scotland. Every summer the streets of many
rural towns in the Scottish Borders region become the sites for the enactment
of public rituals and cultural performances, all of which celebrate and affirm
"the character, value, history, and continuity of local life." [36] At the same time
that regional identity is being rearticulated—and as part of that process—these
local festivals close the borders, so to speak, to outsiders. The dialogue within
the performance is spoken from the positions of both a dominant majority
and of an oppressed minority; racism and community building in this instance
seem to go hand-in-hand. Smith's nuanced reading of the Borderlands festivals
captures much of the ambiguity and the complex, competing meanings of
regional memory, as the English colonial past hovers over the celebrations.
Indeed, it is the festivals' very distinct regional setting—a borderland that is
itself a place on the margin—that not only provides the context for cultural
performance, but also imbues them with meaning.[37]

While performance is all about process and is marked by the centrality
of human actors, artifacts like *landscape* give the impression of stability and
permanence. A landscape, Fred Inglis has noted, provides "the most solid
appearance in which a history can declare itself."[38] Precisely because landscape
is "a concrete, three-dimensional shared reality," its ability to display regional
memory is unparalleled.[39] Individuals and groups erect monuments to fallen
heroes, construct museums at historic sites, and hoist a flag above a state
capitol with the intention of creating and communicating a shared past. It is
because landscapes seem so natural and enduring that they become all the
more appealing for those wishing to invoke regional identity. For even those
landscapes charged with symbolic meaning—spaces, as D. W. Meinig puts
it, that are "part of the iconography of nationhood, part of the shared set of
ideas and memories and feelings which bind people together"—even these

36.   Susan Smith, "Bounding the Borders: Claiming Space and Making Place in Rural
Scotland," *Transactions of the Institute of British Geographers* 18 (1993): 291–308, quote on
p. 293.
37.   Rob Shields, *Places on the Margin: Alternative Geographies of Modernity* (New York:
Routledge, 1991).
38.   Fred Inglis, "Nation and Community: A Landscape and Its Morality," *Sociological
Review* 25 (1977): 489–514.
39.   J. B. Jackson, *Discovering the Vernacular Landscape* (New Haven: Yale University Press,
1984), 5.

spaces that are so clearly meant to communicate national or regional identity are frequently rendered ageless and authorless.[40]

But, this solidity that landscapes seem to personify melts away on further reflection. Landscape's power, and its duplicity, lies in its ability to project a sense of timelessness and coherency, when, in fact, a landscape is anything but timeless and coherent.[41] No less than performance, landscape is the product of specific historical actors working in discrete spatial contexts. W. J. T. Mitchell's suggestion that landscape be approached less as a noun than as a verb seems especially appropriate. His interest in how landscape "*works* as a cultural practice" is shared by many geographers today, who see landscape as "a process by which social and subjective identities are formed."[42] Thus, the prevailing concern among many geographers today is less with describing landscapes that are symbolic of a regional culture—the pyramids of Egypt, the heathlands of Denmark's Jutland, the plantations of the American South— and more with assessing the ways in which regional identity is imaginatively constructed through these landscapes. Local writing, photography, guidebook literature, tourism, film, and cartography are a few of the media through which landscapes are mobilized to construct regional identity.[43]

Although landscape's construction of national identity has generated perhaps the most sustained analysis in this newer literature, regional identity is of growing interest.[44] One of the best regional studies that comes to mind is

40.   D. W. Meinig, "Symbolic Landscapes: Models of American Community," in *The Interpretation of Ordinary Landscapes*, ed. D. W. Meinig (New York: Oxford University Press, 1979), 165.

41.   Stephen Daniels, "Marxism, Culture, and the Duplicity of Landscape," in *New Models in Geography*, ed. Richard Peet and Nigel Thrift (London: Unwin Hyman, 1989), 196–220.

42.   W. J. T. Mitchell, "Introduction," in *Landscape and Power*, ed. W. J. T. Mitchell (Chicago: University of Chicago Press, 1994), 1–4, quote on page 1. See also Don Mitchell, *The Lie of the Land: Migrant Workers and the California Landscape* (Minneapolis: University of Minnesota Press, 1996).

43.   Derek Gregory, "Between the Book and the Lamp: Imaginative Geographies of Egypt, 1849–1850," *Transactions of the Institute of British Geographers* NS 20 (1995): 29–57; Kenneth Olwig, *Nature's Ideological Landscape* (London: George Allen and Unwin, 1984); and Charles Aiken, *The Cotton Plantation South Since the Civil War* (Baltimore: Johns Hopkins University Press, 1998).

44.   At the national scale see Wilbur Zelinsky, *Nation into State: The Shifting Symbolic Foundations of American Nationalism* (Chapel Hill: University of North Carolina Press, 1988); James Duncan, *The City as Text: The Politics of Landscape Interpretation in the Kandyan Kingdom* (New York: Cambridge University Press, 1990); Stephen Daniels, *Fields of Vision: Landscape Imagery and National Identity in England and the United States* (Princeton: Princeton University Press, 1993); and David Matless, *Landscape and Englishness* (London: Reaktion Books, 1998).

Joseph Wood's study of the New England village landscape. With its familiar vista of neat white houses facing a central "common," the New England village stands as a powerful regional icon recognized across the nation. For many, this familiar landscape is the archetypal "city on a hill," emblematic of strong community values, discipline, and economic stability. But as Wood demonstrates in considerable detail, the New England village emerged as an ideal regional landscape only during the Industrial Revolution, and only when members of the old local elite cultivated it as a way to maintain their social authority. That this distinctly rural landscape emerged in precise conjunction with industrial capitalism is far from mere coincidence or irony. In their idealization of the New England village, regional leaders found a powerful medium to argue for their region's cultural superiority, to export their culture to a rapidly expanding republic, and to relieve some of the class tension associated with the nation's unprecedented industrial transformation.[45]

Conclusion

After a long quiescence, region has re-emerged as an essential and vigorous concept within geography. Not that it was ever truly dead, but as the twentieth century wore on, region (and place) moved increasingly to the periphery of social science. As John Leighly, one of the region's earliest skeptics, noted in 1937:

> There is no prospect of our finding a theory so penetrating that it will bring into rational order all or a fraction of the heterogeneous elements of the landscape. There is no prospect of our finding such a theory [of regions], that is to say, unless it is of a mystical kind, and so outside the pale of science.[46]

Because of their inability to find empirical-theoretical, normative, or scientific significance for the concept of the region, regional geographers found themselves speaking to ever shrinking audiences, and inviting critiques by sociologists like Bourdieu.[47]

---

45.   Joseph S. Wood, *The New England Village* (Baltimore: Johns Hopkins University Press, 1997). See also Nissenbaum, "New England as Region and Nation."

46.   John Leighly, "Some Comments on Contemporary Geographic Method," *Annals of the Association of American Geographers* 27 (1937): 125–141, quote on p. 128.

47.   John Agnew, "The Devaluation of Place in Social Science," in *The Power of Place: Bringing Together the Geographical and Sociological Imaginations*, ed. John Agnew and James Duncan (Boston: Unwin Hyman, 1989), 9–28. See also Entrikin, *Betweenness of Place*, 27–108; and "Place and Region."

As this chapter has attempted to show, the concept of region once again occupies center stage for much geographical research, which is characterized by vitality and an interdisciplinary dialogue. Geographers today are less concerned that their concepts of region fit narrowly prescribed boundaries of science as they thrive on the region's heterogeneity that so worried Leighly. If the study of region has received a powerful theoretical boost from the so-called cultural turn in the humanities and social sciences, its growing importance is also due to larger societal trends. Stephen Daniels makes the important point that the current focus on regions is not mere academic fad: region and place are central components of "how the world seems to work."[48]

Rather than disappearing as so many mid-century modernist thinkers predicted, regional differences have persisted and are, in fact, accelerating to an astonishing extent.[49] From rates of incarceration and execution, to patterns of venture capital investment and toxic waste distribution, regional differences remain an ever-present feature of American geography. And, as the Confederate flag controversy in South Carolina shows, those differences are more than simply economic. Regional memory, heritage, and tradition remain a vitally important component of our sense of place.

This chapter offers one perspective on a geographical approach to the study of region, one that focuses on how competing notions of a region's past construct its identity—or, more accurately, its identities. I believe that this admittedly personal perspective captures many of the most fruitful trends in the geographical study of region. A sense of place, after all, is dependent on a sense of time.[50] Recognizing this relationship is an important step in the ongoing effort to understand the construction of regional identity.

---

48.   Stephen Daniels, "Place and the Geographical Imagination," *Geography* 77 (1992): 310–322, quote on p. 311.

49.   Allen, Massey, and Cochrane, *Rethinking the Region.*

50.   John Brinkerhoff Jackson, *A Sense of Place, a Sense of Time* (New Haven: Yale University Press, 1994).

4

The Utility of Regionalism for Comparative Research on Governance: A Political Science Perspective

Andrea Witt

Introduction

Regionalism is a rather complex tool for political scientists as it resists any single-minded definition.[1] While countless publications deal with the phenomena, many lack a well-defined framework and terminological definition. Regionalism is synonymously used as a research tool, to indicate a political level, or to express a certain policy context. Also, most publications shy away from a theoretical definition and instead focus on regionalism's practical impact and its significance for new supranational institutions such as the European Union (EU).[2] Arbitration in focus, scope, or intention is the result, hindering a broader recognition of its research potential. However, if delivered with a clear-cut methodological approach and theoretical framework, political science research on regionalism offers valuable insights into new patterns of participation, structural set-ups and innovative policy contexts. Studying regionalism may reveal emerging forms of governance, thus highlighting changes significant far beyond the specific regional setting.

In an effort to help fulfill this potential, this paper offers a discussion of various approaches to and scholarly interest in regional phenomena. In

---

1.   Andreas Langmann, "Regionen," in *Handwörterbuch des politischen Systems der Bundesrepublik Deutschland*, ed. Uwe Andersen and Wichard Woyke (Opladen: Leske & Budrich, 1997), 482.

2.   A. J. Hingel, "The Prime Role of the Regional Cooperation in European Integration," in *Regional Networks, Border Regions and European Integration*, ed. R. Cappellin and P. W. J. Batey (London: Pion Limited, 1993); Joachim Jens Hesse, ed., *Regionen in Europa*, Vol. I and Vol. II (Baden-Baden: Nomos, 1996); Bernd Groß and Peter Schmitt-Egner, *Europas kooperierende Regionen—Rahmenbedingungen und Praxis transnationaler Zusammenarbeit deutscher Grenzregionen in Europa* (Baden-Baden: Nomos, 1994); Christopher Harvie, *The Rise of Regional Europe* (London: Routledge, 1994); Lynn A. Staeheli, Janet E. Kodras, and Colin Flint, eds., *State Devolution in America—Implications for a Diverse Society*, Urban Affairs Annual Review 48 (Thousand Oaks, CA: Sage, 1997).

addition, it will debate different contexts of research as they relate to political science, including the significance of the so-called "old" regionalism.[3] The main part of this paper deals with regionalism as a tool to analyze multilevel systems of decision-making and structural problems of governance.[4] Special attention is given to the capacity of a regionalism-centered research approach for comparative studies of cross-border cooperation in Europe and North America.[5]

The primary focus of the paper is on regionalism expressing the institutionalization of hierarchies within a political unity. Institutionalization can refer both to formal structures and to informal networks impacting political processes. Regionalism thus represents vertical and horizontal power divisions that indicate different spheres of influence. Such an understanding differs from the broader definition used in some political scientists' analysis[6] but seems the most useful in dealing with questions of governance. It allows research on the emergence of new political levels and actors within modern statehood and international relations and reflects recent literature on developments in Europe and North America. The main justification for the narrower definition lies in its capacity to relate to concepts and structures of federal, supra-and multinational decision-making, and to measure quantity and quality of political integration.

Different Concepts of Region and Regionalism in the Field of Political Science

In addition to the absence of a single dominant definition, political science research faces a second problem: There is no theoretical concept encompassing

---

3.   The term "old" regionalism indicates potentially violent protests against the state's core power structures; for further detail see below.

4.   Arthur Benz, Fritz W. Scharpf, and Reinhard Zintl, *Horizontale Politikverflechtung: Zur Theorie von Verhandlungssystemen* (Frankfurt a.M.: Campus, 1992); Dorothea Jansen, "Policy Networks and Change: The Case of High-Tech 'Superconductors'," in *Policy Networks: Empirical Evidence and Theoretical Considerations*, ed. Bernd Marin and Renate Mayntz (Frankfurt a.M.: Campus, 1991); Fritz W. Scharpf, "Politiknetzwerke als Steuerungssubjekte," in *Systemrationalität und Partialinteresse. Festschrift für Renate Mayntz*, ed. Hans-Ulrich Derlien, Uta Gerhardt, and Fritz W. Scharpf (Baden-Baden: Nomos, 1994).

5.   This paper discusses studies on regionalism in Europe and North America in regard to their specific theoretical approach and not as unique research areas. The various concepts, methodological approaches, and theoretical assumptions seem better represented in a context-dominated structure than in a geographical outline.

6.   Dietrich Fürst, "Region/Regionalismus," in *Lexikon der Politik*, Vol 1, *Politische Theorien*, ed. Dieter Nohlen (Munich: C. H. Beck, 1995).

regional phenomena in general.[7] Consequently, each area of research within the discipline has generated its own understanding and constructed a unique theoretical context. (For example, regionalism from an economically-driven approach is mostly understood as trading blocks formed by states within a certain geographic area, while in the context of political ideologies it is observed as a separatist movement.) Assumptions about intentions, actors, institutions, and frameworks change with the research focus.

To add to the confusion some scholars limit the term "regionalism" to regional movements initiated bottom-up, while top-down strategies to strengthen the incorporation of regional actors in decision-making processes are regarded as "regionalization."[8] Others distinguish between "regionalism" and "decentralization," viewing the former as a point of reference for reflections on political concepts and the latter as the application of theoretically developed regional policies. A specific form of regionalism (termed "old" regionalism in this paper) indicates the "politicalization of the provinces," [9] a synonym for (radical) political claims developed by subnational actors and / or entities. The term is most likely to be associated with demands expressed by its activists.[10]

To add to the confusion, definitions of the term "region" are as numerous as those of "regionalism" and offer a broad variety of possibilities in terms of theoretical potential and practical application. The term "region" is neither confined by the dimension of space nor by its relevance to a people's "identity."[11] Most often, the definition of region is linked to its practical context and/or subjectively composed to match an individual case study.[12] Since its unifying factor changes according to the frame of reference, once again only an exact definition and precise research question can guarantee the value of its research. Random use as a catchword (e.g., the proclaimed "Return of the Region" or the

---

7. Fürst, "Region/Regionalismus."

8. Fürst, "Region/Regionalismus," 540.

9. Dirk Gerdes, "Regionalpolitik/Regionalismus," in *Wörterbuch Staat und Politik*, ed. Dieter Nohlen (Bonn: Bundeszentrale für politische Bildung, 1995), 647; Franz Neumann, "Regionalismus," in *Gesellschaft und Staat: Lexikon der Politik*, ed. Hanno Drechsler (Munich: Franz Vahlen, 1995), 678.

10. Rainer-Olaf Schultze and Roland Sturm, "Regionalismus," in *Lexikon der Politik*, Vol. 3, *Die westlichen Länder*, ed. Dieter Nohlen (Munich: C. H. Beck, 1992).

11. Sturm, "Regionen," 645.

12. Schultze and Sturm, "Regionalismus," 405.

political slogan "Regional Competence vs. Brussels' Bureaucracy") renders the word virtually meaningless.[13]

The actual significance of "region" for research on governance is closely linked to the dynamics between a region's relevance to its inhabitants and its recognition on the macro level.[14] In other words, as long as "region" is experienced as an "imagined community" without structural consequences for the political, social, or economic order, the term is of little use for political science research. Conversely, the more constructed[15] a region is, the more clearly the actors' political competencies are defined, and the more pronounced institutional positions and intentions are—the more visible regions interact within the political system—the higher its research value is for determining governance structures.

In the following sections, regionalism is discussed within different research frameworks to help distinguish terminologies and approaches. To enhance understanding, practical examples are used where appropriate to highlight current German/European and North American research.

"Old" Regionalism

"Old" regionalism is a synonym for (violent) political emancipation processes away from the political unity of a state. It is regarded as a political movement that rises from below and aims at autonomy from superior political levels, or more generally as the 'politicalization of a subnational territorial framework.'[16] Motivations to cause such movements are multiple, including restriction of basic freedoms and oppression of cultural values that shape personal and regional identity (e.g. use of a language or religious freedom).

In its extreme form "old" regionalism emerges as a separatist movement, trying to abolish a state's inner and outer structures and thriving for independence. As a more subtle form, the generated feeling of unity in a region—due to a geographical condensation of certain cultural and linguistic characteristics—produces a lobbying movement striving for broader recognition

---

13.   A particularly devastating example of the careless application of the term "region" without accurate definition is the debate concerning the so-called "Europe of the Regions" or "Regional Europe" (*Europa der Regionen*). Such usages dominated the public debate on European integration in the early to mid 1990s [Rudolf Hrbek and Sabine Weynand, *Betrifft: Das Europa der Regionen: Fakten, Probleme, Perspektiven* (Munich: C. H. Beck, 1994), 9].

14.   Sturm, "Regionen," 646.

15.   Here the term "constructed" relates to a process of political institutionalization and differs from the definition associated with postmodernist debates.

16.   Fürst, "Region/Regionalismus," 540; Gerdes, "Regionalpolitik/Regionalismus," 648.

within the state.[17] This desire for growing independence is generally motivated by the negative dynamics between the center and the periphery.[18] The center of a state—and its elites—traditionally generate policies and dominate politics. Mainstream political, social, and economic values and belief systems are exported to the periphery, even though they often collide with the beliefs and necessities there. This can lead to a so-called 'internal colonization' which is reinforced if the periphery feels neglected in terms of economic development and long-term political investment.[19]

Rainer-Olaf Schultz and Roland Sturm define three factors for the emergence of "old" regionalism: socioeconomic and political development in the state structure that ignores traditional unities and traditions; a common regional culture; and a shared regional history.[20] A lack of regional representation within the state's decision-making processes also fuels dissatisfaction. Political science research regards "old" regionalism generally as a malfunction of the modern state, indicating shortcomings in satisfying essential needs and in providing services for its citizens.[21] In its milder forms the phenomenon is regarded as a compensation for a loss of trust in the governing powers of the state and as a resistance against the decline of identity.[22] It also has a territorial dimension, since it develops from within a geographically defined region and is a reaction to the existing power structures of a state.

Violent forms of "old" regionalism have generated a broad variety of analysis and dominated political science research on regionalism for a while. Some of the more progressive publications have been linked to historic-dialectic theory. From a neo-Marxist perspective, "old" regionalism is often regarded as a protest against the installation of capitalist systems.[23] Since it entails the "emancipation" of subnational actors from a "quasi-colonized status," many political activists have seen "old" regionalism as a desirable political goal and an inevitable reflection of structural blockades produced by

---

17. Langmann, "Regionen," 482.
18. Ibid.
19. Ibid.
20. Schultze and Sturm, "Regionalismus," 406.
21. Michael Keating, *State and Regional Nationalism* (New York: Harvester Wheatsheaf, 1988).
22. Renate Mayntz, "Föderalismus und die Gesellschaft der Gegenwart," in *Die Reformfähigkeit von Industriegesellschaften. Fritz W. Scharpf. Festschrift zu seinem 60. Geburtstag*, ed. Karlheinz Bentele, Bernd Reissert, and Ronald Schettkat (Frankfurt a.M.: Campus, 1995), 133.
23. Fürst, "Region/Regionalismus."

modern governance.[24] It is thus viewed both as a strategy and as an outcome to end long-term suppression. However, this center-periphery model fails to provide answers as to why some economically and culturally neglected regions develop separatist movements while others do not. Recent publications find that dissatisfaction has to be linked to specific programs and a social setting in order to produce a regional revolt.[25] In many cases, "old" regionalism and regional revolts are steered by two sets of actors: a popular—often illegal—movement and an official political party fighting for autonomy or even independence.

In the early 1990s, political science research renewed its 'political focus' on regionalism, this time as an indicator for increased European integration associated with a change of power structures within the member states. The gradual increase of subnational influence was believed to be accompanied with a weakening of superior political levels. Thus, the term regionalism became for a short while a synonym for the decline of the (nation) states within the EU.[26] Some researchers even considered the historic role of the state as fulfilled, labeling it a 'dispensable troublemaker' for the integration process.[27] More recent research on Europe, however, has altered this perspective and focused more on networks of decision-making within the supranational context, [28] as will be discussed later on.

Even though the phenomena of "old" regionalism—both in its stronger and in its more moderate forms—is still alive, it does not reflect dominant political developments in Europe and North America. Nor does it reflect current research perspectives. On the contrary, "new" regionalism has gained attention as subnational levels compete for more pronounced political roles within federal systems. Today's regionalism includes identification with and acceptance of the state's political structures as a given. Plus, it has adapted to supranational and multinational entities as the new relevant frameworks for political action: In the European Union pressure from subnational levels has resulted in the institutionalization of the "Committee of the Regions." In North America pressure from public interest groups and regional actors has

24. Fürst, "Region/Regionalismus," 541.
25. Groß and Schmitt-Egner, *Europas kooperierende Regionen*, 15–17.
26. Elisabeth Fix, *Niedergang des Nationalstaates? Zur konstitutiven Rolle des nation-building für die Genese von Regionalismen* (Frankfurt a.M.: Lang, 1991).
27. Peter-Christian Müller-Graf, "Die europäischen Regionen in der Verfassung der EG," *Integration* 3 (1997).
28. Ursula Männle, "Grundlagen und Gestaltungsmöglichkeiten des Föderalismus in Deutschland," *Aus Politik und Zeitgeschichte*, B 24/1997, Beilage zur Wochenzeitung *Das Parlament*, Bonn, 3–11.

guaranteed their inclusion in trilateral NAFTA-organizations and shaped the trilateral agenda.[29] Finally, regionalism as a top-down instrument to encourage decentralization processes has gained importance in systems undergoing political and economic transformation such as Poland or Mexico.[30]

Region and Regionalism as Synonyms for International Trading Blocs

A different research approach focuses on the region as an economically integrated zone that links political units either through trading patterns and interdependencies or through formal agreements.[31] Regional policies either formalize already existing trading patterns or aim to initiate a more active economic interchange. Accordingly, this approach uses the study of regionalism either to examine the global market in general (with or without acknowledging the role political directions play) or to focus on the nature of multi- and supranational formal trade agreements.[32]

Most recently, research attention has shifted to Foreign Direct Investment (FDI) as a complementary factor to determine economic linkages within and between trading zones.[33] The units in question are generally either states or larger subnational entities with a strong economic or industrial basis. Here, the concept of regionalism is based on increased economic interaction and the exchange of ideas, goods, capital, and people.

To associate regionalism with an economic rather than a political interconnection has become increasingly popular within the framework of

---

29.   Hesse, *Regionen in Europa*. Extended research on the impact subnational levels have had on the formulation of NAFTA-related agreements is published in *Naminews*, an online-magazine published by The North American Institute.

30.   These conclusions are based on interviews conducted with local experts in 1999–2000 along the German-Polish and the United States-Mexican borders; see Andrea Witt, *Die deutsch-polnische und die US-mexikanische Grenze–grenzueberschreitende Zusammenarbeit zwischen regionaler Identitaet, nationaler Prioritaet und transkontinentaler Integration* (http://dochost.rz.hu-berlin.de/dissertationen/witt-andrea-2003-07-08/HTML/).

31.   Jürgen Bellers and Wichard Woyke, eds., *Analyse internationaler Beziehungen* (Opladen, Germany: Leske & Budrich, 1989); Kym Anderson and Richard Blackhurst, eds., *Regional Integration and the Global Trading System* (Hertfordshire: Harvester Wheatsheaf, 1993).

32.   Dieter Nohlen, "Region/Regionalpolitik," in *Lexikon der Politik*, Vol. 7, *Politische Begriffe*, ed. Dieter Nohlen (Munich: C. H. Beck, 1998).

33.   Daniel S. Hamilton and Joseph P. Quinlan, *Partners in Prosperity: The Changing Geography of the Transatlantic Economy* (Washington, DC: Center for Transatlantic Relations, 2004).

globalization.[34] As a significant element of international relations, it is generally discussed in a macroeconomic setting. Trading blocs are examined in terms of their competitive advantages and disadvantages.[35] Economic regions such as the European Union, the North American Free Trade Agreement (NAFTA) or the Association of South East Asian Nations (ASEAN) are studied both in respect to the specifics of their trading agreements and based on the underlying integration philosophy.[36]

Here, regionalism is used to illustrate the institutionalization of economic linkages due to the international market economy. Even though economically linked regions are normally geographically connected, the territorial dimension loses its importance. Traditional interaction and sociocultural connections are helpful but not necessary for the emergence of economic regions. Linkages between economically potent subunits can emerge without a traditional basis, as has been the case in Europe.[37] This specific form of economic regionalism relies heavily on distinct political decisions and aims to integrate traditionally nonpolitical actors, such as the private sector.

In the case of the European Union and NAFTA, the motivation to form economic trading zones connects economic goals and distinct political aims.[38] As economic cooperation has the power to spark political action and vice versa, political scientists debate cause and effect of such regionalism. This debate is

34. Seyom Brown, *International Relations in a Changing Global System: Towards a Theory of the World Polity* (Boulder: Westview, 1992); Ernst-Otto Czempiel, *Weltpolitik im Umbruch* (Munich: Beck, 1993).

35. Lee Bahrin Boon-Thang and Shamsul Tengku, eds., *Vanishing Borders: The New International Order of the 21st Century* (Brookfield, VT: Ashgate, 1998); Harvie, *Rise of Regional Europe*.

36. Alice Enders, "The Europe Agreements and NAFTA: A Comparison of Their Ends and Means," *IPG* 3 (1996): 254–265; Karl Kaiser, "Globalisierung als Problem der Demokratie," *Internationale Politik* 4 (1998): 3–11.

37. An example of cooperation between regions without historic ties is the concept "Vier Motoren für Europa" (Four Engines for Europe), which unites the economically potent regions of Baden-Württemberg (Germany), Catalonia (Spain), Rhônes-Alpes (France), and Lombardy (Italy). Other forms of interregional cooperation within the European Union focus mainly on political lobbying such as the *Versammlung der Regionen Europas* (Assembly of European Regions).

38. Even though the political ambitions of the European Union as expressed in the Maastricht treaty are more obvious, NAFTA also has a political dimension. The ratification of NAFTA has guaranteed that the United States has a lasting influence on Mexico's domestic policies and politics. The extent to which economic interaction can motivate political action was documented in the billion-dollar aid program President Bill Clinton has provided after the Mexican peso crisis in 1994. NAFTA side agreements also linked trading issues with labor standards and environmental concerns.

closely linked to different theoretical concepts, namely a "neofunctionalist"[39] versus a "neorealist" or "intergovernmental" framework[40] and has gained momentum in reference to the ongoing political and economic integration of the European Union within the 1990s. Following a "neofunctional" approach, nonpolitical actors and the private sector are regarded as the deciding forces for economic and political interaction. In contrast, "intergovernmentalists" believe that European political and economic integration has strengthened federal and national executives. They deny a lasting shift of power to the non-political or local/regional and supranational spheres.

Other analysts focus on the implications trading blocs have beyond state structures and democratic transparency.[41] Such studies link economic issues with social integration and international relations with domestic issues, while considering the general trend of globalization as the major influence for any future international agreement.[42] Here, the traditional sovereignty of the state is perceived as an insufficient tool for modern challenges as it has long been surpassed by international businesses, which act as a strong influence in directing the development of transnational regional cooperation.[43] Options and scope of political steering are debated in contrast to the influence of multinational companies or transnationally active nongovernmental organizations (NGOs). Globalization as a whole is viewed as the main impulse for interconnection between states and societies. This research often focuses on "complex interdependencies"[44] between the political and economic sphere: How do regions function that are de-facto borderless for trading purposes and

39.   Wolfgang Schumann, "Vorlesung: Theorien regionaler Integration" (2000, http://www.politik-international.de/vl_integrationstheorie.htm); Beate Kohler-Koch and Martin Schmidberger, "Integrationstheorien," in *Die Europäische Union*, ed. Beate Kohler-Koch and Wichard Woyke (München, Germany: C. H. Beck, 1996), 152–162.

40.   Andrew Moravcsik, "Warum die Europäische Union die Exekutive stärkt: Innenpolitik und internationale Kooperation," in *Projekt Europa im Übergang? Probleme, Modelle und Strategien des Regierens in der Europäischen Union,* ed. Klaus Dieter Wolf (Baden-Baden: Nomos, 1997), 219–277.

41.   David Held, *Democracy and the Global Order: From the Modern State to Cosmopolitan Governance* (Cambridge, MA: Polity Press, 1995); Kaiser, "Globalisierung als Problem der Demokratic."

42.   Allan Rosas, "The Decline of Sovereignty: Legal Perspectives," in *The Future of the Nation State in Europe*, ed. Jyrki Iivonen (Brookfield: Edward Elgar, 1993).

43.   Markus Jachtenfuchs, "Die Europäische Union—ein Gebilde sui generis?" in *Projekt Europa im Übergang?*

44.   Dirk Messner, "Architektur der Weltordnung. Strategien zur Lösung globaler Pobleme," *Internationale Politik* 11 (1998) (http://www.uni-duisburg.de/Institute/INEF/lehre/messner_ss01~1/InternationalePolitik.doc); Robert O. Keohane and Joseph S. Nye, "Globalization:

at the same time experiencing a redrawing of internal and external political borders—as is the case in Europe and in the NAFTA area?[45]

Region and Regionalism as Synonyms for Administrative Functions

A different definition acknowledges a region as a subnational state entity with a distinct administrative function and accompanying tasks.[46] Regions in this sense are normally constructed and formalized within a political system, though they may also rise from voluntary cooperation between communities to better facilitate local tasks. Administrative duties, economic development and planning purposes motivate such delimitation of responsibilities. In itself this provides no information about who has responsibility for services, about the division of political competency, or to what end regions are setting the agenda within the political unity.[47] Also, the set-up of such regional units does not adhere to a uniform dividing pattern. Administrative orders may change constantly, and they often are drawn by coincidence or based on traditions rather than on political reasoning. The complexity of such a division is visible within American federalism. In the United States regional administrative units consist of entities as diverse as counties, municipal cooperation, and special districts. They differ in size and competency not only among states but sometimes also within one state.[48] In Germany, regions as planning units for spatial development are situated between the local level and the states (*Bundesländer*)[49] and coordinate local initiatives. Special financial funds and compensation mechanisms aimed at a cohesive regional development try to provide equivalent standards of

---

What's New? What's Not (And So What?)," *Foreign Policy* (spring 2000): 104–119 (http://fparchive.ceip.org/archive/118/whatsnew-whatsnot.pdf).

45.   Andrea Witt, "National Borders: Images, Functions, and Their Effects on Cross-Border Cooperation in North America and Europe," in *Caught in the Middle: Border Communities in an Era of Globalization,* ed. Demetri Papademetriou and Deborah Waller Meyers (Washington, DC: Brookings Institution Press, 2001), 166–199.

46.   Functions include regional control over fundamental services such as water and telephone providers and the jurisdiction of a police department.

47.   Berhard Thibaut, "Region/Regionalpolitik," in *Lexikon der Politik*, Vol. 7, 550.

48.   James Q. Wilson, *American Government: Institutions and Policies* (Lexington, MA: D. C. Heath and Company, 1989); Arthur B. Gunlicks, "Die Grundzüge der einzelstaatlichen Regierungssysteme," in *Regierungssystem der USA*, ed. Wolfgang Jäger and Wolfgang Welz (Munich: R. Oldenbourg, 1998).

49.   In other European countries the regional level is directly located between local and central actors.

living as required in the federal constitution.[50] In this context, regional policy is understood as an intervention strategy influencing structural data in order to achieve a balanced regional development.[51] To that end regionalism is a comprehensive political goal for the entire state binding local, regional, and federal actors in specific coordination patterns.[52]

Research focusing on this specific form of regionalism is broad and crosses disciplinary lines.[53] Political geographers deal with the impact of spatial planning and infrastructural challenges.[54] Legal experts analyze the relationships among local, regional, and federal or state actors in regard to the constitutional framework.[55] Political scientists have increasingly focused on regional planning and development activities as it is performed in an international environment. It is here that the process of European integration demands the most attention.[56] Based on the notion that infrastructural planning and economic well-being in border communities are strongly interdependent, integrated concepts of transboundary cooperation have gained importance within the research community.[57] Analyzing regional cross-border cooperation also unites researchers from various fields:[58] Legal experts focus on questions of

---

50.   The European Union also committed itself to obtaining regional balance by fostering economic and regional coherence. For an elaborate evaluation of European regionalism see Witt, *Die deutsch-polnische und die US-mexikanische Grenze*, 67–72.

51.   Gerdes, "Regionalpolitik/Regionalismus," 645.

52.   Witt, *Die deutsch-polnische und die US-mexikanische Grenze,* 87–88.

53.   Alan D. Burnett and Peter J. Taylor, eds., *Political Studies from Spatial Perspectives: Anglo-American Essays on Political Geography* (Chicester: John Wiley & Sons, 1981).

54.   Peter Nijkamp, ed., *New Borders and Old Barriers in Spatial Development* (Aldershot, UK: Ashgate, 1994); Jörg Maier, ed., "Netzwerke in der Kommunal- und Regionalpolitik," *Arbeitsmaterialien zur Raumordnung und Regionalplanung*, Heft 150, 1996.

55.   Christoph Mecking, *Die Regionalebene in Deutschland: Begriff—Institutionaller Bestand—Perspektiven* (Stuttgart: Boorberg, 1995); Eckart Meyberg, *Auslandsrelevantes Verhalten auf Gemeindeebene—Grundlagen und Grenzen aus verfassungrechtlicher Sicht.* Juristische Dissertationsschrift (Tübingen: StuWe-Druck, 1990).

56.   Hrbek and Weynand, *Betrifft*; Groß and Schmitt-Egner, *Europas kooperierende Regionen.*

57.   The fields of decentralized cross-border cooperation include common needs such as access to water and waste water facilities, shared economic tasks, and sociocultural events; for a more detailed elaboration see Witt, *Die deutsch-polnische und die US-mexikanische Grenze.*

58.   Ivo Duchacek, *The Territorial Dimension of Politics: Within, among, and across Nations* (London: Westview Press; 1986); S. Erçman, *Cross-Border Relations: European and North American Perspectives* (Zürich: Schulthess Polygraphischer Verlag, 1987); James W. Scott, "Dutch-German Euroregions: A Model for Transboundary Cooperation," in *Border Regions in Function Transition: European and North American Perspectives*, ed. James Scott, Alan

national sovereignties and their impact on subnational cooperation.[59] Political geographers develop transnational infrastructural concepts.[60] Economists study the costs of transaction and consider the benefits and disadvantages of economic cooperation between states with strong differences in economic performance.[61] The Maquiladora industry in northern Mexico is one example a of economic policy with regional and state-wide cross-border influences that offers vast insights into interdependent political and economic linkages for political scientists, economists, human rights activists, and ecologists alike, to name only a few of the disciplines involved.[62]

Regionalism As a Method to Analyze New Forms of Governance

Political regionalism within a federalist framework acknowledges that both central and subnational actors hold responsibilities within the multilevel political system. In that sense, regionalism defines the degree of political decentralization in a system, reflecting both top-down policies and bottom-up movements. The conditions of interaction between stakeholders and the balance of power differ according to the specifics of the given system. Regionalism can serve both as an indicator of dominant power structures and as an explanation for the patterns of cooperation in a specific context. Regionalism as directly linked to the nature of a political system has special relevance for political science research dealing with questions of political steering. Focusing on regionalism is fruitful for the analysis of internal decision-making processes and for an international comparison of federal systems. Since regionalism

Sweedler, Paul Ganster, and Wolf-Dieter Eberwein (Erkner, Germany: Institute for Regional Development and Structural Planning, 1996); Oscar J. Martinez, ed., *Across Boundaries: Transborder Interaction in Comparative Perspective* (El Paso, TX: Texas Western, 1986); Dennis Rumley and Julian V. Minghi, *The Geography of Border Landscapes* (London: Routledge, 1991).

59.   Matthias Oehm, *Rechtsprobleme Staatsgrenzen überschreitender interkommunaler Zusammenarbeit* (Münster: Institut für Siedlungs- und Wohnungswesen, 1982); Horst Christoph Heberlein, *Kommunale Außenpolitik als Rechtsproblem* (Cologne: W. Kohlhammer, 1989); Ulrich Beyerlin, *Rechtsprobleme der lokalen grenzüberschreitenden Zusammenarbeit* (Heidelberg: Springer, 1988).

60.   Yehuda Gradus and Harvey Lithwick, eds., *Frontiers in Regional Development* (Boston, MA: Rowman & Littlefield, 1996).

61.   Sidney Weintraub, "In the Debate about NAFTA, Just the Facts Please," *Wall Street Journal*, 20 June 1997.

62.   Multidisciplinary research on the United States-Mexico border with a strong focus on the Maquiladora industry is published in the online-magazine *Borderlines* at http://www.americaspolicy.org/borderlines.

reflects both constitutional frameworks and political processes, it also helps to explain the gaps among the theoretically defined legal structure of government, the actual procedures of governance, and their final outcomes.

Regionalism offers several research perspectives for the study of governance. As it reflects dominant organizational principles of a political system, it demonstrates a state of being. A region as a constructed subnational entity within the state holds clearly defined rights and responsibilities. Their nature, appearance, and competences, however, reflect the contexts of space and time, since their degree of uniformity differs between systems and changes constantly. In that regard regionalism as an analytic tool helps to locate and define the position regions hold at a certain time within a certain federal system.

Another research perspective may use regionalism to analyze how policies and directives are merged into the regional political agenda and how they will convert into regional reality. Here, horizontal partnerships between political and nonpolitical actors play a crucial role for the set-up of regional policy-circles. Vertical partnerships are also visible as regionalism binds federal and subnational actors together in a common policy goal.[63]

On a different level, regionalism can indicate a normative development, e.g. in the acclaimed "European regionalization." Perceived as a process—from the verbalization to the political recognition of subnational interests—regionalism can be initiated by various factors. As the result of a top-down decentralization, it symbolizes the pursuit of a dominant political philosophy pursued by central decision makers. At the same time, regionalism may be initiated by a bottom-up approach. Such public campaigns may have different motivations, one being an attempt to achieve official acknowledgment of the region as a political entity based on the experience of it as an imagined community.[64] Such regionalism would be an indicator of a well developed civil society.[65] Even though the different initiating processes often produce an equivalent degree of decentralization, potential conflict arises when the boundaries drawn by a top-down regionalization differ from the ones imagined. The motivation to live

---

63. See section *Regions and Regionalism as Synonyms for Administrative Functions.*

64. In order for a society—or parts of a society—to push for the political institutionalization of a region, the notion of connectedness has to be a rather strong form of "imagined community." Here, region is probably already experienced as a substantial political community including social, cultural, and economic links.

65. Very often, however, bottom-up activities in Europe are motivated by economic interest and goals.

up to such a regionalism varies accordingly depending on who initiated the process.

For comparative research on European and North America it seems useful to employ regionalism as a method to gain new insights into the degree of federalism or decentralization in a society at a given time. It is not surprising that regionalism as the institutionalization of political hierarchies is one of the major yardsticks for political science research to systematize governmental styles and political systems. In the United States labels such as "picket-fence," "marble cake," or "new federalism" as well as the contested concept of "devolution," publicly supported by the Republicans in 1994, all refer to the balance of power between the federal government and subnational political levels.[66] The same holds true for research on Europe: Present and future characteristics of European integration are regularly determined according to the relationship between the supranational institutions, the state, and subnational regions within various European organizations and institutions.[67] Accordingly, regionalism is a very useful tool for comparative research, measuring both the degree of integration achieved within a political system and the degree of integration intended or desired.

Regionalism As an Approach to Define Structural Problems of Political Steering and New Decision-Making Processes in Europe

In regard to questions of political steering, political science analysis is driven by the following questions: Who decides what, why, when, and how— and does it matter? Recent research agrees that political decisions are made by a multitude of political and nonpolitical actors from different levels and

---

66.   Jeffrey M. Elliot and Sheikh R. Ali, *The State and Local Government Political Dictionary* (Santa Barbara, CA: ABC-CLIO, 1988); David C. Nice, "The Intergovernmental Setting of State-Local Relations," in *Governing Partners: State-Local Relations in the United States*, ed. Russell L. Hanson (Boulder, CO: Westview, 1998); John Ferejohn and Barry R. Weingast, eds., *The New Federalism: Can the States Be Trusted?* (Stanford, CA: Hoover Institution, 1997); Staeheli, Kodras, and Flint, *State Devolution*.

67.   Heidrun Abromeit, "Überlegungen zur Demokratisierung der Europäischen Union," in *Projekt Europa im Übergang?*; Volker Eichener and Helmut Voelzkow, "Europäische Integration und verbandliche Interessenvermittlung: Ko-Evolution von politisch-administrativem System und Verbändelandschaft," in *Europäische Integration und verbandliche Interessenvermittlung*, ed. Volker Eichener and Helmut Voelzkow (Marburg, Germany: Metropolisverlag, 1994); Michael Keating and John Loughlin, eds., *The Political Economy of Regionalism* (London: Frank Cass, 1997); Fritz W. Scharpf, "Mehrebenenpolitik im vollendeten Binnenmarkt," *MPIFG Discussion Paper* 4/94 (Cologne: Max-Planck-Institut für Gesellschaftsforschung, 1994).

sectors.[68] Researchers are focusing beyond performance, and also on different structures of governance.[69] Analyzing regionalism is a useful tool here. In federal systems—such as those of Germany or the United States—an integrated style of governance is based on a constitutional framework. One distinguishes between institutionalized constraints on cooperation (e.g. based on the notion of a dual federalism such as defined in the German constitution for specific policy fields) and voluntary cooperation (e.g. between or among American states, German *Bundesländer*, communities, or counties).[70]

Many political scientists regard voluntary coalitions as a reaction to structural blockades caused by integrated forms of governance and resulting in inefficiency.[71] Fritz Scharpf sees here a "joint decision trap," related to the structures of cooperative federalism. This leads to a "muddling through," forcing the various political levels and actors to constantly form new coalitions.[72] One answer to such blockades can be voluntary interaction between local and regional stakeholders as a middle- and long-term political strategy.[73] Regional coalitions are often introduced "in response to a growing dispersion of resources and capacities for action among public and private actors."[74] The formation of private-public partnerships has special relevance for economic development and brings together traditionally separated policy fields and actors to promote the economic well-being of the region. Horizontal cooperation between regions and communities is also regarded as a successful instrument for lobbying.[75]

---

68.   Franz Urban Pappi, *Entscheidungsprozesse in der Arbeits- und Sozialpolitik: Der Zugang der Interessengruppen zum Regierungssystem über Politiknetzwerke—ein deutsch-amerikanischer Vergleich*. Frankfurt a.M.: Campus, 1995).

69.   Beate Kohler-Koch, "Interessen und Integration: Die Rolle organisierter Interessen im westeuropäischen Integrationsprozeß," in *Die Integration Europas*, ed. Michael Kreile (Opladen, Germany: Westdeutscher Verlag, 1992).

70.   Fritz W. Scharpf, "Einführung: Zur Theorie von Verhandlungssystemen," in *Horizontale Politikverflechtung—Zur Theorie von Verhandlungssystemen*, ed. Arthur Benz, Fritz W, Scharpf, and Reinhard Zintl (Frankfurt a.M.: Campus, 1992), 63.71.   Scharpf, "Einführung: Zur Theorie von Verhandlungssystemen," 13.

72.   Karlheinz Bentele, Bernd Reissert, and Ronald Schettkat, eds., *Die Reformfähigkeit von Industriegesellschaften. Fritz W. Scharpf. Festschrift zu seinem 60. Geburtstag* (Frankfurt a.M.: Campus, 1995); Heidrun Abromeit, *Interessenvermittlung zwischen Konkurrenz und Konkordanz. Studienbuch zur Vergleichenden Lehre politischer Systeme* (Opladen, Germany: Leske & Budrich, 1993).

73.   Maier, "Netzwerke in der Kommunal- und Regionalpolitik."

74.   Bernd Marin and Renate Mayntz, eds., *Policy Networks: Empirical Evidence and Theoretical Considerations* (Frankfurt a.M.: Campus, 1991), 19.

75.   Benz, Scharpf, and Zintl, *Horizontale Politikverflechtung*, 192.

Regionalism as a top-down approach is of special concern for the European Union. It is a strong feature within European policy-making, both from a conceptual as well as from a more formal perspective. As a result, many studies focus on regionalism and its significance within the European Union. Special attention is given to the structures of European networks and the position regions have within them.[76] Regionalism is analyzed first as the ability of regional actors to form transnational links with each other. The European multilevel system is then examined according to the chances it opens for new horizontal coalitions.[77] This is of lasting interest, since European decision-making consists of multidimensional structures with dynamic character which are constantly changing competences and institutional framework.[78]

For the European Commission, regionalism is an integrated concept of governance which is used to balance deficits of national decision-making and to pursue social and economic cohesion throughout the Union as manifested in the Maastricht contract and its successors. However, such a forced top-down regionalism is potentially dangerous. Rupert Aigner sees a tendency to implement local and regional plans designed by the European Commission without consideration for subsidiarity and special regional situations.[79] Forced regionalism might exclude vital actors and/or lack the convincing power for long-term commitments as well. Plus, by providing regional funds the European Commission acquires further influence over regional competencies and a new tool to promote its own interests. This phenomenon is also visible in the United States, where devolutionary processes often combine a cut of federal funding with a surplus of regional financial responsibility. In addition, U.S. Congress's recent tendency to earmark financial programs for special purposes within the states conflicts with subnational independence.[80] However,

76.   Dorothea Jansen and Klaus Schubert, eds., *Netzwerke und Politikproduktion: Konzepte, Methoden, Perspektiven* (Marburg: Schüren, 1995).

77.   Jansen, "Policy Networks and Change"; Adrienne Héritier, "Innovationsmechanismen europäischer Politik: Regulativer Wettbewerb und neue Koalitionsmöglichkeiten in europäischen Politiknetzwerken," in *Netzwerke und Politikproduktion: Konzepte, Methoden, Perspektiven*, ed. Dorothea Jansen and Klaus Schubert (Marburg, Germany: Schüren, 1995).

78.   Klaus Dieter Wolf, ed., *Projekt Europa im Übergang? Probleme, Modelle und Strategien des Regierens in der Europäischen Union* (Baden-Baden: Nomos, 1997), 18; Jachtenfuchs, "Die Europäische Union," 17.

79.   Rupert Aigner, "Städtenetze im oberzentralen Bereich—das Beispiel LaRoSa," in *Netzwerke in der Kommunal- und Regionalpolitik, Vorträge im Rahmen des Kolloquiums vom 10. November 1995, Europäische Akademie Bayern und Universität Bayreuth Arbeitsmaterialien zur Raumordnung und Regionalplanung*, ed. Jörg Maier, Heft 150, 1996.

80.   Staeheli, Kodras, and Flint, *State Devolution*.

top-down regionalism as experienced within the EU also offers chances for increased subnational influences beyond the financial benefits attached to it: New steering procedures introduce regional actors to different federal and supranational stakeholders and create new networks of decision-making, thus allowing lasting regional inclusion into emerging European systems of governance.

The flexibility of regionalism has advantages since organizations such as the EU rely on flexibility to strike a balance between a broad framework and the duty to stick to subsidiarity.[81] This should enable decision makers to define complex policy goals with ultimate authority while allowing subordinated levels space to find individual solutions tailored to the specific situation. Within the European Union regionalism is directed toward already existing subnational units within the member states, since the supranational level has no legal basis to establish new local or regional entities.[82] Accordingly, regional policies address heterogeneous levels regarding competencies, shape, and nature. This strategy allows a formalization of the different sublevels in respect to European regional policy without interfering with the member state's traditional understanding of regionalism. Thus, subnational actors are unified in regard to their European role and position even though their national functions differ considerably.[83]

Research on Cross-Border Cooperation to Reveal New Decision-Making Structures

Transboundary cooperation as a specific subtext of regionalism has great potential for research dealing with new forms of governance. This is especially true for comparative analysis focusing on integrative concepts that have developed in Europe and North America. In both cases, new patterns of decision-making evolved that cannot be examined by traditional methods of

---

81.   This paper will not discuss the specifics of subsidiarity and its implications for European governance. However, research on subsidiarity is broad and differs strongly, concerning its relevance, actual application and effectivness.

82.   Sturm, "Regionen," 646; Müller-Graff, "Die europäischen Regionen," 147.

83.   The pragmatic understanding of regionalism is reflected within the membership of the Committee of the Regions. Here, German *Bundesländer* as constitutional federal actors are united with Greek and Portuguese mayors [Udo Bullmann, ed., *Die Politik der dritten Ebene* (Baden-Baden: Nomos, 1994); R. Hrbek, *Die Reform der Europäischen Union: Positionen und Perspektiven anlässlich der Regierungskonferenz* (Baden-Baden: Nomos, 1997)].

political science.[84] Multi- and supranational politics are becoming increasingly sectionalized in a way traditionally only associated with internal policy making.[85] Accordingly, it is increasingly important to understand that specific fields of policy are unique in terms of their structures and actors.[86] One solution is for researchers to focus on a limited field, recognizing that the subject they choose defines the political level, structures of interaction, and potential coalitions with other policy fields. Regional transboundary cooperation is such a clearly defined field combining a set agenda, a limited number of actors, and a territorial area. Plus, relevant actors experience this field of policy as an empirical social system.

For political science the regional phenomenon of transboundary cooperation has significance beyond its administrative impact. The significance stems from vertical and horizontal partnerships that have to be formed both within each nation and across the border. Depending on the research approach, transboundary regionalism can be used to examine different legal frameworks for policy making, the overall willingness of states to promote integrated regional development, the state of binational relations—both on the central and subnational level—and the region's ability to participate successfully in binational or supranational structures. It also helps to redefine questions of influence and power within this clearly defined political agenda: Is the state with its sovereign powers still responsible for the emergence of integrated structures, or have the private sector and nonpolitical interdependencies taken over that role? In short, regional transboundary cooperation offers new insights into the three main areas of political science analysis—the issue, the institutional framework, and the actual process of decision-making.

Recent studies in this field have examined transregional cooperation in regard to a possible change of patterns within international relations.[87] Other studies ask to what extent a region can act as a full-fledged international

---

84.   While the European Union with its supranational organizations and multilevel structures obviously indicates the more pronounced change of governance, the ratification of NAFTA and its side agreements also provides a potential for change of power structures in regard to regional participation [Wolf, *Projekt Europa im Übergang?*].

85.   Wolfgang Schumann, "Vorlesung: Theorien regionaler Integration."

86.   Eichener and Voelzkow, "Europäische Integration und verbandliche Interessenvermittlung," 20.

87.   Joachim Blatter, *Entgrenzung der Staatenwelt? Politische Institutionenbildung in grenzüberschreitenden Regionen in Europa und Nordamerika* (Ph.D. diss., Martin-Luther-Universität Halle-Wittenberg, 1998).

actor.[88] The motives for the emergence of bilateral and international decision-making networks and their strategies within a context of regional cooperation are examined as well.[89] A dominant area deals with transboundary interaction as a result of European integration. Such research is a subfield of research focusing on the general role regionalism plays within the European Union. The legal and political role of cross-border regions, their representation, reasons for the European Commission to support interregional cooperation, and the impact regional funds have for cross-border cooperation are examined in interdisciplinary research.[90]

Research in North American, specifically on cross-border cooperation between the United States and Mexico has traditionally analyzed the impact of informal local and regional contacts.[91] The dynamics of local cooperation in the border region and of the relationship between Washington, DC, and Mexico City have been studied by scientists, policy makers, and local experts alike.[92] Since the ratification of NAFTA, research on regionalism has shifted

---

88.   Pertti Joenniemi, "Interregional Cooperation and a New Regional Paradigm," in *Border Regions in Functional Transition: European and North American Perspectives*, ed. James Scott, Alan Sweedler, Paul Ganster, and Wolf-Dieter Eberwein (Erkner: Institute for Regional Development and Structural Planning,1996); Malcolm Anderson, "The Political Science of Frontiers," in *Border Regions in Functional Transition*.

89.   Beck, *Netzwerke in der transnationalen Regionalpolitik*; Markus Perkmann, "Die Welt der Netzwerke," *Politische Vierteljahreszeitschrift* 39 (1998): 870–883.

90.   Oliver Schwab, "Euroregionen an der deutsch-ponischen Grenze—gefangen im Politik- und Verwaltungsnetz?" *Raumplanung und Raumordnung* 55 (1997): 4–13; James W. Scott and Kimberly Collins, "Inducing Transboundary Regionalism in Asymmetric Situations: The Case of the German-Polish Border," *Journal of Borderlands Studies* XII (1997): 97–121; Hesse, *Regionen in Europa*.

91.   Since this border is likely the best researched in the world (Herzog 1996), the following discussion can only give a brief introduction to the richness of research on regionalism and interregional cooperation in North America [Oscar J. Martínez, *Border Boom Town: Ciudad Juárez since 1848* (Austin: University of Texas, 1978); Martínez, *Across Boundaries*; Paul Ganster and Alan Sweedler, *The United States-Mexican Border Region: Essays on Strategy and Diplomacy* (Claremont, CA: The Keck Center for International Strategic Studies, 1988)].

92.   Peter Andreas, "Escalation of U.S. Immigration Control in the Post-NAFTA Era," *Political Science Quarterly* 113 (1998–1999): 591–615; M. Delal Baer, "Obstacles and Progress in Bilateral Cooperation: The Sovereignty and Institutional Capacity Dilemma," Address before the United States Senate Caucus on International Narcotics Control, given by the Director and Senior Fellow, Mexico Project, Center for Strategic and International Studies, Washington, D.C., February 24, 1999 (http://www.csis.org/hill/ts990224b.html); Arizona, California, New Mexico, and Texas Advisory Committees, *Federal Immigration Law Enforcement in the Southwest. Civil Rights Impacts on Border Communities,* Report to the United States Commission on Civil Rights, March 1997; Tom Barry, Harry Browne, and Beth

toward the emergence of a North American community, the degree of public participation, and the impact NAFTA has had on the border region in general.[93] With the NAFTA side-agreement on the environmental development of the United States-Mexico border, a new concept of binational funds for regional development has been introduced in North America.[94] Experts from different fields examine the impact such funds have on infrastructural planning and transboundary cooperation in the border region and the general state of binational relations.[95]

Evidently, political science research on transboundary cooperation is challenged to apply research perspectives and instruments capable of reflecting and processing the inner dynamics typical for cross-border collaboration. Here, regionalism has indeed offered valuable insights into new patterns of participation, structural set-ups and innovative policy contexts revealing emerging forms of governance significant far beyond the individual border region.

Sims, *Crossing the Line: Immigrants, Economic Integration, and Drug Enforcement on the U.S.-Mexico Border* (Albuquerque: Resource Center, 1994).

93.   Sanford Gaines, "Citizenship and Civil Society: The Merging North American Community at the Local Level," *Naminews* 21 (1998); Michelle A. Saint-German, "Re-Presenting the Public Interest on the U.S.-Mexico Border," in *The U.S.-Mexico Border: Transcending Divisions, Contesting Identities,* ed. David Spener and Kathleen Staudt (Boulder, CO: Lynne Rienner, 1998); Mathias Albert and Lothar Brock, "New Relationships Between Territory and State: The U.S.-Mexico Border in Perspective," in *The U.S.-Mexico Border: Transcending Divisions, Contesting Identities*; Susan Kaufman Purcell, "The Changing Nature of US-Mexican Relations," *Journal of Interamerican Studies & World Affairs* 39 (1997): 137–152.

94.   Paul Ganster and Eugenio O. Valenciano, eds., *The Mexican-U.S. Border Region and the Free Trade Agreement* (San Diego: San Diego State University, 1992).

95.   Juan Carlos Belausteguigoitia and Luis F. Guadarrama, "United States-Mexico Relations: Environmental Issues," in *Coming Together? Mexico-United States Relations,* ed. Barry Bosworth, Susan M. Collins, and Nora Claudia Lustig (Washington, DC: Brookings Institution, 1997); Richard Kiy and John D. Wirth, eds., *Environmental Management on North America's Borders* (College Station, TX: Texas A&M University, 1998); Nora Lustig, "NAFTA: Setting the Record Straight," Policy Brief # 20, The Brookings Institution, June 1997 (http://www.brook.edu/comm/policybriefs/pb20.htm).

5

Toward a Progressive Sense of Region: Situating Anthropological Research in Space and Time[1]

Thaddeus C. Guldbrandsen

Contemporary anthropologists have called for a fundamental questioning of the discipline's "sacred categories" of *community, region, area study,* and *culture area*, all of which are considered to be terms in transition or else imminent obsolescence.[2] Over the past four decades anthropologists have increasingly moved beyond simple notions of community as a unit of study.[3] As anthropological research has come to focus on the global flows of goods, ideas, capital, and people, the conventional notion of regional culture areas has been criticized for not reflecting the complexity of human experience.[4] At the same time regional thinking pervades anthropological consciousness and structures research, analysis, and the lives of anthropologists. Critical interrogations of the treatment of region (and other "sacred categories") seem to be disconnected from the unspoken reigning paradigm in the professional

1.   I would like to thank the Mellon Foundation and the University Center for International Studies (UCIS) at the University of North Carolina whose support made this essay possible. In addition to the lively discussion with scholars at the Concepts of Region I workshop, this essay benefited from dialogue with participants in the Mellon-Sawyer Reading Regions Globally seminar hosted by UCIS.
2.   Sidney Mintz, "The Localization of Anthropological Practice: From Area Studies to Transnationalism." *Critique of Anthropology* 18 (1998): 117–133. Mintz himself does not question these "sacred categories" but offers an elegant assessment of current scholarly debates.
3.   Arjun Appadurai, "Discussion: Fieldwork in the Era of Globalization," *Anthropology and Humanism* 22 (1997): 115–118; Edward Bruner, "Return to Sumatra: 1957–1997," *American Ethnologist* 26 (1999): 461–477; James Clifford, "Spatial Practices: Fieldwork, Travel, and the Disciplining of Anthropology," in *Anthropological Locations: Boundaries and Grounds of a Field Science* (Berkeley: University of California Press, 1997), 185–222; George Marcus, "Ethnography In/Of the World System: The Emergence of Multi-Sited Ethnography," *Annual Reviews of Anthropology* 24 (1995): 95–117.
4.   James Clifford, "Diasporas," *Cultural Anthropology* 9 (1994): 302–308; Rena Lederman, "Globalization and the Future of Culture Areas: Melanisianist Anthropology in Transition," *Annual Reviews in Anthropology* 27 (1998): 427–249.

development of anthropologists that is still structured by underinterrogated notions of regionalism. To put it simply, concepts of region have an ambivalent relationship to contemporary anthropology, one that a brief historical discussion will help clarify.

This essay provides an overview of anthropological concepts of region in order to identify opportunities for interdisciplinary collaboration. I give a broad historical sketch of a discipline that appears to be moving away from the rigidly bounded concepts that were popular from colonialism through the Cold War toward more flexible concepts of region. In arguing for a more "progressive sense of region," this essay considers innovative anthropological contributions and draws on the contributions of sociologists, planners, and geographers.[5] Such a progressive concept of region should enhance discussions about globalization and transnational processes by helping spatialize social relations and ground otherwise abstract processes in specific times and places.

In a review article Lederman shows that anthropology in both North America and Europe has, from its inception, been organized around regional specialization, which is a product of disciplinary convention and the field's relationship to wider political economic trends, including European colonialism.[6] The concept of region is tied to the idea of culture area, which, by the turn of the twentieth century, had emerged as a central organizing concept for the discipline.[7] Lederman explains that in the research, writing, and museums of the first half of the twentieth century, anthropologists used concepts of geographical regions and culture areas in an attempt to understand (through a comparative approach) cultural patterning, cultural history, cultural diffusion, human universals, cross-cultural typologies, and developmental progress.[8] These notions of "culture areas were, from the outset, less simply about areas than about culture theories. They operated as heuristic bases of generalization; they organized local ethnographic particulars for theoretical and comparative ends."[9] As Arjun Appadurai notes, the designation *culture area,*

---

5.   Doreen Massey, "Power-geometry and a Progressive Sense of Place," in *Mapping the Futures: Local Cultures, Global Change,* ed. Jon Bird et al. (London: Routledge, 1993).

6.   Lederman, "Globalization and the Future of Culture Areas."

7.   See, for example, Franz Boas, "The Limitations of the Comparative Method of Anthropology," *Science* 4 (1896): 901–908.

8.   Examples of this are: ibid.; Alfred Kroeber, *Cultural and Natural Areas of Native North America* (Berkeley: University of California Press, 1939); Heskovitz 1955; Murdoch 1951; and Sahlins & Service 1960.

9.   Lederman, "Globalization and the Future of Culture," 431.

has been less about specialization in a geographic area, than a connotation of a set of topical or theoretical concerns.[10]

The middle part of the twentieth century saw a reinvigorated interest in the scholarly conceptualization of *region* and of the study of regions. World War II generated new interest in studying different parts of the world as a matter of national security.[11] Specifically, the Japanese bombing of Pearl Harbor in 1941 inspired new scholarly interest in East and Southeast Asia. The United States government, Social Science Research Council, Carnegie Foundation, Rockefeller Foundation, and other funding agencies increased their commitment to scholarly research on specific regions of the world. New language training programs, interdisciplinary research institutes, and research projects took over where a previous generation of colonial agents, missionaries, and anthropologists left off. This interest focused largely on nation states and their interconnectedness, but *region* emerged as an important concept for understanding variability within and among nation states. At this time, *region* was mostly construed as a bounded category. Regions were cultural wholes in themselves or distinctive parts of larger nation states that could be compared to each other. Interest in researching regions and nation states as a matter of national security continued and expanded through the Cold War, and problem-oriented research dominated anthropology and other American scholarship.[12]

At the end of the 1950s, as anthropologists became more interested in complex societies, scholars turned from a focus on community studies and called for a reorientation toward relatively small-scale regional systems. In 1956 Robert Redfield suggested:

> I think we should come to study regional systems. We shall study such systems, not, as we now tend to do, from the viewpoint of some one small local community looking outward, but from the viewpoint of an observer who looks down upon the whole larger regional system.[13]

---

10.   Arjun Appadurai, *The Social Life of Things: Commodities in Cultural Perspective* (Cambridge: Cambridge University Press, 1987). For example, the South Pacific (especially New Guinea) was seen as a good place to study exchange (especially of yams). Anthropologists went to Africa for "gentle foragers." South Asianists have often been concerned with social hierarchy; thus mastery of the anthropological literature of South Asia meant mastery of the theoretical concepts of social hierarchy.

11.   Joan Vincent, *Anthropology and Politics* (Tuscon: University of Arizona Press, 1990).

12.   Vincent, *Anthropology and Politics*, 283–296.

13.   Robert Redfield, "Societies and Cultures as Natural Systems," *Journal of the Royal Anthropological Institute* 85 (1956): 28, cited in Carol Smith, "Analyzing Regional Systems," in *Regional Analysis*, vol. II: *Social Systems*, ed. Carol Smith (New York: Academic Press, 1976).

Into the 1960s and 1970s one dominant movement in anthropological research was central place theory, which aimed to understand "complex societies as nested regional systems, discrete in some aspects and overlapping others at each level, with specific institutions, functions, and processes."[14] Central place theory employed a spatial model, which took as its object of study regional systems that were oriented around a city, town, or other nucleated center dependent on a market system.[15]

During the late 1970s and through the 1980s, American anthropology went through a period of introspection that transformed the way that many anthropologists conceived of research and objects of study. Heavily influenced by literary studies and new directions in social theory (what some people call "the postmodern turn"), many underpinnings of the discipline were called into question, and the resulting debates dominated the field for more than a decade. Among the foundational concepts of anthropology being debated were notions of *culture* and *cultural wholes*, which had strong implications for notions of *community* and *region* as objects of study. Part of the critique revolved around the simplicity with which culture and community had been treated. "Culture," James Clifford noted, is "always relational, an inscription of communicative processes that exist historically, between subjects in relations of power," and could not be treated as having some coherent essence.[16] By 1994 James Clifford could make the fairly safe assertion that "it is now widely understood that the old localizing strategies—by bounded community, by organic culture, by region, by center and periphery—may obscure as much as they reveal."[17]

Today anthropology, as a discipline enmeshed in and subject to larger political economic trends, maintains an ambivalent relationship to regionalism, and it is not possible to give a straightforward assessment of the role of regionalism in contemporary anthropology. For some anthropologists the concept of region is considered of little use in an integrated world of "flows" and "scapes."[18] For others, regionalism is a defunct legacy of the field's relationship to colonialism. Recent anthropological works on globalization and transnationalism have challenged the saliency of cultural boundaries (See, for

14.   Smith, "Analyzing Regional Systems," 4.

15.   William G. Skinner, "Marketing and Social Structure in Rural China: Part I," *Journal of Asian Studies* 24 (1): 3–43.

16.   James Clifford, "Introduction: Partial Truths" in *Writing Culture* (Berkeley: University of California Press, 1988).

17.   James Clifford, "Diasporas," 303.

18.   Arjun Appadurai, *Recapturing Anthropology: Working in the Present*, ed. Richard Fox (Santa Fe: The School for American Research, 1991), 191–210.

example, Eric Wolf's *Europe and the People without History* and Ulf Hannerz's article "The World of Creolization" and book *Transnational Connections.*), but this is not the entire story.

On closer inspection Clifford's assessment of the "widely understood" demise of localism and regionalism needs greater explanation. It is true that notions of bounded communities have been handily discarded. However, reflection on the professional organization of the discipline—the departments, journals, and professional associations—exposes a field that is still largely structured around concern with local interactions and regional specializations. If one looks through the *Anthropology Newsletter* or the American Anthropological Association's *Guide to Departments*, one will get a view of anthropology that complicates Clifford's pronouncement. Advertisements for job openings, professional organizations, journals, and faculty descriptions all identify regional specializations and boldly highlight the enduring importance of the concepts of *region* and *regionalism* in contemporary anthropology. Indeed regional specialization continues to be a major organizing principle for professional journals, professional associations, job announcements, course offerings, language training, and the socialization of new anthropologists into the field.[19]

While older notions of *region* and regional designations are left over an earlier era in anthropological scholarship, new ideas about *region* have emerged as part of contemporary research programs. Paradoxically, concepts of *region* and new regional designations are as important as ever in anthropological scholarship. The North American Free Trade Agreement (NAFTA) and the European Union and its Committee on Regions have emerged from the same context as recent scholarly projects examining concepts of *region* with new perspectives. The National Endowment for the Humanities embarked on an ambitious new program to establish new regional research centers at ten universities across the United States. Private foundations have recently funded projects that focus explicitly on regions and concepts of *region.*[20] Plans for redefining the concept of *region* maintain a connection with previous interest in regionalism. The "bounded region" is a relic of World War II and Cold War geostrategics; the "flexible region" is both an artifact of post Cold War sensibilities and a strategy of studying a world defined by movement, fluidity, and ubiquitous boundary transgressions.

19. Perhaps if anthropology's professional organization was more closely in line with theoretical innovation, this aspect of the discipline would be less pronounced.
20. Vincent, *Anthropology and Politics.*

Anthropological research reflects larger political-economic trends in that the field has moved from a comparative study of regions to a study of "regions of flows."[21] While much contemporary ethnographic research recognizes the permeability of localities, regions, and nations, anthropological study continues to focus its attention on specific human interaction in specific places, thus grounding abstract ideas in concrete relationships. Transnational flows of people, capital, commodities, and ideas call for defining regional boundaries as flexible and permeable, but that does not obliterate the importance of place. In that regard numerous examples of anthropological work offer historically and spatially grounded ways of studying often abstract and seemingly free-floating processes of globalization.

Anthropological theory, particularly in the realm of conceptualizing space and place has been heavily influenced by geographers, such as Doreen Massey.[22] Massey's concept of a "progressive sense of place" offers a productive way of thinking about the concept of *region* that is useful for the contemporary moment of "transnationalism," "global capitalism," and "post-industrialism." Massey's notion of *place* can include household, locality, region, nation, and other spatial designations. She notes that concepts of *place* are often disparaged by scholars, and the term has certainly been subject to considerable debate in geography and other disciplines. A major problem with notions of *place* (especially if one is discussing a "sense of place") is the tendency toward nostalgia, "reactionary nationalism," "competitive localisms," and "sanitized, introverted obsessions with 'heritage.'"[23]

However, place matters, in spite of the challenges of capital mobility, telecommunications, and speed of travel. Place matters especially because people across time and space experience social processes differently. Places have unique histories and specific social relations and relations of power. Indeed people do harbor nostalgic sentimentalities for their place in the world (regions included), they are willing to kill and die for them, and powerful memories of a "lost cause" can linger for generations.

Massey devised a "progressive sense of place" (as opposed to a reactionary, or nostalgic one) that can be adapted for the purposes of this discussion to consider a "progressive sense of region." She identifies four components of

---

21.   Manuel Castells, "The Reconstruction of the Social Meaning in the Space of Flows," in *The City Reader*, ed. Richard T. LeGates and Frederic Stout (London: Routledge, 1996).

22.   Doreen Massey, *Space, Place, and Gender* (Minneapolis: University of Minnesota Press, 1994).

23.   Massey, "Power-geometry," 64.

such a categorization. First, a progressive sense of place should be considered "non-static" as places are comprised of dynamic social relations. Second, there are no simple boundaries dividing one place from another (though for some studies it may be useful to temporarily consider fabricated boundaries). And the inclusion of "newcomers" to an area should not be considered a threat to social relations in that place. Third, since there are always internal differences and conflicts, places should not be considered to have a singular identity. Fourth, progressive notions of place need to acknowledge historical specificity. Globalization is not simply a set of homogenizing processes; it also reproduces difference and often exacerbates uneven development. Particular places are tied to global flows and relationships in different ways. These premises, when applied to the concept of *region*, yield a concept that is sensitive to the complexity of the contemporary human condition and has a capacity to generate understanding of social processes that would not otherwise be possible.

Regional designations help organize anthropological studies of global and national trends in uneven economic development. Corporations, governments, nongovernmental organizations, and tourists conceptually construct regions of the world and then invest in them differentially. For example, regions such as the Pacific Rim, Sunbelt, and Caribbean are given positive connotations while others such as Sub-Sahara Africa and the Rust Belt are given negative ones.[24] From this research it is evident that, while transnational capitalism touches every part of the world, not all parts of the world are not integrated into the world system in the same way. Regions are not treated equally by capitalist interests, governments, and nongovernmental organizations.

Other contributions to anthropological thinking on region come from sociology and urban and regional planning. Two scholars from those fields in particular have added to understandings of region by thinking productively about regions within regions. Ann Markusen, a scholar in planning and public policy, has made important contributions to understanding economic restructuring and its differential impact on regions in the United States.[25] Markusen's more recent scholarship on "second tier cities" builds on her previous work by thinking about smaller-scale subnational regions (such as

24. See Smith's discussion of "global redlining" in his 1995 book; Dudley 1994; Collier 1994.
25. Ann Markusen and Virginia Carlson, "Deindustrialization in the American Midwest: Causes and Responses" in *Deindustrialization and Economic Transformation in the United States*, ed. Lloyd Radwin and H. Sazanami (Winchester, MA: Unwin Press, 1989).

North Carolina's Research Triangle Region and California's Silicon Valley).[26] Sociologist Sharon Zukin offers a way of understanding unequal capitalist development with her concepts of "landscape of consumption" and "landscape of production" (or, alternatively, "landscape of devastation").[27] Such concepts offer models for understanding heterogeneity with a larger region of study while maintaining a sensitivity to the importance of place.

If social research is to have any degree of specificity, it should be grounded in actual places of social interaction, as much current anthropological work is. Transnationalism, after all, should not be treated as an abstract, free-floating process that defies spatialization. Places—and regions are a kind of place— entail social relations, structures of power and domination, economics, and political relations. *Region* provides a heuristic tool for understanding the intersection of spatial variation with historical specificity and, drawing on Massey's notion of a "progressive sense of place," makes the concept even more useful.

Anthropology's primary contribution to the study of region revolves around its notion of fieldwork. One of the defining features of anthropological (especially sociocultural anthropological) inquiry is the primacy of the on-the-ground particulars that put theory to the test and (literally) ground interpretation.[28] Methods that were developed for studying local, small-scale societies have been revised periodically over the past hundred years and are currently being retooled alongside transnational transformation, which makes them relevant to broader scholarly discussions of globalization and regionalism.

Ethnographic fieldwork entails on-the-ground research with real people engaged in real social relations, struggling within systems of power, constructing meaning, living, dying, creating, and re-creating the world. Through formal and informal interviews with people, participating in daily life, and understanding life histories and visions of the future, anthropologists test social theory and attempt to understand the world from different perspectives. At their best ethnographic investigations put the researcher in a position to learn something entirely unexpected about the everyday substance that comprises the human experience. In that regard ethnographic fieldwork offers a useful set of methods to use in conjunction with the hallmark methods of history, literary

26.   Ann R. Markusen et al., eds., *Second Tier Cities: Rapid Growth Beyond the Metropolis* (Minneapolis: Minnesota University Press, 1999).
27.   Sharon Zukin, *Landscapes of Power: From Detroit to Disney World* (Berkeley: University of California Press, 1991).
28.   Clifford, "Spatial Practices," 185.

studies, geography, linguistics, and other disciplines in order to examine the meanings of globalization, region, or any other situation in which people find themselves.

In the wake of the vigorous debates of the 1980s current anthropological research illustrates ways of "writing against" any assumed homogeneity, boundedness, and stagnation of locality or region (though this is not always practiced).[29] In response to the reconsideration of the cultural homogeneity of regions anthropologists have developed novel ways of approaching fieldwork and other foundations of anthropological knowledge production. Innovative concepts of "global archipelagos" with their islands of wealth amid seas of poverty, refashioned models of core-periphery, the incorporation of media studies, and oral history have all enlivened contemporary anthropological inquiry.[30] In his study of the Mexican-United States border region Robert Alvarez calls for an "anthropology of borderlands," which is itself a kind of regional designation, one that defies clearly demarcated boundaries.[31] Borderlands are those places in which the dynamic interaction of populations, nation states, and capital are most visible. Marcus calls for a "multi-sited ethnography" that is flexible enough to study complex flows of people, ideas, capital, and issues.[32] His models for research are not bound to any particular place or region, though research is inevitably conducted in particular places, strategically constructing units of analysis. Through the study of relationships among places, processes, and people, contemporary ethnography contributes to the understanding of global and regional variation and social processes.

If they are to be useful for understanding the complexity of human experience, regions should not be considered "fixed" or "bounded" entities. Rather should be viewed as dynamic, discontinuous sites of social interaction in loose, but identifiable and methodologically practical units of space-time. Regions need not necessarily be considered sites of nostalgic images of "Lost Causes" or better days gone by. If we see that regions have lasting

---

29. Lila Abu-Lughod, "Writing Against Culture," in *Recapturing Anthropology: Working in the Present*, ed. Richard Fox (Santa Fe: School of American Research Press, 1991); Edward Soja, *Postmetropolis: Critical Studies of Cities and Regions* (Oxford: Blackwell, 2000).

30. Donald Nonini, "Disposing of Today's 'Trash': Teaching Marx's Concept of the "Industrial Reserve Army," paper presented at the Annual Conference of the Canadian Anthropological Society (CASCA) and American Ethnological Society, Toronto, Canada, May 8, 1998.

31. "The Mexican–US Border: The Making of an Anthropology of Borderlands," *Annual Reviews in Anthropology* 24 (1995): 447–470.

32. Marcus, "Ethnography in/of the World System."

legacies, but ultimately are constructed and reconstructed as unique places with internal heterogeneity, then the concept of region may endure, not only as a salient social construction, but as a useful conceptual tool in the mesoscale of human interaction. Concepts of region need to be open enough to accommodate the constant flow of people, capital, commodities, and ideas. They need to acknowledge the importance of information technology as a factor in reproducing and redefining social relationships. Acknowledging such complexity, concepts of region offer themselves as social constructs and units of study that allow for the specificity of place, the relevance of history, and the primacy of space as dynamic, contested, grounded sites of social interaction.

6

Dynamism and Gatekeeping in the Study of Regions: An Anthropological Approach

Celeste Ray

C hapel Hill, North Carolina, is a most appropriate venue for an interdisciplinary gathering of scholars to discuss the study of regions and regionalism. It was in Chapel Hill that regional sociologist Howard Odum and cultural geographer Carl Sauer met in the 1930s and enthusiastically shared their approaches to regional studies. Together with ecologist Robert Park, their convergent interests shaped what Nicholas Entrikin has called the "guiding ideas and controlling metaphors" of regionalist research for much of the twentieth century.[1] Since their cooperative exchange, regional studies have diverged along disciplinary lines. Re-establishing interdisciplinary communication and collaboration requires exploring our varied uses of "region" and likewise relocating common frames through which we have continued to conveniently, and often statically, define regions.

In this paper I address the concept of region from an anthropological perspective. I begin with a brief note on the history and importance of regional specializations within anthropology and then consider how scholars define and validate regions. After suggesting that we can expect regions—and perhaps the theoretical or popular metonyms through which we have bounded them—to endure, I discuss regional memories and identities through my own research, and conclude by commenting on what anthropology can contribute to a much needed interdisciplinary approach to regions and regionalism.

Regions in Anthropology

Regional specializations characterize anthropology. Entrance to graduate programs often depends on the region to which a student is already committed, jobs are described in regional terms, and frequently the allocation of titled teaching and research positions directly relates to regions of study. How

---

1. Nicholas Entrikin, "Place, Region, and Modernity," in *The Power of Place: Bringing Together Geographical and Sociological Imaginations*, ed. John Agnew and James Duncan (Boston: Unwin Hyman, 1989), 36–37.

did region become one of the key concepts shaping the discipline and anthropological careers?

Anthropology initially approached regions through the same schools of thought as did other social sciences before we carved the study of society and culture into specialized fields. Friedrich Ratzel's late nineteenth-century anthropogeography argued that habitat differences could alone explain cultural diversity. Although reductionistic, his were the first systematic attempts to relate ethnographic data to geographical explanations. Anthropological responses to Ratzel's school include Clark Wissler's concept of "culture area" (1917), which contended that the mode of subsistence, rather than the habitat alone, made certain types of cultures "possible" in a given environment.[2] Pointing to a correspondence between natural and cultural areas, Wissler's "possibilism" ignored the potential for human-environmental relationships to change over time, and could not adequately explain how contrasting cultures with different subsistence strategies could exist within the same habitat. Despite trends toward ethnographic particularism in which scholars focus narrowly on a particular village or community and inductively attempt to integrate their work into more general theoretical concerns, we still employ Wissler's idea of culture areas.[3] We continue to draw boundaries around areas that share religions, languages,

2.   Clark Wissler, *The American Indian: An Introduction to the Anthropology of the New World* (New York: D. C. McMurtrie, 1917).

3.   Further reifying culture as the "Superorganic," Alfred Kroeber argued in the first half of the twentieth century that cultures, histories, and environments are too variable for any generalization, and that each "particular" cultural phenomena was a product of other cultural phenomena [Alfred Kroeber, *Cultural and Natural Areas of Native North America* (Berkeley, CA: University of California Press, 1939)]. Kroeber was a student of Franz Boas, the acknowledged "father" of American anthropology. Boas stressed the importance of fieldwork (the process of which made the student both an anthropologist and an area specialist), and he stressed the ethic of cultural relativism—that all cultures, as bounded wholes, must be explained only in their own terms [Franz Boas, "The Limitations of the Comparative Method in Anthropology," in *Race, Language and Culture* (New York: Macmillan, 1940), 270–280]. Characterizing cultures as "non-comparable," particularism and relativism produced a lingering wariness about making cross cultural comparisons. As Michael Lambek and Andrew Strathern note, anthropologists still struggle to distinguish incomparability from incommensurability [Michael Lambek and Andrew Strathern, *Bodies and Persons: Africa and Melanesia* (Cambridge: Cambridge University Press, 1998), 21–22]. The legacy is a discipline in which scholars have focused on the uniqueness of "their people" and inductively attempted to apply their specific findings to general questions [Richard O'Connor, "Agricultural Change and Ethnic Succession in Southeast Asian States: A Case for Regional Anthropology," *The Journal of Asian Studies* 54 (1995): 968–969]. In many disciplines, publications have increasingly focused on the most discrete units of analysis possible in our attempts to study the "as-yet-unstudied." We would benefit from a return to more comparative and deductive analyses.

patterns of gender relations, material cultures, or particular environments (e.g., arctic, desert, Mediterranean), but we have yet to redeem fully the culture area concept through a diachronic perspective and a recognition of the fluidity and dynamism of regions.

What Are Regions?

Edward Royle writes that a region is "no less an imagined community than is a nation."[4] How we bound a region depends on analytical purposes, though in reality they are always mutable, with cores and peripheries shifting and redefining themselves over time. Carole Crumley notes that we can view regions "as homogeneous, heterogeneous or both depending upon our goals as researchers."[5] Michael Lambek and Andrew Strathern concur that regions emerge not just from geographic proximity or common historical origins, but from the act of studying them.[6] Regions are environmentally, historically, and culturally created, but they are also constructed through the scholarly lens.

We each define "our" regions as they relate to our particular studies so that the term regionalism can apply to our research strategies as well as to indigenous sentiment and popular movements.[7] Arjun Appadurai and Rolph Trouillot note that novel and thorough investigation of particular regions is often blocked by what Appadurai has called "gatekeeping concepts" or theoretical metonyms such as caste in India, filial piety in China, and honor-and-shame in the Mediterranean.[8] Trouillot suggests these concepts have acted as theoretical simplifiers and ahistorical means of bounding the object of study. In the American South slavery, Jim Crow, and racism have been gatekeeping concepts on the one hand, while magnolias, benevolent mammies, and the plantation legend of the Old South have been their opposite pole.

---

4.   Edward Royle, "Introduction: Regions and Identities," in *Issues of Regional Identity*, ed. Edward Royle and J. D. Marshall (New York: St. Martin's Press, 1998), 4.

5.   Carole Crumley, "Three Locational Models: An Epistemological Assessment for Anthropology and Archaeology," in *Advances in Archaeological Method and Theory*, ed. Michael Schiffer (New York: Academic Press, 1979), 143–145.

6.   Lambek and Strathern, *Bodies and Persons*, 21–22.

7.   See Charles Reagan Wilson, *The New Regionalism: Essays and Commentaries* (Jackson: University Press of Mississippi, 1998).

8.   Arjun Appadurai, "Theory in Anthropology: Center and Periphery," *Comparative Studies in Society and History* 28 (1986): 356–361; Michel-Rolph Trouillot, "The Caribbean Region: An Open Frontier in Anthropological Theory," *Annual Review of Anthropology* 21 (1992): 21–23.

In the past decade especially, after "invention of tradition" studies and "deconstruction," it has become popular to dismantle such concepts in relation to political or cultural hegemony as a way of studying region. I am more interested in examining the historical evolution of such gatekeeping concepts as an interesting process in itself and asking why they endure as foci of both popular culture and scholarly work. With historical perspective, such concepts can continue to help us define regions. By examining their changing role in shaping regional identities and memory, we may also trace regional core and periphery shifts.

For example, in studying the South, do we include only those eleven states that were in the Confederacy? Or do we include states or parts of states that have at some point considered themselves southern (Kentucky, Maryland, and the "Little Dixies" established in the 1870s and 1880s in Missouri and southwest Oklahoma)? In the 2000 U.S. Census, the South includes Delaware, Maryland, West Virginia, Oklahoma, and the District of Columbia, although historically these were not part of the Confederacy and culturally they were not a part of the Old South's plantation mythology. The diachronic study of regions reveals the evolution of cultural and historical memory. Tourist brochures for southern and western Kentucky now portray these areas as the "gateways" or "strongholds" of the Old South, even though Kentucky was not part of the Confederacy.

The American South is a creole of African, European, and Native American cultures. For example, bluegrass music, which we think of as typically Southern, is really a mix of Celtic fiddle and African banjo. All regions of America have diversity; it is the patterns of cultural blending that define the South as unique. The whole is greater than the sum of its parts. Even with desegregation and dramatic changes in politics, economics, and the ways in which Southerners interact with each other, cultural constants remain—certainly a feeling of cultural identity and distinctiveness persists.

Do Regions Have a Future?

As we increasingly theorize about globalization, will regions remain? Culture's flexibility has perhaps enabled its seeming stability and cohesiveness within regions. Entrikin reminds us of Clifford Geertz's reference to primordial attachments—that our attachments to places endure despite change in those places. Entrikin suggests that sense of place remains "important despite increased mobility of the population and the production of standardized landscapes."[9] Even these have local interpretations and significance. Seemingly identical American street corners punctuated with Taco Bell, McDonald's, Texaco, and Wal–Mart franchises may have different patterns of associations for different communities. In some places the Wal–Mart might be a gathering place for older community members to have coffee, visit, and look at gardening supplies. Maybe Taco Bell is a center for youth cruising in one town while different youth cliques stake claim to a McDonald's or a Burger King in another. These chain businesses look the same and provide the same services and mostly the same goods, but their employees and consumers may interact in regional styles. Though shifts from local to national or international merchandisers and restaurateurs obviously change regional lifestyles, regional interpretations are nonetheless imposed on what may seem standardized, generic, or even resistant to any local or regional cultural meaning.

Earlier than Geertz or Entrikin, Norwegian anthropologist Fredrik Barth emphasized that cultural boundaries are more stable than culture. Considering ethnic identities, Barth suggested that ethnicity lay in the boundary-making process itself, rather than in the cultural ideas associated with each group, so that while the cultures of ethnic groups evolve, the boundaries between them remain.[10] Similarly, Mary Steedly notes that continuity is not "something that just happens in the absence of change," but rather is "something that has to be produced and reproduced in the face of change."[11] Gatekeeping concepts (perceived cultural constants) have shaped our definitions of regions, yet while culture changes, regional boundaries remain. Regional cores and peripheries may shift and resettle over time, but they endure.

Regional Memories in the Celebration of a Hyphenated Identity

In the past two decades anthropologists have begun turning their attention to our own society. As I began fieldwork with what my fellow graduate students assumed would be "unexotic" Americans, I did not expect to be told "we want you to meet our chief—the one over there with three feathers on his cap." I chose to study southern Scottish Americans who celebrate a tribal past by, among other things, joining clan societies and wearing clothing (tartans) that they feel represents their clan identity. They actively identify themselves as

---

9.   Entrikin, "Place, Region, and Modernity," 41.

10.   Fredrik Barth, ed., *Ethnic Groups and Boundaries: The Social Organization of Cultural Difference* (Boston: Little, Brown, 1969).

11.   Mary Margaret Steedly, "The State of Culture Theory in the Anthropology of Southeast Asia," *Annual Review of Anthropology* 28 (1999): 441.

Celtic Americans rather than as Anglo-Saxons, and though their celebrations are in some ways reactions against the southern gatekeeping concepts I mentioned above, they also reiterate and renegotiate those for a politically correct, multicultural present. The Scottish identity American celebrants embrace today is a regional Highland Gaelic identity—celebrated equally by Americans of Highland Scots, Lowland Scots, and Ulster Scots descent—that became representative of the Scottish national identity only after the ancestors of many Scottish Americans left Scotland. This regional identity further evolves in different American contexts.

Underneath the Scottish dress and rituals are paradigms that seem very familiar. Those who express strong feelings about their Scottish heritage in interviews and at heritage events also communicate a deep attachment to their southern heritage and usually draw explicit links between the two. Both Scottish (Highland) and southern identities play on a sense of historical injuries and lost causes, on links between the senses of place and kinship, on connections between militarism and religious faith, and on symbolic material cultures.

What has intrigued me most is the selection and reworking of tradition and the blending of two regional identities in the creation of a heritage for our current time. Heritage is a rhapsody on history. We strike the chords we wish to hear. The value of heritage lies in its perennial flexibility and the strength of emotions it evokes. Celebratory and commemorative reflections on ancestral experience merge historical incidents, folk memories, invented traditions, and often sheer fantasy in order to interpret a past in a form meaningful for a particular group or individual at a particular point in time. The bits of the past that seem most significant change continuously relative to the present.

In the United States we take for granted that generation upon generation has blended intellectual, cultural, and historical legacies in the making of an American heritage, but modern Americans have attempted increasingly to sort out and reclaim particular cultural memories that they feel make them unique and hyphenate their identity to reflect this belief. As a nation we seem somewhat confused about demanding individualism, yet facing alienation; challenging conformity, yet decrying our lack of community. We want to embrace difference but want to do so in groups; so that communities based on difference, ease of transportation, the Internet, and so forth, fill in for our lack of "good neighbors." Claiming particular dress or food customs as an inheritance provides the feeling of uniqueness but not aloneness.[12]

12.   See Celeste Ray, *Highland Heritage: Scottish Americans in the American South* (Chapel Hill: University of North Carolina Press, 2001); Celeste Ray, ed., *Southern Heritage*

The Scottish-American heritage movement is just one example of the many American groups celebrating an "old country" yet also revealing a strong sense of American regional identity and, in fact, layering regional culture and memory within a hyphenated heritage.

What Can Anthropology Contribute to an Interdisciplinary Approach to Regions?

Anthropologists especially promote our most basic technique, ethnography: describing the activities and beliefs one encounters through simultaneous participation and observation within a given setting. Ethnography also involves formal and informal interviewing, the collection of oral histories, and, often, ethnohistorical attempts to reconstruct cultural and ethnic histories through archival and library research. Such qualitative research is essential to measure what surveys can not. Fieldwork reveals the correspondence and contradictions between what people say they believe and what they actually do. Anthropologists take a labor- and time-intensive approach to the study of culture. Clifford Geertz has given us the metaphor of "reading culture as text," but did not suggest that cultural texts could be understood without fieldwork as many "cultural studies" presume.[13] One must engage the actors rather than interpret or gleefully deconstruct from afar.

Event-centered ethnography seems particularly useful for regional scale studies. As Sally Falk Moore notes, "Events situate people in an unedited and 'preanalyzed' context, before the cultural ideas they carry and the strategies they employ are extracted and subjected to the radical reorganization and hygienic order of anthropologists' analytic purpose."[14] My work with Scottish Americans has focused on attending events both across the South and beyond for comparative purposes. Event ethnography allows the fieldworker to examine first-hand the public rituals and the production and renegotiation of communal memories that define ethnic and regional identities. It also allows one to meet a large number of possible consultants at one time; arrange later, more extensive interviews, and eventually create a network of contacts on a regional scale.

---

on Display: Public Ritual and Ethnic Diversity within Southern Regionalism (Tuscaloosa: University of Alabama Press, 2003); Celeste Ray, ed., *Transatlantic Scots* (Tuscaloosa: University of Alabama Press, forthcoming).

13.   Clifford Geertz, *The Interpretation of Cultures* (New York: Basic Books, 1973).

14.   Sally Falk Moore, "The Ethnography of the Present and the Analysis of Process," in *Assessing Cultural Anthropology*, ed. Robert Borofsky (New York: McGraw-Hill, 1994), 365.

In the creation of disciplines and careers we have reinvented and renamed each other's wheels and often made our work unintelligible and unserviceable across disciplinary boundaries. While the regional scale still seems strategically and intellectually the most appropriate from which to address globalization and global problems, the challenge before us requires a dialectical and an interdisciplinary synthesis of theory and methods. Geographic Information Systems (GIS) holds enormous promise for regional scholars if an effective strategy can make information accessible across disciplines. Shaping a cooperative approach to regions and regionalism requires an abiding awareness of scalar variation through time. The French Annales have long offered a historical model applicable at the regional scale for considering *conjonctures* (trends), *structures* (enduring societal institutions that check shorter-term processes), and changes over longer periods (the *longue durée*).[15] An Annales approach to *mentalité* and regionalism offers a valuable and diachronic perspective for rebridging regional studies within the social sciences, geography, and the humanities.

We could further benefit from a common lexicon. As a start, "landscape" has resurfaced as one of the most popular buzzwords since the 1980s in many of our disciplines.[16] Archaeologists Carole Crumley and William Marquardt define landscapes as the spatial manifestations of relations between human groups, and between humans and their environments.[17] Anthropologists who study the human shaping and perception of landscapes call themselves ethnoecologists. Ethnoecologists consider phenemonological aspects not generally included in scientific endeavors—such as feelings of attachment, cognitive mapping of landscapes, and religious values.[18] They conduct ethnography under the assumption that humans and their environments interact in dynamic and mutually constitutive ways.

---

15. See Ferdinand Braudel, *The Mediterranean and the Mediterranean World in the Age of Philip II* (New York: Harper and Row, 1972).

16. See Eric Hirsch and Michael O'Hanlon, eds., *The Anthropology of Landscape: Perspectives on Place and Space* (Oxford: Clarendon Press, 1995); John Winberry, "The Geographic Concept of Landscape: The History of a Paradigm," in *Carolina's Historical Landscapes: Archaeological Perspectives*, ed. Linda Stine et al. (Knoxville: University of Tennessee Press, 1997).

17. Carole Crumley and William Marquardt, eds., *Regional Dynamics: Burgundian Landscapes in Historical Perspective* (New York: Academic Press, 1987), 6.

18. See Kay Milton, *Environmentalism and Cultural Theory: Exploring the Role of Anthropology in Environmental Discourse* (London: Routledge, 1996).

In my work with Scottish Americans I have found that the places chosen for Scottish heritage celebrations are often those that Scottish-Americans perceive as looking "Scottish," or believe they can modify to meet such expectations. One of the largest Scottish "clan gatherings" is the Grandfather Mountain Highland Games in the Blue Ridge Mountains that participants describe as "a wee bit of the Scottish Highlands in North Carolina." Scottish Americans claim that the locations of such events themselves become pilgrimage sites as "clan lands" in America. Landscape is a powerful element in evoking and celebrating a regional identity. A sense of place for the Scottish Highlands is transferred and cultivated in a "new" space, remaking the meaning of place for a particular purpose and period. Celebratory discussion and oration about regional "character" often link perceived characteristics to landscape and environment. Clearly anthropogeography is alive and well in popular culture. Ethnographic methods offer one way to unravel its enduring appeal and the way it continues to shape visions of regional identity and heritage.

We now commonly speak of landscapes as palimpsests, human creations that are edited and rewritten over the ages. As we attempt to reevaluate the "gatekeeping concepts" through which we have synchronically defined regional cultures, we should likewise consider specific spatial and temporal scales of cultural memory and the flexibility and dynamism that often suggest stability.

7

Regionalism in Global Societies: A Contradiction?

Kornelia Hahn

The question raised in this article's title was actually the problem that first came to mind when I started to think about regionalism in the modern— or better, "late-modern"—world. There are confusing phenomena to observe: New technologies provide opportunities to communicate "interactive" and "real time" around the world but do not replace the desire for face-to-face contact and association. Already in the 1960's Marshall McLuhan pointed out that new media provoke "the extension of Man" in two ways. We all gather— via television—in a *global village* that will cause a retribalization: On the one hand, the extension allows a worldwide participation in communication; on the other, this newly shaped community is structured like a tribe. We are aware that communication did not become global nor did the world turn into a giant tribe. However, we should obviously consider McLuhan's focus on the changing frame of communication created by the *forms* of media and its impact on social life. Similarly, there is a great deal of mobility as tourists travel around the world in order to either try to dive into the "typical life styles" of foreign regions or get away from daily life by relaxing in artificially constructed "regions," such as Club Meds and other amusement centers. In both cases travelers try to pick up daily life "as before." Being away from home, being "outside," may increase the understanding of what is going on differently in the locale; however, it is very doubtful that this experience really leads to an *internal* understanding of a foreign region. Thus, as Dean MacCanell points out, the "term 'tourist' is increasingly used as a derisive label for someone who seems content with his obviously *inauthentic* experiences."[1]

Like people and information products, too, circulate worldwide. Of course, globally produced and distributed goods are consumed locally. There are some good reasons to regard this phenomenon as a significant factor in the creation of a standardized lifestyle. Do we not observe, for example, a

---

1.   Dean MacCannell, *The Tourist: A New Theory of the Leisure Class* (Berkeley: University of California Press, 1999), 94.

unified sense of fashion among young people all over the world? On the other hand we have to consider that the use of any product is embedded in a specific constellation of local customs and practices. Therefore, we always have to find out whether eating with, say, chopsticks is someone's traditional practice or a demonstration of being familiar with different eating instruments, a means of symbolical distinction from traditional practice.

Of course, even in the most important social systems such as politics and economy it is becoming increasingly obvious that global efforts for balancing political interests, laws, economic transactions, stock markets, and so forth have a lot to do with being able to control and observe every local event carefully. Moreover, the specifics of regions and conflicts within an area or among regional cultures are certainly a focal point in contemporary politics. One may conclude that the awareness of regional cultures across the globe is due to the broader perspective of a so-called "global world." This general perspective encourages us to observe every region as a part of something bigger or as an area surrounded by something different from it.

This consideration may lead to the idea that regionalism and globalization are unified aspects of a single, ongoing phenomenon of social transformation. It may also lead to the idea that any rethinking of regions should include phenomena represented by the terms "space" and "place." For example, *Newsweek* refers to NY-LON (New York-London) as a "single city inconveniently separated by an ocean." Therefore, the inhabitants of NY-LON often have to use a plane to reach their working places and homes. A characteristic of NY-LON is its role as a leader in film, television, and pop music production; publishing; and the new economy in general. People all over the world who are involved in these sectors of the economy are increasingly choosing NY-LON as their activity center. But even in this context the image of NY-LON is confusing. The "city" is not spatially united, but united by *money*, the report points out. As a famous businessman puts it: "*In terms of our business*, the cities are beginning to melt into one massive whole" (italics added). This is a *symbolic* kind of unification. However, it is reported that both halves of NY-LON, New York and London, "remain quite unlike each other in *spirit*" (italics added). What can we derive from these observations? I submit that insofar as spatial distances are relatively shrinking due to innovations in transportation and communication technologies, "place" may no longer be defined necessarily in reference to "space."

This possibility of a region existing outside a fixed geographic space raises the question of what terms we would then use to define "region." "Money," as a symbolic medium that circulates among persons and creates certain types of relationships, should certainly be taken into account. Even the perceived and experienced "spirit" within a place may be considered. Therefore, we must determine what "spirit" stands for. Peter Burke remarks that in the late eighteenth-century famous philosophical terms such as "spirit", "genius" and "humor" (*Geist, Stimmung, Genie* in German; *ésprit general, ésprit humain, génie* in French) were replaced by the term "culture," first used by German philosophers. The term "culture," like "spirit,"[2] indicates "a sharper awareness of the links between changes in language, law, religion, and the arts and sciences."[3] Nowadays, when referring to "spirit" we mean "culture" in this sense.

Therefore, the "spirit" of a region, is usually used as a synonym for the "whole of cultural objectives." Culture can be regarded as a synonym for the "whole"[4], just as religion ("the holy") etymologically refers to "the whole" and masks the objectives a social group wishes to preserve in order to evoke its identity.[5] However, this identity can be conserved and even *detected* when something emerges that has to be rejected by symbolic interaction. So, in the most general terms a region is shaped by a boundary made of symbolic categories that do not belong to it. Subsequently, two questions emerge: Which categories should any definition of a region include? Who/what is the defining force of symbolic categories? These questions have to be considered in any analysis of a region. We should take into account three general assumptions when examining Regions:

1. Regions should be formally subdivided in terms of "inside" and "outside";

2. There is a steady exchange among regions (between the "inside" and "outside") through communication, migration, consumption, financial transactions, and so forth;

---

2.   This statement should not be confused with Max Weber's term "geglaubte Gemeinsamkeit." [Max Weber, *Wirtschaft und Gesellschaft* (Tübingen: Mohr, 1972), 237.] Here Weber stresses that the phenomenon of "geglaubte Gemeinsamkeit" may support the birth of a community, but that it is a term describing a community that does not exist in reality despite this phenomenon.

3.   Peter Burke, *Varieties of Cultural History* (Cambridge: Polity Press/Blackwell Publishers, 1997), 20.

4.   Burke, *Varieties of Cultural History*, 31.

5.   Karl-Heinz Kohl, *Ethnologie—die Wissenschaft vom kulturell Fremden* (Munich: C. H. Beck, 1993), 72.

3. Due to constant exchange and the changing characteristics of regions, it may be very helpful to consider a local, or spatial, reference point to carry out the analysis.

As Maurice Halbwachs observes, space *conserves* the cultural memory, perhaps better than other media of memory such as rituals or records.[6] A certain "space" therefore becomes a meaningful "place" through the significance actors ascribe to it in the course of their symbolic interacting. A region is always a "place" in this sense. When Erving Goffman pointed out: "A region may be defined as any place that is bounded to some degree by barriers of perception," he was referring to situations of face-to-face communication.[7] But the usefulness of this definition should allow it to extend to a broader concept of region. The community is shaped by boundaries perceiving each other, this means by boundaries of communication. This general statement is not affected by new communication technologies. Even the most advanced technologies, those allowing a large- scale distribution of communication in time and space create certain (new) barriers of perception in comparison with face-to-face situations. Moreover, we have to stress the application and specific utilization of media instead of focusing solely on media's technological scope. This may lead to the observation that regional communities should be interpreted as a result of their *imagined* boundaries. In addition we can even point out that a (regional) culture always consists of *hybrid* structures preserving *selective* communication processes from the past. So all traditions stand for an extension in time and space and the distribution of a common sense within communities.

From this point of view it is not very useful for us to focus on "inside" and "outside" in observing regions, but it is true that "outside" may involve a global extension. Regions may be influenced by cultural patterns of former immigrants, the importation of foreign products, or even sociocultural techniques developed in a distant society. Asking about regions and regionalism means contrasting the characteristics of an area's social structure with those of the surrounding environment. But we should keep in mind that these specifics do not stem from

6. Maurice Halbwachs, *La mémoire collective* (Paris: Michel, 1997). This can be clarified by two phenomena: (1) the changing of spatial conditions of life (e.g., rural reforms) are causing a cultural turnover; and (2) communities that have lost or abandoned their spatial roots may try to reconstruct the former, even spatial, organization elsewhere (e.g., a group of emigrants).

7. Erving Goffman, *The Presentation of Self in Everyday Life* (New York: Anchor Books, 1959), 106.

the characteristics of the area or territory as such. Social homogeneity derives from cultural and behavioral patterns and habits and the collective rules of conduct encoded in common symbols. Therefore, the concept of regionalism is of special interest to sociologists because the embedding of social interactions in a certain social structure is usually explored in connection with a local reference point. In this context "globalization" is placed on the one side and "localization" on the other.

"Globalization" can be specified as a worldwide spatial extension of cooperation in economy, politics, consumption, production, and the division of labor. Globalization includes global ecological risks and *unintended* consequences.[8] This definition is supported by new technologies in communication and transportation systems as well as the origination of "global cities" as centers of international investment, communication, production, and distribution.[9] Societies and cultures can no longer be seen in terms of the boundaries of nation-states. New development cuts across former sociopolitical systems and may newly shape both supranational and subnational areas. We are observing a dissolution of temporal and spatial constraints in communication, and this dissociation of time and space greatly affects social contacts. Social relations have now been seen in the light of continual inputs of "external" (outside local communities) information, knowledge and restrictions. However, "[a]t the same time as social relations become laterally stretched and as a part of the same process, we see the strengthening of pressures for local autonomy and regional cultural identity."[10] As a result, social life in a "region" is influenced by the intensification of worldwide relations and formed by events occurring many miles away. This process links distant localities in such a way that even local happenings may move in a different direction from the very distanced relations that form them.[11] Therefore, this process is now described as "glocalization" (Roland Robertson), which puts more emphasis on the mutuality of changes in regard to both global and local structures.[12]

---

8.   Ulrich Beck, *Was ist Globalisierung? Irrtümer des Globalismus—Antworten auf Globalisierung* (Frankfurt a.M: Suhrkamp, 1997).

9.   Ludger Pries, "Transnationale soziale Räume: Theoretisch-empirische Skizze am Beispiel der Arbeitswanderung Mexico–USA." In *Zeitschrift für Soziologie* 6 (1996): 456–472.

10.   Anthony Giddens, *The Consequences of Modernity* (Stanford: Stanford University Press, 1990), 65.

11.   Giddens, *Consequences of Modernity*, 64.

12.   Although this process started two to three hundred years ago, it has developed an extraordinary dynamism in the last few decades. But we should keep in mind that not every part of the world is influenced by this process to the same degree.

The characteristic of "glocalization," therefore, is not the decline of regional cultures and the rise of an apparent convergence toward a global culture—a phenomenon nicknamed the "McDonaldization" of the world (a term introduced by Ritzer). First of all, McDonalization focuses on a standardization of social interactions developed first in the industrial mass production of goods, then transferred through the organization of fast-food restaurants to every exchange between the customer and those offering products and services. At some point globalization became empirically demonstrated by the consumption of hamburgers. A famous example of the success of the McDonald system of organization was the opening of a McDonald's restaurant in Moscow. But, as I once heard during an academic lecture from a critic of the convergence thesis, a Big Mac in Moscow does not taste like a Big Mac in the United States. Ritzer himself gave an interesting example of the *merging* (and *not* the uniqueness) of organizational systems: One characteristic of the McDonalds' in Moscow is the long queue of clients waiting at its entrance but another is the "service people" providing clients with Big Macs within fifteen minutes for a small additional charge. So the obviously enormous attraction of this fast-food restaurant seems a consequence of its image rather than its function. Getting a meal at the Moscow McDonald's is not as fast as promised in the home country; the price for a meal is now increasing, too, which also contradicts the original marketing strategy of McDonald's. However, these discrepancies do not cause confusion because the integrating culture has already found a means of preventing long lines (and providing some persons with profit). The ironic result is the complete mixture of the two systems, American and Russian. In Moscow providing somebody with something is first a matter of contacts and right relationships; here, originally, "time is not money," but now creative actors have melded the two systems, constituting a new logic of interaction. Similarly, before putting their products on the market the creative directors of companies with a global market ("global players") consider regional specifics and try to develop local bonds. Coca-Cola and Sony describe this task as "global localization."[13] We are observing a powerful paradox: on the one hand the need for standardization for global organizational purposes and on the other the search for "authenticity" within regions. The impact of this has not yet been determined.

This ambivalent situation may be clarified by considering the essence of what C. Wright Mills has called "the sociological imagination," or what Georg Simmel termed "the sociological view" of societies. In its most

---

13.   Beck, *Was ist Globalisierung?*, 86.

general conception sociology refers to the discovery of structures in social life. These structures are created by networks of contacts among people and are usually intended consequences of these interactions. This strengthens the focus on communication processes, which can be seen in terms of a spectrum between two poles, local communication (face-to-face) and the so-called mass communication. The coexistence of these two forms of communication is of special importance.

Recent sociological theories can help us analyze the social effects of modern means of communication on regions in a context where regions can no longer be regarded bounded space or territories. I introduce three key terms in discussing these theories: "ethnoscape," "glocalization," and "inclusive distinction."

1. The neologism "Ethnoscape" refers to the fact that the origination of cultural identities is not inevitably linked to with their presence in a certain area.[14] On the contrary, multiple cultural identities may develop within the same region. What is of special significance when describing an ethnic group or a culture cannot be derived exclusively from the internal conditions of the group's life. The modern world is often regarded as a variety of transitional or mixed communities instead of as a certain number of national societies. Here, the organization of social relations and day-to-day life is not based on regional—in the meaning of spatial—classification. Furthermore, a region is now determined by its specific cultural mixture, and the specific ways global events are interwoven with local structures.

2. The region is a "mélange" of transnational and local social relations. The process of "glocalization" notes that the region is still the place where global events and influences are intermediated and experienced. The variety of regions and cultures is not "spaceless," but people pay special attention to the openness of their social spaces and environments.[15] This view holds that residents "selectively 'appropriate' elements from metropolitan cultures in order to 'construct' a hybrid medium in which to articulate their

---

14. Arjun Appadurai, "Global Ethnoscapes: Notes and Queries for a Transnational Anthropology" in *Recapturing Anthropology: Working in the Present*, ed. Richard G. Fox (Santa Fe: School of American Research, 1991).

15. Beck, *Was ist Globalisierung?*, 118–119.

own, historically and socially specific, experience."[16] This view stresses the active, creative role of people as producers of culture rather than representing them as passive victims of globalization.

3. This leads to the question of how to perceive boundaries between cultural groups now that spatial borders are no longer valid. Here we can point out the argument of "inclusive distinction." This means that boundaries are not constructed by "exclusion" or "separation" but—more practically—by not having the chance to participate in all groups or to absorb all the information at one's disposal. "Inclusive distinction" dictates a certain means of observing social life. These means subordinate the separation between social categories or groups to highlight intersections that create new relations between social categories or groups. In linking local social structures and culture "inclusive distinction" does not distinguish between "either/or" but rather accentuates "as well as."

These theories and arguments suggest ways of analyzing regionalism or "regional cultures" within global societies. They indicate that most of the time we should *not* make an "exclusive distinction" and should *not* look for boundaries and dissimilarities that have not yet shifted as a result of the increasing assimilation of cultural groups.

Due to the fact that globalization appears in a new *crossing over* of global structures and identity, the contradictions of globalization will be detected mainly in the course of individual lives. As Ulrich Beck said: We are living "glocal," and we experience this phenomenon in multicultural family lives, business, interactions with friends, watching movies, shopping, and listening to music.[17] "Modern" biographies, therefore, give expression to a compromise between all the individual ideas about chances and challenges within an "open" environment (of actions) and what can actually be realized. This influences the interpretation of regionalism. At first we can say that the value and appreciation of a region can only be developed if there is a chance to experience the "time-

---

16.   Karen Barber and Christopher Waterman, "Traversing the Global and the Local: Fújì Music and Praise Poetry in the Production of Contemporary Yorùbá Popular Culture" in *Worlds Apart: Modernity through the Prism of the Local*, ed. Daniel Miller (London and New York: Routledge, 1995), 240, quoting Ulf Hannerz 1987 Africa 57 (4), pp. 546–559
17.   Beck, *Was ist Globalisierung?*, 129.

space dissociation" of contacts or a certain "alienation" from the locale.[18] Therefore, discussing a region means *at any time* discussing its *image* or how the region is described from the point of view of its residents. Anthony Giddens writes: "In conditions of modernity, place becomes increasingly phantasmagoric. . . . What structures the locale is not simply that which is present on the scene; the 'visible form' of the locale conceals the distanciated relations which determine its nature."[19] Consequently, an awareness of "ethnoscape" requires the development of new methods that take into account that the culture of a social group combines a number of regional and transregional criteria, including changing reflections of what is characteristic of the region. When Robertson explained the process of glocalization, he found out that within this process particularity is becoming a *global* value.[20] This makes identity a complicated construction. On the one hand, people clamor for local loyalties and for reassurance of the familiar in a globalized world. On the other they appreciate cosmopolitan ideas and participating in cosmopolitan life styles.[21] Before focusing on empirical methods I would like to complete our discussion by giving some empirical results. Daniel Miller writes:

I have been working with several colleagues to try and understand why Christmas has managed to expand around the world . . . . We noted that this festival is both beloved of folklorists, who constantly find parochial local customs associated with it, and yet has also developed as potentially the first truly global festival encompassing many non-Christian countries. . . . While philosophers struggle with the question of what is called "being at home in the world" the celebrants of Christmas take this phrase literally. The festival enshrines the home as pure domesticity, the only place one should really be at Christmas time. It then uses the domestic microcosm to encompass the sense of a globe, that is envisaging the peoples of the world all conducting the same rite at the same time as a global family. As such the festival both symbolically and actually creates commensurability between the largest social (or for the religious—cosmological) universe we are

---

18.   Roland Robertson, "Glokalisierung: Homogenität und Heterogenität in Raum und Zeit" in *Weltgesellschaft*, ed. by Ulrich Beck (Frankfurt a/M: Suhrkamp, 1998), 215.

19.   Giddens, *Consequences of Modernity*, 18–19.

20.   Roland Robertson, *Globalization: Social Theory and Global Culture* (London: Sage, 1992).

21.   Beck, *Was ist Globalisierung?*, 91; Giddens, *Consequences of Modernity*, 140.

called upon to imagine and the smallest social universe we tend to assume.[22]

This observation contradicts the popular theory of Joshua Meyrowitz, which he compressed into the words: "No sense of place." Meyrowitz underlines this statement by explaining how the information distributed by mass media influences face-to-face relationships.[23] Certainly, the huge output of films and television series in Hollywood studios that are transmitted all over the world has to be considered when valuing interactions and experiences in the locale. But in this context empirical research gives us hints of the specific *perception* of media contents.

In order to show how empirical research provides an indication of how people perceive media material, I want to bring in the results of a project about "crosscultural readings of *Dallas*." The authors Tamar Liebes and Elihu Katz tried to explain the "export of meaning" by the popular series *Dallas*.[24] But they showed instead the impossibility of exporting meaning via television. They concretely accentuate the characteristic of *perception*, which first constitutes meaning and may vary according to social group membership. When Liebes and Katz tried to find out what people of different ethnicities (Russians, Arabs, Japanese, Americans, and Jews living in a kibbutz) "have seen" when they watched *Dallas*, they became aware that their interpretations were contradictory. For example, in one episode Sue Ellen leaves her husband, J. R. in order to go back to her former lover and live with him in his father's house. When the authors discussed this event, the Arab group all believed that Sue Ellen was escaping from J. R. and returning to her own father's house. This "misinterpretation" shows the dominance of both the local readings and the stability of forming shared experiences in social groups. The slogan "no sense of place" can be discussed in an even more macrostructural way. Blakely and Snyder remark that "[u]sing physical space to create social place is a long and deep American tradition."[25] This tradition is applied to a modern form of residentship, the "gated communities."

---

22.   Daniel Miller, "Introduction: Anthropology, Modernity and Consumption" in *Worlds Apart*, 18.

23.   Even he does not follow McLuhan in his assumptions.

24.   Tamar Liebes and Elihu Katz, *The Export of Meaning: Cross-cultural Readings of Dallas.* (New York: Oxford University Press, 1990).

25.   Edward J. Blakely and Mary G. Snyder, *Fortress America: Gated Communities in the United States* (Washington, DC: Brookings Institution Press, 1999), 1.

This kind of community preserves a characteristic of social organization insofar as its residents look for distinction when segregating their real estate. On the other hand the regionalization of gated communities shapes a somewhat new characteristic, even though community is dissolved. The separation (for whatever reasons) actually yields a bond uniting the residents and allowing them to live incognito as singles or isolated families (as long as they respect the long list of rules and prescriptions of how to style the front of their houses and even their behavior outside their walls). In short, gated communities in their specific organization of space allow life *without* contact with the people living around them. However, this leads to the question: Do the residents of gated communities arrange their social relationships with no regard to physical space (as NY-LON short for), only supported by spatial mobility and "cyberspace" communication? Yet living according to no sense of place in an old-fashioned manner follows the European tradition of creating social distinction. Instead of subdividing the (more limited) space, social distinction is organized by different practices or by the demonstration of consumption patterns that symbolically indicate the commitment to a certain status or class among people within a spatial unit.[26] Even here an investigation of the impact of glocalization would be an extremely attractive topic for further research.

Now, we can conclude that the methods of analyzing regionalisms in a globalized world must provide a means of observation in response to these questions: How can regionalism be *experienced* in a world of "time-space dissociation? How can the effects and the reflections of the "time-space dissociation" be described in connection to experiences of the locale? From this point of view we see the need for a link between the micro and macro perspectives of analysis as well as the need to emphasize the subjective interpretation patterns of actors. Moreover, the process of glocalization can only be mastered by investigating social situations, *local* interactions, or symbolic tokens that *refer* to global conditions.

Some promising methods have been developed recently in cultural studies, based on complementary approaches first developed in different disciplines. In addition to the classical empirical research in sociology that is usually based upon macrodata of socioeconomic structure, there is a special need to consult the methods used in other fields. For example, biographical research or oral history, interpretations of literature, methods in geography and linguistics, and descriptions of ethnomethodology or anthropology all offer means of accessing

---

26. See the still instructive work of Thorstein Veblen, *The Theory of the Leisure Class* (Fairfield, NJ: Kelley, 1991). [Originally published in 1899.]

individuals' experiences. With regard to the importance of considering the mutual influence of the micro- and macrolevels of data, I want to put special emphasis on two research methods. These methods link microdata and macrodata so that they can complement each other. Each method represents a paradigm of sociological analysis of regional cultures.

The first approach was developed by R. T. McKenzie, who was part of a group of sociologists in the 1920's and 1930's that later became known as the Chicago School of Sociology. McKenzie worked out a number of rules in connection with the Chicago School's famous theory of social ecology that are still useful as a classical analysis of social space. The theory is devoted to a functional approach for strengthening the macroperspective. In his concept of "social ecology" McKenzie points out that the ecological concept covers processes (created by interactions or institutions) *within* a space. More specifically it analyzes how the distribution of people and their activities in space correspond to the special forms of organization within an area and to forms attached to that particular space. Therefore, different "ecological units" can be distinguished according to principles of internal organization. In order to specify these principles McKenzie identifies the following fundamental categories of social space:

- *Mobility and fluctuation*: changing positions of residents, working places or goods due to the dynamic of technological and cultural progress;

- *Distance*: spatial expansion and transportation depending on a balance of time and cost;

- *Concentration*: density of persons during a certain period;

- *Centralization*: centers of special attraction that are temporarily frequented by large numbers of people;

- *Segregation*: shifting density among residential groups to shape either a more homogenous or heterogenous community according to financial means, linguistic facility, ethnicity, and so forth;

- *Invasion*: dislocation of residential groups as a result of segregation;

- *Succession*: a circular process of change in making use of a space so that different types of residents or different forms of utilization of the space follow successively (even as a result of invasion).

These categories are still valid when conducting a structural analysis, but should converge with a closer view on the microcosm. The second approach, drawing on the concept of symbolic interactions, comes from Clifford Geertz. Geertz worked out the method of "thick description," which can help complete "superficial" macro data by including the micro perspective of actors.[27] Contrary to McKenzie's approach stressing the social organization of space, Geertz's "thick description" focuses on the symbolic dimensions of social action or the meaning actors themselves ascribe to symbols while interacting. Therefore, the method is based on Max Weber's *verstehen* approach, one of the most famous methodological foundations in social sciences. Accordingly, Geertz explains "that man is an animal suspended in webs of significance he himself has spun," and that each web can be regarded as a "culture."[28] For that reason he submits that the main task of the researcher is to *interpret* constructed social expressions in search of *meaning*. The aim is to arrive at an ethnographic description that covers three characteristics: "it is interpretive; what it is interpretive of is the flow of social discourse; and the interpreting involved consists in trying to rescue the 'said' of such discourse from its perishing occasions."[29] The flow of discourse in every social situation intensifies the web of significance, and the analysis should sort out its structure. But most of the time the ethnographer is faced with "a multiplicity of complex conceptual structures, many of them superimposed upon or knotted into one another."[30] Geertz interprets data collection as a text, with the implication that the method approaches that of a literary critic.[31] Difficulties develop here both in determining the social ground and import of textual interpretation and—in connection with this task—being aware of or at least keeping in mind that *observation* and *interpretation* cannot be separated ideally or practically. So the conclusion is that *thick* description means "the writing out of systematic rules. . . which, if followed, would make it possible so to operate, to pass . . . for a native."[32] At the same time, gaining

---

27. Clifford Geertz, "Thick Description: Toward an Interpretive Theory of Culture," in *The Interpretation of Culture: Selected Essays by Clifford Geertz* (New York: Basic Books, 1973).
28. Geertz, "Thick Description," 5.
29. Geertz, "Thick Description," 20.
30. Geertz, "Thick Description," 10.
31. Geertz, "Thick Description," 9.
32. Geertz, "Thick Description," 11.

this competence validates the method of approach and is an expression of overcoming the interpretative description's mere subjective point of view. These two approaches can complement each other. Moreover, they may help to hybridize local experiences and global impacts methodologically.

8

The Evolving Meaning of Region in Canada

Gerald Friesen

C anadians have recognized the existence of regional communities within their nation-state since its founding in 1867. However, what constituted a region and determined its boundaries has not been consistent from one generation to the next. A widely accepted notion in European and American writing in the nineteenth century, and one that circulated in Canada, held that every human society was shaped by its environment. It was complemented in Canadian public discussion by the recognition that differences in political and economic interest also defined regional communities. Both approaches, environmentalism and political economy, contributed to the assumption that regions were influential forces in Canadian public life and probably in the shaping of individual Canadians' identities. At some point in the twentieth century such broad interpretations were called into question. The challenge came in part from social scientists who replaced environmentalist (or "formal") interpretations with "functional" approaches to social analysis. An equally important dissent originated with scholars in the humanities whose increased attention to language and communication resulted in widespread interest in "imagined communities" and a postmodern skepticism about seemingly timeless or essentialist constructs. Yet Canadian citizens and the popular press continued to refer to regions, though with less frequency and emphasis than in previous generations. This paper surveys the evolution of these various perspectives. It argues that not only the federal state and divergent economic interests but also the physical world and the historic bonds of community influence the contemporary understanding of regions in Canada. This paper suggests, to put its message in the most general terms, that those who wish to understand the region should not forget place and history in their efforts to come to terms with its continuing relevance.

I

Northern North America is a vast territory, about six thousand kilometers from east to west and a comparable distance from south to north, based on the drainage systems that once served as aboriginal and fur trade communication routes. Before the seventeenth century the land supported a relatively small population of aboriginal people, probably fewer than one million, who followed several different economic and cultural patterns in adapting to disparate environments. Aboriginal perception of place was associated with the resources on which the people relied for their existence and was affirmed by the stories and other arts that communicated their experience. Space was indivisible from place—that is, from specific locations on the earth's surface— but it was also indivisible from the spiritual qualities embedded in this world's physical attributes. In other words the link between human experience and the natural world was so immediate that reference to two spheres, human and natural, would have seemed incongruous. This unification of the human with the natural, given the assumption in many cultures that the two are entirely separate, has important consequences in both Canada's present and past.[1] At the very least, it established a strong association between specific aboriginal peoples and specific physical zones.

Over the next two hundred years small numbers of settlers from Europe, some of whom intermarried with the First Nations, also sustained their households on the fruits of the earth. Whether aboriginal, European, or métis, these communities—fewer than four million inhabitants in the mid-nineteenth century—communicated regularly only with their nearest neighbors though they also maintained intermittent contact with distant centers where imperial governments, church leaders, and markets for staple exports were located. In the absence of systems of intensive administration and trade encompassing a larger territory, the notion of region had little or no relevance. Nonetheless, limited public identities were coalescing during these centuries, notably as a consequence of war.[2] What could be clearer than the fact that, in the battles between the French and English empires for control over northern North America, residents who belonged to one empire identified with its fortunes and fought against the other? Both established lasting enclaves of settlement and thereby introduced another source of regional difference.[3]

---

1.   Royal Commission on Aboriginal Peoples, *Final Report*, vol. I, *Looking Forward, Looking Back* (Ottawa: Supply and Services Canada, 1996), 1–33.
2.   Margaret Conrad and James Hiller, *Atlantic Canada: A Region in the Making* (Oxford: Oxford University Press, 2001), chapter 7.
3.   Useful perspectives are offered in André Siegfried, *The Race Question in Canada* (Toronto: McClelland and Stewart, 1966, first pub. 1906); Carl Berger, *The Sense of Power: Studies in the Ideas of Canadian Imperialism 1867–1914* (Toronto: University of Toronto Press, 1970); and Ronald Rudin, *Making History in Twentieth-Century Québec* (Toronto: University of Toronto Press, 1997).

The European newcomers also brought a Christian and literate culture to the new land. Their worldview introduced notions of an unbridgeable divide between the human and natural worlds and of a print-encased body of knowledge that addressed all things temporal and spiritual. Moreover, by the closing decades of the eighteenth century thriving presses in the British North American colonies, as in the rest of the Americas, reported the views of colonial business, military, and church leaders as well as the opinions of the editors themselves. In this sense, as Benedict Anderson has suggested, the colonial community was made real by its members' articulation of distinctive perspectives.[4] The emergence of "creole nationalism" provided another potential source of regional sentiment.

Despite their roots in this text-based culture, most of the ordinary people of northern North America were several steps removed from the courts and governments where print prevailed. Their relations with aboriginal neighbors and the natural environment itself were more immediate. They responded to the rhythms of the day and the season and, like their aboriginal neighbors, they exploited the resources of the land. Their specialization in particular export staples also shaped the communities differently because each product required a different kind of infrastructure for its harvest and shipment. Thus, fish and timber from the Maritime provinces, lumber and wheat from Québec and Ontario, furs from the Northwest, and gold from British Columbia provided foundations for both growing economies and the apparently distinct societies built on them. The very character of the land was imprinted on human communities, a physical difference expressed as a social and "regional" quality. It constituted yet another potential foundation for regional identity.

The decision to create a single state, Canada, introduced a different version of region, a conceptualization based not on the environment or print but rather on political institutions. When Sir John A. Macdonald, George Brown, and their colleagues launched the national project, they faced the task of reconciling within the framework of a single administrative and electoral system distinct communities that had acquired a defined status within the British Empire during the previous century. Each of the five British colonies in eastern North America

---

4. Benedict Anderson, *Imagined Communities: Reflections on the Origin and Spread of Nationalism* (London: Verso, 1991). Anderson emphasizes the views of the newspaper writers. However, as other scholars have argued, while the emergence of colonial nationalism may have been partly due to the ideas recorded in newspaper columns, it also owed a great deal to the legislation of colonial politicians and even more to the economic and strategic interests of the people. After all, journalists and politicians typically articulated views that prevailed in the communities they represented.

differed from its counterparts in the size and composition of its population as well as in history and outlook. The Fathers' solution to this political and administrative puzzle was to adopt the federal principle. The creation of two levels of government, one of which—the province—was constructed precisely on the colonial boundaries of the preceding century, confirmed the regional qualities of the new national community. So, too, did the creation of two chambers of Parliament, a House of Commons and a Senate, the former based on representation by population and the latter based on a principle of "regional equality." Provinces might well be considered regions. But so, too, might larger territories. Thus, the notion of regions was reinforced by the allocation of twenty-four seats to Canada West (Ontario), Canada East (Québec), and the Maritimes (Nova Scotia and New Brunswick). In later years this version of the regional principle was extended when the four western provinces were allocated six seats each, twenty-four in all, to match the representation provided the three original sections.[5]

The forces that underlay later notions of Canadian regions were deeply entrenched by the time of Confederation. Aboriginal cultural history and aboriginal-white relations, imperial wars, enclaves of language and staple production, and distinct colonial administrations all reinforced the perception that the new nation embraced a number of spatially distinct communities. And the introduction of print capitalism with its power to shape public sentiment reinforced the people's identification with these colonial—soon to be regional—identities. Region, in short, was already employed in a "functional" sense. Moreover, these aboriginal and settler households maintained direct, immediate relations with the natural environment. Thus, the various physical landscapes of northern North America—"formal" regions—were engraved on the minds of an overwhelming proportion of ordinary citizens. The federal state established in 1867 and the references to sections that can be discerned in its constitution simply recognized what was evident to everyone about northern North America's public identities. Both peoples' relations with each other across a span of several centuries and peoples' relations with the physical environment shaped perceptions of region in the nascent Canada.

---

5.   John A. Macdonald's speech in Canada *Parliamentary Debates on the Subject of the Confederation of the British North American Provinces*, Third Session, Eighth Provincial Parliament (Québec: Hunter, Rose, and Company, 1865), 35.

II

More regions, and more deeply entrenched regional images, became commonplace in discussions of Canada during the seventy-five years after Confederation. By the 1940s and 1950s Canadians accepted as conventional wisdom that the local territory in which they lived—often termed a region—was a defining force in their lives and in their nationality.

As in other European and Europe-descended lands, writers in the new Canadian nation assumed that the environment was a powerful force in human society, and that the distinctive physical character of various regions—often read as an east-to-west-to-north sequence of ocean, forested lowlands, Shield, plains, mountains, and tundra—molded both individual character and entire communities. In the 1930s historian D. C. Harvey described the Atlantic Ocean as "the first heritage of the Maritimes and their first contribution to the Dominion." Similarly, a few years later W. L. Morton attributed prairie citizens' sense of distinctiveness to the land: "So domineering is this environment that it must change people, and greatly, from those of the humid forest regions of the East." Thus, formal regions remained the foundation of stereotypes in Canadian popular thought.[6]

The importance of region as a quality of the new nation was strengthened by political experience, economic interest, and administrative fiat. Annexation of the western and northern interior in 1870, the absorption of British Columbia in 1871 and Prince Edward Island in 1873, and the noisy emergence of the Yukon Territory during the Klondike gold rush of 1898 all represented the addition of regions in the making. A parallel phenomenon was the development of intense conflicts over public issues. The entire history of Canadian politics can be interpreted as a wellspring of regional sentiment, including such well-known episodes as the Nova Scotia secession resolution of 1885–1886, the French language and Roman Catholic school rights debates between the 1870s and 1920s, and the struggles over Canadian contributions to wars overseas.

Regional images actually became fixed in popular opinion. Between the 1850s and the 1920s the West acquired a touch of glamor as a free and untrammeled frontier, an image sustained by paintings and photographs of the Rockies, stories of the exploits of the North West Mounted Police, and by such political "firsts" as Manitoba's legislation to grant women the vote.

---

6.   D. C. Harvey, "The Heritage of the Maritimes," *Dalhousie Review* 14 (April 1934): 2; and W. L. Morton, "Clio in Canada: The Interpretation of Canadian History," *University of Toronto Quarterly* (1946), reprinted in A. B. McKillop, ed., *Contexts of Canada's Past: Selected Essays of W. L. Morton* (Toronto: Macmillan, 1980).

In the early twentieth century the stereotype of the "conservative Maritimes" also came into general circulation. Closer investigation reveals what was evident at the time and then forgotten: The economies of the three Atlantic provinces had been undermined by developments in the rest of the country and federal government policy choices, and this decline in status sustained a strong regional "Maritime Rights" sentiment that was just as forcefully espoused as its western analogue. Yet the West, imagined as a frontier, became the "radical" region, and the Maritimes, rooted in deeper family lineages and local loyalties, became "conservative." On her tour of Canada English visitor E. B. Mitchell was surprised to discover a widespread Canadian opinion about dynamic West and conservative East: "I wonder how many untravelled [sic] Britons have a picture in their minds quite adequately representing the barrier at Lake Superior between Down East and Out West."[7] What is amazing in retrospect is that such stereotypes endured for decades, muddying the ongoing debates about political choices.[8]

More subtle analysts referred not just to landscape or to the spatial distribution of economic activities but to a range of social factors that distinguished Canada's major communities. Thus, W. A. Mackintosh, an economist, writing on sectional voting patterns in the federal election of 1921, started with a list of conventional observations such as the physical distance between West and East, the economic differences between staple and manufacturing zones, and the racial and religious uniqueness of Québec: "In spite of the work of sixty years, the union of regions is but partially accomplished and the sectionalism apparent in election returns is no mere surface phenomenon but rooted deeply in the fundamental facts of geology, topography, climate, and resulting industrial conditions." He then observed that, given this list of differences, "sectionalism"—the struggle between a frontier and a longer-settled region—was "always characteristic of a new and expanding country."[9] In other words a spatial characteristic molded first by

---

7.   E. B. Mitchell, *In Western Canada before the War: A Study of Communities* (London: John Murray, 1915), ix; H. H. Stevens in Canadian Club of Vancouver, *Addresses and Proceedings* (1912–1913), 55, 53; R. L. Borden in Canadian Club of Toronto, *Addresses and Proceedings* (1910–1911), 133; H. W. Wood in Canadian Club of Montreal, *Addresses and Proceedings* (1916–1917), 269.

8.   Ernest Forbes, "In Search of a Post-Confederation Maritime Historiography, 1900–1967," in *Challenging the Regional Stereotype: Essays on the 20th Century Maritimes*, ed. Ernest Forbes (Fredericton: Acadiensis Press, 1989).

9.   W. A. Mackintosh, "Current Events," *Queen's Quarterly* 29 (1921–1922): 311–316. O. D. Skelton, Mackintosh's colleague, made a similar, but less nuanced, observation earlier in the same year: "The sectional cleavage between east and west . . . is in some measure a

community experience over a long period of time—the distinctive stage of social development in each of Canada's constituent parts—must be added to a discussion of physical factors if one was to properly comprehend the character of Canada and its regions.

The concept of Canadian region was perceived by several observers in the 1940s to be a fundamental descriptive category analogous to another type of territorial community, the nation. Thus, W. L. Morton, in his oft quoted 1946 declaration of prairie uniqueness, asserted that the prairie region had to "work out its own identity in terms of its own historical experience. It must realize its latent nationalism, a nationalism neither racial like the French nor dominant—a 'garrison' nationality—like that of Ontario, but environmental and, because of the diversity of its people, composite." If "alternative nationalisms," Morton's phrase, sounds extreme, note that André Laurendeau used similar words during his initial speech to the Québec Assembly in 1944. As the leader of the newly founded Bloc Populaire he pledged to "defend and restore the sovereignty of Québec in areas of its own competence within Confederation. Québec, in my view . . . is a true State, a people, a nation. [It should make] . . . laws suitable to our interests and our provincial ideals." Laurendeau perceived four public identities—province, nation, state, and people—where Morton saw a fifth—region. The dissonance must have been noted at the time but it seemed to cause little unease before the middle of the twentieth century.[10]

The notion of region conveyed powerful meanings to the listener. It was not simply a term intended to define physically distinct, physically homogenous units of settled territory—a "formal" region—but was also employed in "functional" terms as a relatively subtle and realistic assessment of the political and social differences created over a certain span of time by the spatial patterns of language, religion, and economy and by popular discussion of community stereotypes. The decisive quality in Canadians' approach to region in the first half of the twentieth century was the firm attachment that they perceived between the social experience and the specific territory—that is, between people and place—as well as between present and past.

---

cleavage of temperament, but essentially it is a cleavage of occupation, the divergence between predominantly agricultural and predominantly industrial communities, one instance, therefore of the grouping on class lines." *Queen's Quarterly* 29 (1921–1922), 203.

10.   Morton, "Clio in Canada," 110; and Laurendeau is quoted in Simonne Monet Chartrand *Ma Vie Comme Rivière: Récit autobiographique II 1939–1949* (Montréal: Les editions du remue-ménage, 1982), 229 (my translation).

III

The region was discussed often in the popular media and in scholarly writings of the last half of the twentieth century. Despite the frequency of the references, it no longer conveyed a clear, spatially defined image whose essence could be easily identified. Region as public identity remained influential, however, despite serious differences over the term's meaning within the scholarly world and the lack of a common understanding of its implications in academic and popular discussion.

From today's perspective events in the late twentieth century present an interesting dualism. On the one hand televisions, computers, and global trade have worked their homogenizing magic in Canada, as elsewhere. In the words of a misleading cliché they have annihilated space and time. On the other, world events have presented a remarkable tapestry of local democratic struggles in which former colonial states seek national sovereignty, and minority or subordinate populations assert their claims to equality. One might have said that Canadians' resistance to a global, homogenized, consensus society was very strong, and that popular consciousness of region had never been greater. Certainly, Atlantic and Western protests figured prominently in news reports. However, one would have to add that the most publicized of the new reform movements were not regional—far from it. Rather, the leading issues in the public conversation included government-market relations, the sovereigntist movement in Québec, aboriginal peoples' quest for "self-government," and policies concerning women, the family, sexuality, ethnicity, color, and multiculturalism. Region remained prominent in discussions of Canadian life, but it was not as central as in earlier generations.

The clarity of people's understanding of these social differences contrasted with the increasing ambiguity in scholars' analysis of Canadian regions. Two tendencies, an economic and a linguistic one, developed in academic interpretations of regional realities. Some scholars contended that the link between territory and citizenship, or between space and place, was dissolving forever. Others believed that they could define region in whatever manner they chose. The discipline of geography was the first to lodge noteworthy reservations about the concept of region in Canada. Its practitioners had been influenced by environmentalist visions from the late nineteenth century and one of its leaders, Griffith Taylor, published a monumental study based on environmental assumptions as late as 1947. However, the environmental approach to geography was under siege even then.[11] What replaced the old geography was, in fact, the new economics—or, at least, the increasingly influential economic approach to social study. This widely held understanding assumed that societies were shaped not by the land itself but, in a world where primary production occupied fewer and fewer workers, by the modern equivalent, the economic forces associated with industrial and cultural production. The perspective of neoclassical economists, who took the lead in this redefinition of social knowledge, was evident in "spatial microeconomics," which defined a version of region quite precisely because it adopted an enclosed, circular conceptualization of the world. The father of regional science, Walter Isard, illustrated this conceptual shift from environmentalism to economic abstraction when he suggested that regions should be seen as "simple generalizations of the human mind." Another subdiscipline, spatial macroeconomics, that addressed problems of regional underdevelopment, won prominence in Atlantic Canada because it emphasized spatial variations in economic growth. In its Marxist variant the "uneven" spatial dynamics of the economy were said to be concomitants of capitalist development. And an urban studies variant, which found favor in Canada during the 1970s and 1980s, focused on the "regularities of urban form" or on striking differences among major cities. These increasingly specialized and even technical studies set out new "functional" regions, defined them in a similarly enclosed and circular way, and offered policy advice couched in the language of the economist.[12]

Postwar historians followed geographers in suggesting that Canadian regions were distinguished by underlying urban patterns and by class and ethnic composition. They went beyond earlier geographic formulations, however, by noting the importance of social values and group identities to the development of regional consciousness. This was the beginning of notions of "imagined communities" in Canadian historical study. The idea, an extension of Morton's

---

11.   A. H. Clark, "Contributions to Geographical Knowledge of Canada since 1945," *Geographical Review* 40 (1950): 258–308; F. Kenneth Hare, "Canada," in *Canada: A Geographical Interpretation*, ed. John Warkentin (Toronto: Methuen, 1968), 3–12; and Barry Kaye and D. W. Moodie, "Geographical Perspectives on the Canadian Plains" in *A Region of the Mind: Interpreting the Western Canadian Plains*, ed. Richard Allen (Regina: Canadian Plains Research Centre, 1973).

12.   Cited in Frank Stilwell, *Understanding Cities and Regions: Spatial Political Economy* (Leichhardt: Pluto Press Australia, 1992), 47; Margaret Conrad, "The Politics of Place: Regionalism and Community in Atlantic Canada," in *The Constitutional Future of the Prairie and Atlantic Regions of Canada*, ed. James N. McCrorie and Martha L. MacDonald (Regina: Canadian Plains Research Centre, 1992); note the birth of the *Urban Studies Review* and works by Alan Artibise, Gilbert Stelter, and Paul-André Linteau among others.

approach to the prairies and George F. G. Stanley's remarks in the 1950s, was discussed in a more rigorous and influential way by J. M. S. Careless at the 1967 meeting of the American Historical Association.[13] Following Ramsay Cook, Careless suggested that the distinctiveness of Canada should not be imagined as a uniform national identity but, paradoxically, as the *absence* of a national identity—as the "limited identities" of class and ethnic group and, particularly, region: "The experience of regionalism," he wrote, "remains prominent and distinctive in Canadian history—and time has tended less to erode it than to develop it." Careless went beyond environmental factors to argue that Canadian regions were distinguished by urban patterns, class and ethnic composition, and the very workings—here he cited sociologist John Porter—of "the Canadian value system." In sum, Canadian society made greater room for regional experience than did its American counterpart: "The distinctive nature of much of Canadian experience has produced a continent-wide entity identifiable in its very pluralism, constraints, and compromises."

Careless had shifted the ground of the discussion. His innovation was to move the study of region—what created and defined these communities—from environment to values, from the influence of topography to the power of social arrangements and the workings of mind and emotion. Yet as a practical and politically conscious historian, Careless did not take the leap into an exclusively linguistic approach to social study. He contended that the new scholarly interest in values and culture must be married to the old understanding of political economy: "The implicit aim of every regional community has been maximum autonomy for itself consonant with the maximum advantage to be gained from an overriding central regime." In this, he suggested, the regions were simply repeating the experience of Canada itself in its earlier relations within the British Empire. He offered a historian's approach to region—functional

13.　J. M. S. Careless, " 'Limited Identities' in Canada," *Canadian Historical Review* 50 (1969): 1–10; George F. G. Stanley, in a paper presented to the American Historical Association in 1958 and later published as "Regionalism in Canadian History," *Ontario History* 51 (1959): 163–171 wrote: "In some countries regionalism may begin as a state of mind and become an actuality; in Canada it began as an actuality and has developed into a state of mind. Community of purpose, then, is the touchstone." Though his reasoning commenced with traditional assumptions about environment and history, Stanley shifted the focus of study from the place itself to the peoples' self-image: "One feature common to all regions—and by this feature we may recognize it—is its consciousness of its own identity as such in terms of community of purpose." See also George Rawlyk, "The Maritimes and the Canadian Community" and Morris Zaslow, "The Yukon: Northern Development in a Canadian-American Context," in *Regionalism in the Canadian Community 1867–1967*, ed. Mason Wade (Toronto: University of Toronto Press, 1969).

regions, to be sure, but rooted in the inherited concepts of earlier days and the workings of the political system.[14]

Where historians turned to matters of "regional consciousness" and "regional protest," political scientists focused on income and institutions. Some concentrated on government's responsibility for development strategies and the uneven distribution of wealth that such policies produced. Others examined the institutions designed to mediate interregional tensions in the field of federal-provincial and municipal-provincial relations. In either case the political scientists did not challenge the prevailing scholarly assumptions: Regions, whether city-based, single-province or larger, continued to offer a relevant analytical category in discussions of Canadian society, and such territorial loyalties influenced Canadian political activity and citizens' public identities.[15]

Janine Brodie followed the lead of other political scientists by insisting that "the spatial dimension of Canadian politics overshadows most other social cleavages, such as social class, in our collective political experience." Moreover, unlike many other societies, Brodie wrote, spatially based political conflict actually increased in Canada during the 1970s and 1980s. The reason for its primacy, she suggested, was conflict over "where economic activity has and will be located." Thus, Brodie's approach to region was not based on the physical features of the land but remained pre-eminently economic. In her analysis regions had "concrete political and social dimensions that are deeply embedded in our collective historical experience" and required a political theory of regional imbalance to be understood properly. Thus, regions were:

> political creations that state development strategies cumulatively impose upon the geographic landscape. These policies represent the crystallization of underlying class forces and political compromises and are forged in an atmosphere of shifting international contexts and uncertainties. . . . While uneven spatial development may be a necessary condition for the emergence of spatially based politics, it

14. G. R. Cook, "Canadian Centennial Cerebrations," *International Journal* 22 (Autumn 1967): 659–663; John Porter, *The Vertical Mosaic* (Toronto: University of Toronto Press, 1965).

15. Janine Brodie, *The Political Economy of Canadian Regionalism* (Toronto: Harcourt Brace Jovanovich, 1990).

is not a sufficient condition. Regional politics . . . is a response to historical contingencies associated with each development strategy.[16]

As in the new economic approaches to region, so in this political science version, the view of region had broken with the old "formal" definitions but continued to assume that regions were "real forces" in a "real world" and were shaped primarily by economic circumstances.

Another view of region in Canadian political science, articulated by Donald Smiley, David Elkins, Richard Simeon, and Roger Gibbins, among others, proposed that the province should be seen as the important territorial alternative to nation. They argued that the impact of Canada's electoral system and the changing roles of the provinces consequent upon court rulings and the elevated profile of such provincial responsibilities as schools, health care, and roads had increased provincial power relative to that of Ottawa. There had been a corresponding decrease, they suggested, in the relevance of region. There is merit in this approach. However, to propose that the province is the next alternative to nation is also just another way to draw a regional boundary and describe territorial loyalties. Moreover, as Brodie properly notes, there is more to the Canadian region than this narrow approach acknowledges.[17]

These social scientific approaches focused on economic fortunes, social imaginings, and political institutions and asserted the "reality" of the regional forces they addressed. Students of literature, by contrast, contended that imagination and identity had little or nothing to do with material reality. Poet and critic Eli Mandel represented the Canadian version of the linguistic turn in scholarship by arguing in reference to the outpouring of imaginative literature from the Prairie provinces that the "literary and academic overtones [of these works] tell us that essentially the world being observed is a mental one." Noting that cultural historians had hitherto been environmentalists, Mandel commented that Canadians tended to read regional literature as the product of a distinctive environment, "possibly because we tend to equate regions with particular space." But he was not convinced:

---

16.   Brodie, *Political Economy of Canadian Regionalism*, 3, 5, 12, 17, 77; also her "The Concept of Region in Canadian Politics," in *Federalism and Political Community: Essays in Honour of Donald Smiley*, ed. David P Shugarman and Reg Whitaker (Peterborough: Broadview Press, 1989), 33–53.

17.   David J. Elkins and Richard Simeon, *Small Worlds: Provinces and Parties in Canadian Political Life* (Toronto: Methuen, 1980); Donald Smiley, *The Federal Condition in Canada* (Toronto: McGraw Hill Ryerson, 1986); Roger Gibbins, *Prairie Politics and Society: Regionalism in Decline* (Toronto: Butterworths, 1980); Ramsay Cook, "Regionalism Unmasked," *Acadiensis* 13 (1983).

To say, then, as [novelist] Robert Kroetsch says, that we have no identity until someone tells our story, that fiction makes us real, is not paradoxical but tautological. The statement surely means identity is fictional: it exists only in stories, in dreams, in fantasy. About this, we may say one of two things: fantasy plays no historical or social role *or* its role is much stranger than anything we yet know.

Mandel pondered the two possibilities during the 1970s and eventually declared that the relation between them must be sought in "the spiritual enterprise that is western culture." Ironically, Mandel and many of those who have followed him in the study of prairie literature contended that the region remained important—a region of the mind, to be sure, but a region all the same. Mandel can be seen as one of the first of his generation in Canada to insist that the cultural could be separated completely from the physical and economic, and that identity belonged uniquely in the realm of the imagined.[18]

Canadians did not agree about the notion of region in the closing years of the twentieth century. And yet regional generalizations abounded both in their daily conversation and scholarly discussions. In these exchanges region might refer to the unequal distribution of wealth, social and political differences, or esoteric artistic perspectives. In becoming subtler and more nuanced as a category of analysis, region had also become ambiguous.

IV

Does this mean that region is now irrelevant? Is it possible to reconceptualize the relation between social processes, cultural expression, and spatial form to make the concept clearer? How does region relate to nation given that, in Canada but probably in other countries as well, the link between the two concepts is confusing? Is place, the physical referent behind region, still a relevant concept? These questions remain.

Let us suppose that the fundamental dimensions of space and time may be subject to drastic change, but that they continue to exist as reference points in daily life. Assume, too, that the historian's task is to explain how and why they have changed and illustrate the process of transition. In northern North

---

18.   Eli Mandel, "Images of Prairie Man," in *A Region of the Mind*, and "Romance and Realism in Western Canadian Fiction," in *Prairie Perspectives 2: Selected Papers of the Western Canadian Studies Conferences, 1970, 1971*, ed. A. W. Rasporich and H. C. Klassen (Toronto: Holt, Rinehart, and Winston, 1973). Perry Anderson, *The Origins of Postmodernity* (London: Verso, 1998), traces the development of such notions to earlier decades in the twentieth century.

America there evolved a peoples' sense of place and region that commenced with aboriginal peoples' recognition of the different environments in which they sustained their existence. Their stories and art reflected local places. This sense of place was duplicated, if not reinforced, by immigrants' identification with the places in which they settled and the distinctive staple economies they built. The sense of region acquired greater relevance, however, only when a broader vision of a transcontinental society was constructed in the nineteenth century and literate communications—print capitalism—made specialized, abstract social analysis possible. The political arrangements of Confederation recognized, but also entrenched, the regional identities that already existed. In the next three or four generations, peoples' relations with place and environment, and their public loyalties, became increasingly rooted to the point that they could be recognized as essential elements of individual and group character.

Then around the middle of the twentieth century this unity of vision began to crumble. Social scientists introduced regional concepts based on an enclosed universe in which the existence of regions and merit of regional categories were demonstrated by means of a variety of circular analyses. Students of literature contended that their world existed on its own. Neither approach, neither the "functional" nor the "imagined" region, despite the creativity and precision of the individual works, quite captured the subtlety and depth of the Canadian attraction to region. Yet their very existence demonstrated that the regional notion survived in Canada. Its appearance in popular conversation and scholarly writing testified to a prosaic truth: Canadians had not yet left the dimensions of space and time, whatever science fiction or certain strains of postmodern thought might tell them. They still believed that location was important, not just in political activity or economic policy making, though these mattered a great deal, but also in terms of their appreciation of place and history.

Part of the problem with the functional and imagined approaches to region lies in the conceptualization of place.[19] Does it any longer have physical

---

19.   Celia Applegate describes place as the created, self-reproducing, nondeterministic context of collective life: "A Europe of Regions: Reflections on the Historiography of Sub-National Places in Modern Times," *American Historical Review* 104 (1999): 1181, citing Alexander Murphy, "Regions as Social Constructs: The Gap Between Theory and Practice," *Progress in Human Geography* 15 (1991): 23–36. She also cites the recent work of several German scholars, including Beatrice Ploch, Heinz Schilling, Wolfgang Lipp, and Karl Rohe on "regional culture and industrial society," and scholars studying France including Winnie Lem, Charlotte Tacke, and Heidi Kelley, whose studies of regional identity emphasize local communities' resistance to and accommodation with national hegemony. One guide to

dimensions? Arjun Appadurai suggests that a territorial identity such as locality should be understood as "primarily relational and contextual rather than as scalar or spatial." Though he argues convincingly that "space and time are themselves socialized and localized through complex and deliberate practices of performance, representation, and action," he also observes that "virtual neighborhoods" have emerged in contemporary society. Thus, he leaves an element of uncertainty in his discussion of physical places. One can agree with Appadurai to this extent: A contemporary society's sense of place does indeed include familiarity with a particular history, recognition of group boundaries, and identification with imaginary lives and worlds communicated in ritual as well as in such media as film, radio, print, and paint. In Appadurai's terms all these approaches are relational and contextual. One might differ from him by insisting on the addition to this list of both commonsense notions of political space—usually territorial in definition—and, among some citizens at least, an intimate knowledge of physical location—the angle of the light or the touch of the air or the sound of the background hum or the particular quality of the silence—that seems like an epiphany when it strikes. Both types of experience, the political and the physical, are at least as important as the relational and contextual, in fixing a notion of locality and of region—of place—in the public mind. Taken together all four constructs sustain the relevance of region in Canadian affairs.[20]

Another problem concerns the relation between region and nation. Of course, the nation is a sovereign entity in a single space whereas there are many possible regions. The absence of a single, fixed institutional role for "region" is, in the Canadian case at least, a useful and flexible quality that contributes positively to the conduct of local and national conversations because it introduces more complex approximations of reality. Nonetheless, the widely-circulated but mistaken notion that regions can only be transitional moments in a society's growth to nationhood has caused some misunderstanding, especially for Canadians' appreciation of the challenge posed by Québec sovereigntists.

---

these questions is David Harvey, "Between Space and Time: Reflections on the Geographic Imagination," *Annals of the Association of American Geographers* 80 (1990): 418–434 and "From Space to Place and Back Again: Reflections on the Condition of Postmodernity," in *Mapping the Futures: Local Cultures, Global Change*, ed. Jon Bird et al. (London: Routledge, 1993).

20.   Arjun Appadurai, *Modernity at Large: Cultural Dimensions of Globalization* (Minneapolis: University of Minnesota Press, 1996); David Harvey, *Justice, Nature and the Geography of Difference* (Oxford: Blackwell, 1996); Yi-Fu Tuan, *Space and Place: The Perspective of Experience* (Minneapolis: University of Minnesota, 1977).

Regions and nations are not necessarily contradictions or enemies. Lord Acton's dictum about the value of many "races" (or public identities) within one country has long been pointed to as an appropriate recognition of the useful tension that region introduces into national life. That Québec can be a nation and a region of Canada, and yet not be a sovereign entity equal to and separate from Canada, is a notion that has been difficult to establish in Canadian popular discourse.[21]

Behind these issues of place and nation lies a different conundrum, the contemporary understanding of time. In nations such as Canada the scale of historical time is foreshortened, whether viewed from the perspective of Europe and its print-capitalist culture or of Asia and its ancient traditions associated with literacy and memory. It is true that extended aboriginal-European contact in northern North America began only in the early seventeenth century. The Industrial Revolution and print-capitalism became a substantial cultural force only in the mid-nineteenth century. And universal literacy only became possible in the early twentieth century. In other words, though few Canadians live on the land today, their neighbors and perhaps even their recent ancestors probably did so. The aboriginal and settler views of time and space, though remote when viewed in the abstract, are not far removed from daily life. Canadians encounter the children of this history in the streets around them. Such connections can have a bearing on contemporary society, even though the obvious links between present and past have not been communicated with sufficient effect to establish a coherent, articulated historical consciousness among ordinary citizens.[22]

Richard White has noted that, after the linguistic or postmodern turn in the humanities and social sciences, the categories of our thought must be given the same careful analysis that the characters and events once received.[23]

---

21. Jean-Marie Fecteau, "Between Scientific Enquiry and the Search for a Nation: Québec Historiography as Seen by Ronald Rudin," *Canadian Historical Review* 80 (1999): 641–666. The concept of public identities is discussed by Charles Tilly, "Citizenship, Identity and Social History," in *Citizenship, Identity and Social History*, supplement 3 *International Review of Social History* (Cambridge: Cambridge University Press, 1996).

22. Gerald Friesen, *Citizens and Nation: An Essay on History, Communication, and Canada* (Toronto: University of Toronto Press, 2000), 36, 48–49. The condition of timelessness is puzzling. Does it prevail in most contemporary societies? Perhaps it is a cultural failing peculiar to today's generation and not an absence that will prevail for generations. The loss of the dimension of public time is often seen as the source of the ahistorical tenor of today's community conversations. See Eric Hobsbawm, *Age of Extremes: The Short Twentieth Century 1914–1991* (London: Michael Joseph, 1994), 16.

23. Richard White, "Is There a North American History?" (unpublished paper, Stanford University, 1995).

By understanding the history of the regional category in a given society, one is better able to appreciate what is being said in daily discourse and better-equipped to understand contemporary circumstances. This history of "region" in Canada has demonstrated that place mattered in previous generations; that regions are not simply nations in waiting; that land and place continue to play an important role in daily life; and, though it must make room for many other pressing concerns, that region continues to offer insights into economic, political, social, and cultural difference.

9

Decentering the Region: Spatial Identifications and Differentiations in Postmodern Regional Narratives

Michaela Röll

Narrative literature provides insight into the perspective of one or several individuals. The same holds true for regions in narrative literature. Furthermore, regions in literature are not only seen through different perspectives, they also carry different meanings. They are semanticized, like all places in narratives. Literary critics therefore investigate how regions are viewed by their literary inhabitants, and what regions really mean to those situated in them. Literary critics less quantify than qualify the various processes of regional identifications. Because of its specificity, the literary perspective is very important for interdisciplinary regional studies: It views the region in its specific impact on the individual, and the individual's attitude toward the region. The manner in which place is represented through fictional characters might tell us something about how we represent and perspectivize places in the life world. Literary critics have an invaluable advantage over sociologists, anthropologists, and philosophers: They have the unique chance of slipping into the mind of regional characters and assessing regions simultaneously from without and within.

Departing from the study of contemporary North American novels, I analyze the mechanisms of representation and interpretation of regions in postmodern literature. My main concern is with the decentered perspective on literary regions and characters' search for a home region. I show how postmodern regions result from a new concern with spatiality. Postmodern regions are also closely connected to movement, new perceptions of time, and memory.[1]

Regions are either viewed through the narrator's eyes, or they are filtered through one of the fictional characters' perspectives. And, of course, they are

---

1.   This essay is closely connected to my doctoral thesis, which I completed at the University of Bonn. In the thesis I explore postmodern regional identities in contemporary novels from New England and eastern Canada.

presented as perceived by the author. As a result literary regions are neither defined in their overall extensions, as they might be by the geographer, nor are they comprehensively described, in the manner of a social scientist. They exist through their importance for the literary characters only. If there is no author who writes about the region, and no character who experiences the region, it does not exist for the literary critic.

In narrative texts places do not exist independently of and externally to characters. Narrated action takes place somewhere. Therefore, setting, as a location of the characters' movement, as a "place of action," is a defining feature of this genre. In fact, as the philosopher Edward Casey points out, the location of bodies is a defining feature of place as opposed to space. He explains: "Place . . . serves important locatory purposes—a given body must, after all, be located *somewhere*, in the infinity of space, occupying some locale within its capacious embrace—and it still bears qualities that no other entity or medium exhibits so completely: qualities of directionality, fit, density, contiguity and interstice."[2] Even if the fictional body is not material in the philosophical sense, it is at the center of the fictional world. A lot of attention has been paid to the importance of body for the analysis of fictional texts, following the philosophical ideas of Michel Foucault, Jacques Lacan, Gilles Deleuze, and Félix Guattari. The body is intentional and directional, fits or does not fit into its surroundings, coexists with other bodies, and experiences the qualities of its place.

Two concepts of place are central to regionalism in literary studies. First, regions as sociocultural phenomena are seen as spatial manifestations of cultural networks or political units with a common history.[3] These regions have names such as New England, Québec, or the South in North American regional fiction. They are often, but not necessarily, smaller than a nation but bigger than a local community.[4] They are seen in relation to other regions, and they are

2.   Edward S. Casey, *The Fate of Place: A Philosophical History* (Berkeley: University of California Press, 1997), 199. For Casey the main difference between space and place is that "as vacuous, even if not a perfect vacuum, space lacks those specific attributes or qualities that would tie it to place as the specific setting of material bodies," 198.

3.   Richard Pieper, *Die Neue Sozialphysik: Zur Mechanik der Solidarität* (Frankfurt a/M: Campus Verlag, 1989), 340ff.

4.   "In general, the region presents itself as a middle space, less extended than the nation and the great space of civilization, but wider than the social space of a group." A. Frémont, *La région, espace vécu* (Paris: Presses Universitaires de France, 1976), 138, translated in Roberto M. Dainotto, *Place in Literature: Regions, Cultures, Communities* (Ithaca: Cornell University Press, 2000), 8.

connected to a certain geographic extension and undergo a certain historical process. This is where literary critics can use the approaches of sociologists, cultural geographers, and historians. Once a region's name is dropped, readers know more or less where the action takes place and can draw upon their own historical or geographical knowledge.

On the other hand, places in literature are often presented as fuzzy surroundings of the characters, stylized by the author to correspond to the highly selective perception of a subject at their center. In this sense they are closely connected to the philosophical concept of "environment." Bodies move and organize the places in which they move as larger units. These units cannot be pinpointed. Their fuzziness results from the movement of the human body, its changing positions, and the manual use of tools.[5] The human body places itself through its action in the center of its own environment. In the philosophical sense subjects are always at the center of their personal places of action, organizing place around themselves. Without this center, any orientation whatsoever is unthinkable. Place is divided into a "here," the region of the subject's influence, and a "there," the area beyond its reach. Mobility involves the act of making the "there" (the distant, the unknown) into the "here" (the close, the known). In her novel *Lives of Girls and Women* Alice Munro describes the coming of age of Del Jordan, who slowly extends her notions of "here" by crossing her perceived borders and moving into hitherto unknown territory.[6] Through this movement she reassesses her former center of perception, and this reassessment is indissolubly bound to her personal and artistic growth. Without movement action is not possible.

The phrase "decentering the region" in my title involves both concepts of place: the socio-cultural concept of cultural networks located in certain regions and the philosophical concept of personal "environment." As I see it, the act marks the free movement of individual perspective within a larger cultural and geographic region. It thus takes into account the increasing mobility of subjects and draws attention to the importance of differentiation for the construction of postmodern regional identities.

Because perception and representation are central elements of literary regionalism, a phenomenological approach is the most able to grasp the specific mechanisms of interaction between the human and the region. Since regions involve communities or an individual's notion of community, the literary approach to regionalism has to bridge the gap between individual

---

5.   Casey, *The Fate of Place*, 21.
6 .   Alice Munro, *Lives of Girls and Women* (Toronto: McGraw-Hill Ryerson Limited, 1971).

perception and its cultural consequences. Individual perspectives contribute to the cultural shape of the region. They are not just a passive reception of the region but can also shape a region's cultural images. The approach I propose, therefore, considers philosophical ideas as well as methods derived from social and cultural studies. It is important to stress that communities are not viewed as homogenous or monolithic. They are constructed and questioned by each individual, and they are thus structured according to the individual's mode of identification with the communities.

According to Martin Heidegger, the basic mode of existence is "being in the world," by which he means a specific situatedness in place and time.[7] It is therefore not the Cartesian philosophy of "cogito ergo sum" underlying today's interest in regions and regionalism, but rather, "Hic et nunc sum, ergo sum" (I am here and now, therefore I am), introduced by existential philosophers. Many recent theories of being and place are based on this philosophy. For example, Edward S. Casey writes: "To live is to live locally, and to know is first of all to know the places one is in."[8] We all find ourselves situated in a place at a time. Both provide a basic orientation for us. We can assess the importance of both elements to our notion of self if we imagine waking up one day without remembering where and when we went to bed, and how long we slept. Heidegger claims that we become aware of our regions of orientation through misplacement, and that our orientation becomes visible once it is threatened.[9]

While existentialists observed the intrinsic failure of finding meaning in place and time as well as an anthropological disorientation resulting in ontological insecurity, the postmodern predicament is slightly different. Subjects are displaced, and this displacement draws attention to human orientations. But postmodern authors are acquainted with the idea that orientation is fragmented, and displacement is not necessarily identical with misplacement any longer. There is a multitude of different visions of place and time, which makes places multifarious. A knowledge of these different visions is the prerequisite for postmodern communities and regions. The sense of uneasiness and loss of a home place observed by the existentialists remains,

---

7.   Martin Heidegger, *Being and Time*, trans. John Macquarrie and Edward Robinson (New York: Harper and Row, 1962), 79ff.

8 .   Edward S. Casey, "How to Get from Space to Place in a Fairly Short Stretch of Time: Phenomenological Prolegomena," in *Senses of Place*, ed. Steven Feld and Keith H. Basso (Santa Fe: School of American Research Press, 1996), 18.

9.   See Heidegger, *Being and Time*, 138: "Often the region [Gegend] of a place does not become accessible explicitly as such a region until one fails to find something in *its* place."

even increases, through globalization. Today's regional authors, however, dramatize the search for the place, the struggle to render meaningful one's place. In doing so they uncover various layers of meanings attached to places and trace the dynamic interrelation between places.[10]

Regions provide for human societies what sociologist Pierre Bourdieu calls "habitus."[11] Habitus is people's conception of their communities. Habitus influences and shapes communities, which in turn shape people's conceptions of them. It therefore describes the process of representing and individually conceiving one's sociocultural context. Humans thus construct both place and time, and their communities. The knowledge of this constructedness of their world is one of the major elements of postmodern subjectivity. Not every place, however, makes such an active constructing possible.

The human search for existence is therefore strongly connected to a search for one's place. Regions have long been important units for human orientation, because they are connected to the idea of closeness and familiarity.[12] Furthermore, regions are sociocultural areas with a history, and they are strongly connected to the idea of home. The present concern with global networks and the consequent decline of the nation as a unit of identification coincide with a stronger appreciation of place and regions.[13] Regions are semantic networks connected to a specific locale that may provide a meaningful place to live for their inhabitants. They make the experience of specificity and difference tangible. Therefore, they are a much more useful counterweight against postmodern disorientation than the more abstract concept of a nation. Cultural anthropologist Arjun Appadurai uses a very similar concept when he speaks about neighborhoods, by which he means "the actually existing social forms in which locality, as a dimension or value, is variably realized. Neighborhoods, in this usage, are situated communities characterized by their actuality, whether spatial or virtual, and their potential for social reproduction."[14]

---

10. This interrelation between places is not least one of power structures. The postmodern discourse about displacements and multiculturalism should not obscure the fact there still are cultural hegemonies connected to place. Cf. Dainotto, 3ff. Although Dainotto uses "place" in a rather archaic sense, this attention on cultural hegemony is nevertheless justified.

11. Pierre Bourdieu, *Distinction: A Social Critique of the Judgement of Taste*, trans. Richard Nice (London: Routledge, 1984), 169ff.

12. Heidegger, *Being and Time*, 135ff. See also Casey, *The Fate of Place*, 243–284.

13. Ibid., xiiiff.

14. Arjun Appadurai, *Modernity at Large: Cultural Dimensions of Globalization*, 4th ed. (Minneapolis: University of Minnesota Press, 1998), 178.

With the increase of global mobility home is no longer guaranteed by birth and no longer grounded in earthbound traditions. Homes are no longer locales that guarantee a continuum of generations and provide meaning through this continuum. Global mobility disrupts the cultural memories located in one home place. As Homi Bhabha puts it: "The borderline work of culture demands an encounter with 'newness' that is not part of the continuum of past and present."[15] People find themselves in places that are not connected to their personal past and in times in which change is a stronger value than continuity. Because homes are no longer guaranteed by birth, people have to render meaningful the places in which they live. Because of the mobility of their ancestors and themselves, they do not have access to a home as a center around which place can be organized. They often find themselves dislocated, displaced or in between. Therefore they begin to search for something that could become a home. The search for a home region thus becomes the central quest in many contemporary narratives, precisely because mobility and dislocation are major conditions of postmodern existence.

In many regional novels the center of action is moved throughout the region, often even beyond its limits. In Margaret Atwood's *Alias Grace* the protagonist immigrates to Toronto from Europe. Grace's attempts to find a new home, to render meaningful her new "here," are always counterbalanced by her traumatic experiences, and this rupture ultimately leads to her schizophrenia and confinement in prison. After her release she moves out of Ontario, south of the national border, to the United States. This is a story of social, cultural, and psychological border crossings, and at the same time a vivid description of Ontario's settlement history.[16] The border crossings in this novel problematize the idea of home, and the region is assessed through the protagonist's movement into and ultimately out of the region. The spatial border crossings parallel her rupture of identity, the psychological homelessness of her self.

Regions in many contemporary novels are presented from different points of view or from various angles. These multiple perspectives point to different functions of a regional location. This, too, is a way of decentering the region. While every subject is the center of his/her own place of perception, we know that there are other subjects and thus other centers of perception. The regional novel can contextualize these multiple centers of perception and explore the varied meanings of a region. This is the case in Jane Urquhart's novel *The Whirlpool*, which is set in the town of Niagara Falls in 1889. For

15. Homi K. Bhabha, *The Location of Culture* (London, New York: Routledge, 1994), 7.

16. Margaret Atwood, *Alias Grace* (Toronto: McClelland and Stewart, 1996).

the town's historian the region around Niagara Falls and the Whirlpool is a historic site, demarcating the border between Canada and the United States as an outcome of the War of 1812. It is therefore a vessel of Canadian identity from his historical perspective. The visiting poet views the Whirlpool as a romantic landscape, at the same time horrible and sublime, and ultimately as a projection of his spiritual yearnings. He enters the current in search of an aesthetic experience and in admiration of the British Romantics. For the local undertaker the hazardous river signifies business, and for the people from the region it provides a sensation. Gradually, these different readings mix like the waters of the current, revealing a people's struggle to make sense of their lives, their past, and their possible future.[17] These different views on the landscape in Urquhart's novel highlight the strong evocative powers of place. At the same time it becomes clear that place cannot guarantee a collective memory.

Regions in literature are often set into relation with other regions and defined through their difference. More often than not this serves to dramatize the protagonist's quest to belong somewhere. In Austin Clarke's *The Origin of Waves* a Barbadian immigrant literally bumps into a childhood friend in Toronto. Searching for a relief from homesickness, he tells his friend about his feeling of misplacement. Although he has become part of Toronto, he always measures his environment against his place of origin, which he thinks of as home. Together the two Barbadians confront the fact that "there ain't no goddamn home back home!"[18] They are both displaced, but they realize they have to learn to accept their displacement and give up their idealized vision of Barbados. The metropolis of immigration is counterbalanced against the immigrants' place of origin, and out of this tension arises the city's specific atmosphere in the book. Novels such as Michael Ondaatje's *In the Skin of a Lion*[19] explore how rural regions differ from urban lifestyles. In Atwood's *Cat's Eye*[20] Ontario is contrasted with the West Coast, and the relationship of modern Toronto to the Toronto of the past is explored. These novels dramatize the protagonists' quests for emplacement, tracing their various dislocations and journeys between potential home regions. The regions in these novels are questioned and asserted at the same time: questioned, because their value is evanescent, and because sufficient meaning to grasp them cannot always be constituted; asserted, because their image emerges out of the context of

---

17. Jane Urquhart, *The Whirlpool* (Toronto: McClelland and Stewart, 1986).

18. Austin Clarke, *The Origin of Waves* (Toronto: McClelland and Stewart, 1997), 70.

19. Michael Ondaatje, *In the Skin of a Lion* (Toronto: McClelland and Stewart, 1987).

20. Margaret Atwood, *Cat's Eye* (Toronto: McClelland and Stewart, 1988).

dislocations, and because the protagonists do not give up their search for them.

What distinguishes regions from mere geographic areas is that regions have a history. Regions exist and change over time. Looked at sociologically, people(s) continuously create and re-create representations of their regions. These representations are held together by the threads of individual and cultural memory. And memory itself is closely connected to real places, as Cicero was one of the first to point out. According to his mnemotechnics, memory is stimulated by the images of existing places and is structured in analogy to real places. It serves to keep the tradition of the ancestors, which is indissolubly bound to the specific locale.[21] Of course, the meaning of memory has undergone substantial changes in the course of history, as has the concept of the human mind itself.

With the increase of mobility the ties between traditions and their places have become unstable.[22] In early Europe a place tied people to their ancestral history. Consequently, people felt they belonged to the place. The European settlers in North America, however, proposed a concept of place as something one can obtain and that has to change in order to serve its new inhabitants. The strong unifying tie connecting different generations, which bound people to their home regions, was cut. Even though this model of earthbound traditions still exists, mostly in indigenous and francophone literatures, the concept of North American regions was from the beginning one that allowed for human mobility and spatial renegotiations. Regions have become the sites of various reinscriptions of memory, and therefore several groups and societies may now claim certain areas for their respective traditions and memories. This is part of the region's decentered nature. It also means that a region cannot guarantee the continuity of its memories any longer; people actively have to keep it alive.

One of the most effective means of keeping a region's memories alive is the writing of regional literature. Writer and reader draw upon known locales, each of them having in mind their proper representation of the specific region. Both fields of experience converge in the text. The text mediates between all the different individual perceptions of region. Through the individual perceptions it presents the text then becomes a new source of experience for the reader. Thus, literature can strongly influence the modeling of regional

---

21.   Marcus Tullius Cicero, *De Oratore: Über den Redner*, ed. and trans. Harald Merklin, 2ⁿᵈ ed. (Stuttgart: Reclam, 1976), 431–439.

22.   Cf. Aleida Assmann, *Erinnerungsräume: Formen und Wandlungen des kulturellen Gedächtnisses* (Muich: Verlag C. H. Beck, 1999), chapter 5.

identifications. Henry David Thoreau's book *Walden* is an example of what literature can do to a real place.[23] Thoreau's literary description of Walden Pond was such a popular model of New England nature experience that the real pond became a mecca for many visitors from New England and even from all over the United States. Paradoxically, the place now also monitors the change in the relationship between people and their nature. Whereas for a long time it signified a refuge for the lone transcendentalist, it has become a tourist attraction for globetrotters—and has, miraculously, still retained some of its evocative powers.

These observations on postmodern regions should make it clear that today's regional novels have nothing to do with parochial novels or local color texts. In local color texts the sketched regions function as a mere backdrop, an idyllic setting. Such texts do not generate a dynamic that really motivates the action. In parochial novels regions are conceived as secluded islands that do not fit into a larger frame but work, much like the limited place on a stage, as a representative space for the world in general.[24] The individual surroundings in this case correspond to the region in general, and the fictional character is always in its center. The space beyond the protagonist's reach is also beyond the regional boundaries, marked only by being unknown. Neither of those types can appropriately describe the cultural dynamics of a real region, especially a postmodern one. Regional heroes often transcend borders, they move their point of view beyond known borderlines, and they transform their "here" into a "there." That way they can perceive their home region from a new angle. Or they feel disoriented and are only able to find their home region after a long journey, as in Annie Proulx's *The Shipping News*, in which Quoyle, the protagonist, searches for his complicated family ties in Newfoundland.[25] Or they constitute their identity being situated between two cultural regions, as the protagonist in Clark Blaise's story "North," whose mother wants him to grow up in Montreal's anglophone part, while his father wants to raise him as a Catholic in the city's francophone part.[26] Or they have to abandon the idea of home altogether, as the Barbadians in Austin Clarke's *The Origin of Waves*.

While social sciences quantify regions, literature monitors their quality. It is therefore necessarily much more selective. Literature offers an insight into

---

23.   Henry David Thoreau, *Walden: An Annotated Edition* (Boston: Houghton Mifflin, 1995).

24.   Cf. Norbert Mecklenburg, *Erzählte Provinz: Regionalismus und Moderne im Roman* (Königstein: Athenäum, 1986), 46.

25.   E. Annie Proulx, *The Shipping News* (Toronto: Maxwell Macmillan Canada, 1993).

26.   Clark Blaise, "North," in *Resident Alien* (Markham, ON: Penguin Books Canada, 1986), 77–105.

the perspective of one or several individuals. As such, it can obtain the status of a model experience. To put it in a nutshell: The writers and readers of a book think globally, because their protagonists act regionally. And by "act" I mean that they make full use of their fictional "place of action." They make the region come alive, because they move away from its center. They make visible the semantic networks that connect to regions by experiencing difference in place and time. And they fathom region's changing memories. Contemporary regional fiction tries to make visible the multitude of possible identifications with a region. Regional experience today is not so restrictive to people, but it must be sought after, sometimes in a long and painful journey. Because this search for a place is paradigmatic for postmodern identity, no one can seriously claim any longer that regional fiction is meant for regional readers only.

10

The Role of Community and Regional Structure in Language Shift[1]

Joseph Salmons

The process whereby speakers stop speaking one language and start speaking another, language shift, remains in many ways ill understood. While it cannot be captured easily in terms of the categories used in sociolinguistic work (ethnicity, gender, class, religion, and so forth) or along the areal lines typically explored by dialectologists, I argue that it is ultimately driven by changes in the structure of region.

Most human languages are dying rapidly today, as speakers shift from about six thousand minority languages toward a few numerically large languages. This has focused the attention of linguists increasingly on the problem of shift, and it brings a few linguists onto the foreign territory and unfamiliar landscape of regionalism, normally inhabited by historians, geographers, and others. We come carrying some working hypotheses about regions and language shift: This paper seeks to show how a certain notion of region is important and directly relevant in linguistics. It is part of the ongoing work of the Max Kade Institute at the University of Wisconsin–Madison to tie shift to a basic change in community and regional structure, in some sense a change in the meaning of region in the lives of many Americans. We argue that language shift among immigrant languages in the United States has been driven by a process of "verticalization," or shift of political, social, and economic control from the local or regional to the state or national level.

"Region" is a definitional moving target, not only as a socially constructed notion, but because we find dramatic changes over time with regard to what spaces are directly relevant to a community. This paper explores an approach to language shift that builds on notions of region laid out by Robert Ostergren and Steven Hoelscher in this volume, as well as a definition from Paasi:

1.   I would like to thank the following people for various discussions on this topic and comments on earlier drafts: Mary Devitt, Steve Geiger, Rob Howell, Julia Karolle, Mike Lind, Mark Louden, Monica Macaulay, and Bob Ostergren. Comments by James Peacock were particularly helpful in sharpening the thesis. All the usual disclaimers apply.

Regions and communities are spatially constituted social structures and centres of collective consciousness and sociospatial identities. ... [B]elonging to a locality or community is mediated by affiliations with its more fundamental (face-to-face) structures: kinship, friendship, neighbourhood, which are constituted in various "larger scale" institutional practices in which people are involved in their daily routines.[2]

Language is powerfully connected to these kinds of structures, and shift can be driven by the historical transformation of regions, particularly "instituted" or "functional" regions. I thus suggest that a change in regional structure drives shift in minority-language communities.

Despite the long tradition of dialectology (and/or linguistic geography) and the more recent growth of sociolinguistics, most linguists have largely neglected region.[3] Sociolinguists explore how linguistic innovations spread across physical and social space, but also at the most local level, from one individual to another.[4] Sociologists of language such as Joshua Fishman and other social scientists such as Walter Kamphoefner typically focus on the broadest macrolevel, analyzing national demographic data, for example.[5] The present project aims to contribute a different, intermediate piece of the puzzle, namely the role of changing regional social structures in language shift, to which I now turn briefly.

Since the second half of the nineteenth century, the United States has seen a dramatic restructuring of community life toward increasingly nonlocal, centralized structures.[6] Roland Warren treats this as a shift from horizontal (local) social organization and structure to vertical (regional or national) ones.[7] I argue that Warren's framework and his notion of a "Great Change" can

2.   Anssi Paasi, "Deconstructing Regions: Notes on the Scales of Spatial Life," *Environment and Planning* 23 (1991): 239–256.

3.   A subject search of "region" on the electronic *Linguistics and Language Behavior Abstracts* yielded no titles, for instance.

4.   Lesley Milroy and James Milroy, "Social Network and Social Class," *Language in Society* 21 (1992): 1–27.

5.   See, for example, Joshua Fishman, "Language Maintenance and Language Shift as a Field of Inquiry," in *Language Loyalty in the United States*, ed. J. Fishman (The Hague: Mouton, 1966); Joshua Fishman, *Reversing Language Shift* (Clevedon, England: Multilingual Matters, 1991); Walter Kamphoefner, "German American Bilingualism: *Cui Malo*? Mother Tongue and Socioeconomic Status among the Second Generation in 1940," *International Migration Review* 28 (1994): 846–864.

6.   Note the contrast here to contemporary European efforts at increasing regional autonomy, such as discussions of "subsidiarity."

7.   Roland L. Warren, *The Community in America* (Chicago: Rand-McNally, 1978).

provide fresh insight into one of the most salient regional phenomena of earlier American society—the decline and eventual loss of minority languages as local cultures increasingly fell under the control of national-level institutions. While the data here come from immigrant languages in the United States (particularly German in Wisconsin), the same basic argument holds, it seems, for Native languages and cultures in North America and for shift in at least many other societies beyond North America.

What Is Language Shift, How Do We Track It Historically, Why Does It Happen?

As already indicated, language shift refers to situations where a population abandons one language for another over time, so that former speakers of X become speakers of Y, generally with an intermediate period of bilingualism. For example, the massive immigration of German speakers to Wisconsin up until the turn of the twentieth century led to the creation of German-speaking islands across the state. A conservative estimate of speaker numbers is the sum of the number of German-born residents and the number of children of two parents born in Germany.[8] Table 1 gives that calculation:

Total population	1,693,330	
German-born	259,819	15.34%
Children of 2 German-born parents	293,039	17.31%
Estimated German speakers	552,858	32.65%

Table 1: Estimated German speakers in Wisconsin, 1890
(Based on the U.S. Census, as compiled by Seifert[9]).

---

8.   Such an estimate could be either high or low on several counts. First, it is possible that people from Germany were not speakers of German, and that children of two German-born parents were not speakers either. I assume the former was uncommon. The latter was certainly the case for some, but probably not that many. Even in 1940, when the German-to-English shift was greatly advanced, Kamphoefner reports that over seventy percent of such children grew up speaking German. It is safe to assume that number was considerably higher in 1890s Wisconsin. Second, many German speakers came from outside of Germany, and thus would not be captured here. Finally, we entirely miss all German speakers beyond the second generation. Both these last groups were sizeable in Wisconsin. It is likely, in short, that more than one in three Wisconsinites spoke German natively, leaving aside the many fluent nonnative speakers in the state.

9.   Seifert, Lester W. J. 1949. "The problem of speech mixture in the German spoken in northwestern Dane County, Wisconsin." Transactions of the Wisconsin Academy of Sciences, Arts and Letters. 39.127–139.

Often several generations in heavily German communities spoke German natively, and many used it in every sphere of life. Today, those populations have largely adopted English, with essentially everyone under the age of fifty now being English monolingual. Aside from Old Order Amish and recent immigrants, few speak German regularly: 61,929 reported using German as home language in the 1990 U.S. Census, 1.36% of the state's population. In the last century a range of institutions—religious, educational, social, political—conducted business in German; today almost all have switched to English. This is a clear case of a shift nearing completion.

Previous analyses of communities throughout the United States usually treat such shifts as failed radication or extirpation of imported cultures. That is, shift happened because the immigrant language simply never took root or because the Anglo-American dominant culture somehow pulled up an established language by the roots. Too often studies attribute German-to-English shift to characteristics of the particular culture and language at hand. Standard accounts for German typically appeal to anti-German sentiment before and during World War I, lack of cultural and political unity among German Americans, and the presence of a range of dialects rather than a single uniform standard language. Such explanations are incomplete and fail to expose the social, historical, and linguistic roots of shift. Worse, they miss the profound parallels across many instances of shift in different communities where many different languages were spoken under many different social and political circumstances. Indeed, these accounts are poorly situated in any kind of broader social, cultural, historical, or linguistic theories.

Some more theoretical work on language shift has sought to identify possible social correlates of shift. A classic example built around German in the United States are the factors listed by Kloss:[10]

1. Religio-societal isolation;

2. Time of immigration: earlier than or simultaneously with the first Anglo-Americans;

---

10.   Heinz Kloss, "German-American Language Maintenance Efforts," in *Language Loyalty in the United States*. See Lenore A. Grenoble and Lindsay J. Whaley, "Toward a Typology of Language Endangerment," in *Endangered Languages: Language Loss and Community Response*, ed. Lenore A. Grenoble and Lindsay J. Whaley (Cambridge: Cambridge University Press, 1998) for a more modern and more general typology of what brings about the "decreased efficiency" of a language in a community.

3. Existence of language islands;

4. Affiliation with denominations fostering parochial schools;

5. Preimmigration experience with language maintenance efforts;

6. Former use as the only official tongue during pre-Anglo-American period.

Joshua A. Fishman notes, specifically in reference to work by Kloss, that "many of the most popularly cited factors purportedly influencing maintenance and shift have actually been found to 'cut both ways' in different contexts or to have no general significance when viewed in broader perspective."[11] That observation certainly applies to Kloss's list. Fishman ultimately found that valid crosscultural and diachronic generalizations about language shift had not been made in the literature to that time. A third of a century later several excellent case studies have brought us further toward understanding the process of shift in particular communities, but we still have no really workable general theory of why and when shift will or will not happen.[12]

General progress has been made, however, especially in putting the social correlates of shift on a firmer quantitative basis. As compared to ethnic Germans who had switched to English, Kamphoefner, for example, finds that those who still spoke German in 1940 were associated with more traditional behavior, larger families (by half a child per family on average), lower divorce rates, greater residential stability, and higher rates of home ownership.[13] Theresa G. Labov has recently found, among other things, that geographical concentrations of speakers of a given immigrant language correlate with

---

11. Fishman, "Language Maintenance and Language Shift," 441.

12. Li Wei, *Three Generations, Two Languages, One Family: Language Choice and Language Shift in a Chinese Community in Britain* (Clevedon, England: Multilingual Matters, 1994); Michael Clyne and Sandra Kipp, *Pluricentric Languages in an Immigrant Context: Spanish, Arabic and Chinese* (Berlin: Mouton de Gruyter, 1999); Susan Garzon et al., *The Life of Our Language: Kaqchikel Maya Maintenance, Shift, and Revitalization* (Austin: University of Texas Press, 1998). The closest to date is probably Fishman's 1991 notion of geographical, social, and cultural "dislocation" of language communities, but even that needs more precision and can be better situated in a notion of community. Perhaps the closest thing to a weakness in this approach is that Fishman tends to see shift in terms of the *loss* of a language, while speakers clearly often perceive themselves to be gaining in the process. A complete theory of shift presumably needs to balance these two aspects.

13. Kamphoefner, "German American Bilingualism."

lower rates of acquisition of English.[14] Such findings pave the way for more explicit and testable hypotheses about why shift happens, ideally linking the community/regional level with the local focus of sociolinguistic work and the broad societal focus found in other research.

A New Approach

I break with traditional accounts to argue that the German-to-English shift (and shift in other communities across North America) was driven by changes sweeping across almost all of American society during the late nineteenth century, changes almost entirely external to and independent of German-speaking communities. Warren's theory of community structure is useful here. He sees the assorted interests and activities—economic, religious, or educational—of any given community as being carried on by groups with specified functions. A community does not usually act as a single unit, but parts of it operate more or less independently. These groups and their functions can be defined along either horizontal or vertical dimensions. Warren defines these patterns of interaction as "two rather distinct types of systemic ties: The relationships through which they are oriented to the larger society beyond the community constitute the community's vertical pattern, and those that local units share with each other on the local level constitute the community's horizontal pattern."[15] Figure 1 gives a schematic, highly simplified example of such connections, using only two institutions, religion and education, and only two vertical levels.

This paper argues that horizontally structured communities will typically maintain a minority language, while verticalization will lead to shift to the majority language.[16]

Warren defines the Great Change as a situation where connections among various local institutions (horizontal ties, in Warren's terms) give way to ties

---

14.   Theresa G. Labov, "English Acquisition by Immigrants to the United States at the Beginning of the Twentieth Century," *American Speech* 73 (1998): 368–398.

15.   Warren, *Community in America*, 240.

16.   Fishman's concept of "boundary maintenance" in linguistic minority communities (briefly laid out in Fishman, *Reversing Language Shift*, 66–67) is the closest parallel to this hypothesis I am aware of. Majority and minority languages are clear enough in an American context, where English is typically the former in the nineteenth and twentieth centuries (at least at a national or regional level) and all other languages are the latter. Settings where minority languages receive systematic and substantial institutional support from governments (Belgium, Canada, and many other cases around the world) would require far more discussion on this count.

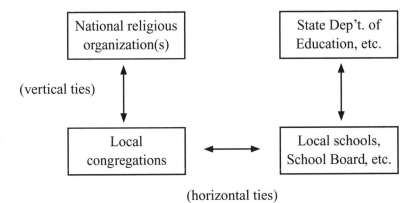

Figure 1: Vertical vs. horizontal patterns, exemplified by religion and education

between a given institution and its regional, state or national counterpart (vertical ties). He makes this case convincingly for a number of communities and a full set of institutions across the United States. For example, before the Great Change local schools were more closely connected to local religious, political, and other institutions; after the Change they were more closely connected to a state board of education and national educational policy. This systematic transfer of power and authority weakened local ties almost everywhere in American society, including minority-language communities, unraveling the institutional threads of a social fabric indispensable for language maintenance.

Note the parallel to Paasi's ideas of regional "institutionalization" and "regional transformation":

> Institutionalisation is a sociospatial process in which a territorial unit emerges as part of the spatial structure of the society concerned, becomes established and identified in various spheres of social action and consciousness, and may eventually vanish or deinstitutionalise in regional transformation. The process is a manifestation of the goals established by local or nonlocal actors and organisations and the decisions made by them.[17]

In the nineteenth century, immigrants created communities and regions in this sense and in more recent times those units have been virtually transformed out of existence—although scholars such as Steve Geiger and Mike Lind point to some hints of the survival or revival of the earlier patterns in communities where German is still spoken.

---

17.   Paasi, "Deconstructing Regions," 243.

In recent and forthcoming work I document in some detail patterns of verticalization among Wisconsin's German-speaking communities in education, religion, and the press, as well as politics, economics, and elsewhere.[18] Here I sketch very briefly a couple of points in this process of relevance to regionalism. Kathleen Conzen treats German-American history in terms of "ethnic persistence and transformation."[19] Her view has been paraphrased (in a commentary published in the same volume) this way: "The endurance and strength of the ethnic subsociety rose in proportion to its ability directly and indirectly to create its own effective institutions." In the nineteenth century, Germans in Wisconsin were remarkably successful in creating and maintaining their own institutions, which directly supported language maintenance until they were vitiated by the Great Change.

In many cases verticalization is expressly tied to institutional language shift: Nonlocal control typically forces a switch to English, even while such changes in language policy were hard fought in many cases. The processes in different domains were very much interconnected, but each institution followed its own path: In religion linguistic verticalization was hotly debated within churches and denominations at the local, regional, and national levels. In education laws mandating English in schools were often passed early, but states did not or could not enforce those laws until much later. Thus the shift in schools was slow and gradual, lasting well into the 1930s even in public schools. In the early twentieth-century press, general national economic pressures drove vast numbers of small papers out of business, including most of the foreign-language press. Shift, then, is a result of the dismantling of community structures needed for language maintenance and the replacement of local structures by higher-level organizations. The correlates of maintenance and shift identified by Kloss, Kamphoefner, Labov, and others can be seen as manifestations of those same community structures, and changes along those parameters are thoroughly consistent with an analysis in using Warren's framework. Indeed, the few communities that are successfully maintaining languages in the United States today are precisely the groups that have maintained horizontal community

---

18.   See "The Shift from German to English, World War I and the German-Language Press in Wisconsin," in *Menschen zwischen zwei Welten: Auswanderung, Ansiedlung, Akkulturation,* ed. Walter G. Rödel and Helmut Schmahl (Trier: Wissenschaftlicher Verlag Trier, 2002), 179–193; "Community, Region and Language Shift in German-Speaking Wisconsin," in *New Orientations in the Study of Regionalism,* ed. James Peacock, et al. (Madison: Monographs of the Center for the Study of Upper Midwestern Cultures, forthcoming).

19.   Kathleen Neils Conzen, *Making Their Own America: Assimilation Theory and the German Peasant Pioneer* (New York: Berg, 1990).

structures, most notably Pennsylvania German among the Old Order Amish and Mennonites and Yiddish among ultra-Orthodox Jews.

Conclusion

A basic restructuring of community and regional life undermined the maintenance of German in Wisconsin. Language shift is one of the most salient consequences of this regional transformation, and this brief paper suggests that *region* is central to understanding the shift. That verticalization drives shift in key institutions might be easily accepted by many scholars looking at German-to-English shift. More notable is that these processes are widespread, nearly universal, in North America and elsewhere during the last century. The relevant change is distinctly regional and falls squarely between the extremely local, speaker-level studies of sociolinguistics, and the societal-level social science approaches to the problem. This project aims to develop a significantly new model for how, when, and why minority language communities abandon their languages for a majority tongue in a way tied closely to changes in regional structure. Warren's verticalization, as a kind of antisubsidiarity, provides a link to contemporary issues of region in Europe.

In closing here are a few brief responses to questions posed for the UNC workshop out which these volumes on regionalism have emerged:

- What does region and / or regionalism mean in the context of linguistics? What approaches and theories on region and regionalism exist in linguistics?

   Region has been ignored in modern linguistics, especially in North America.

- In which way are the concepts of region and regionalism important for linguistics?

   This paper suggests that *region* proves more useful a concept for understanding language shift than other concepts previously used.

- Where do you see opportunities for interdisciplinary research on region and regionalism in the context of the approaches and theories linguistics offers? In which ways could the approaches and theories on the region and regionalism of linguistics contribute to an inter-disciplinary approach?

The view of language shift sketched above relies entirely on work from history, geography, and community studies, and a fuller statement would embrace anthropology and other fields from sociology to print culture studies.

11

Region and Regionalism in Linguistics: A Brief Survey of Concepts and Methods

Klaus P. Schneider

Introduction

The present paper aims to provide a concise overview of concepts of region and regionalism in linguistics, which have changed considerably in the course of the history of this academic discipline. Accompanying developments in methodology are also discussed. Given the limited space available, this survey remains necessarily sketchy. However, the literature referred to provides ample material for further reading. The present overview is addressed to nonlinguists in particular.[1]

Two Approaches to Language: Uniformism and Variationism

A discussion of the role and status of region and regionalism in linguistics presupposes an understanding of a fundamental divide in the study of language. In the most general terms two alternative, mutually exclusive, approaches to language can be distinguished, for which the labels "variationist" and "uniformist" can be used. Even though these terms are not generally accepted (particularly the latter), they neatly capture the essential difference between the two approaches.[2]

The crucial distinction involves different conceptualizations of language. Variationists view language as a heterogenous continuum, whereas uniformists treat language as a homogenous whole, thereby abstracting away all variation that exists in natural languages. The uniformist approach is based on Ferdinand de Saussure's notion of language as an abstract relational system of

1.   I would like to thank Anne Barron for discussing and improving the contents and language of this paper. Needless to say, I alone remain accountable for any inaccuracies that may still exist.

2.   A similar basic distinction is made in Michael C. Steiner and Clarence Mondale's multidisciplinary survey of American regionalism, in their chapter on "Language": Steiner and Mondale, *Region and Regionalism in the United States* (New York: Garland Publishing, 1988), 316–317.

linguistic signs.[3] This approach was adopted in twentieth-century mainstream linguistics, particularly in structuralism, between the 1930s and the 1960s and in generativism, where it has been a dominant paradigm ever since, especially in theoretical linguistics.[4] By contrast the variationist approach has a long pre-Saussurean tradition. In particular it involves dialectology, one of the oldest disciplines in linguistics, which originated in early nineteenth-century Romanticism in Germany, and sociolinguistics, which developed in the second half of the twentieth century.[5] Among living linguists major representatives of uniformism and variationism are the generativist Noam Chomsky and the sociolinguist William Labov respectively.[6]

In Saussurean terms structuralists study "langue," the systems of individual languages such as English, German, or Chinese, while generativists primarily investigate "langage," the biologically founded human capacity for language. Variationists, on the other hand, investigate "parole," i.e. manifestations of language in speech. Furthermore, variationists acknowledge that variation exists in language, and more particularly that speech varies according to a number of factors including region, social class, ethnicity, and gender. In other words generativism attempts to describe and explain an ideal speaker's language competence in terms of universal grammar, whereas variationism aims at understanding variation in language by analyzing the verbal behavior of real speakers. Finally, while uniformists often focus on standard languages alone, variationists analyze the substandard varieties of a language, commonly referred to as dialects or vernaculars, and the differences between them.

While uniformists perceive language as static, variationists perceive it as dynamic, i.e. as varying in both space and time. From a variationist perspective all languages are constantly undergoing changes, and variation at a given time

---

3.   F. de Saussure, *Cours de Linguistique Générale* (Lausanne: Payot, 1916).

4.   Structuralism describes language in terms of (formal) structures in systems, whereas generativism models linguistic competence in terms of algorithms for generating (grammatical) structures.

5.   Traditionally, dialectology has examined regional variation in language, while sociolinguistics, the interface between linguistics and sociology, has investigated social variation in language.

6.   See, for example, N. Chomsky, *Aspects of the Theory of Syntax* (Cambridge, MA: MIT Press, 1965); N. Chomsky, *Lectures on Government and Binding* (Dordrecht: Foris Publications, 1981); N. Chomsky, *The Minimalist Program* (Cambridge, MA: MIT Press, 1995); W. Labov, *The Social Stratification of English in New York City* (Washington, DC: Center for Applied Linguistics, 1966); W. Labov, *Principles of Linguistic Change*, Vol. I *Internal Factors* (Oxford: Blackwell, 1994); W. Labov, *Principles of Linguistic Change*, Vol. II *Social Factors* (Oxford: Blackwell, 2001).

can be explained, at least partially, as a reflection of such changes. Therefore there are obvious links between dialectology and sociolinguistics on the one hand, which examine linguistic variation in geographical and social space, and historical and diachronic linguistics on the other hand, which investigate varieties of a language at different times and processes of linguistic variation in time. Traditionally, however, there is a clear division of labor between these disciplines.

A further difference between the uniformist and variationist approach to language concerns methodology. Uniformism in its present form is essentially nonempirical, predominantly relying on "introspection," the researchers' intuitions about (their native) language. By contrast variationism is strictly empirical. Variationists collect instances of naturally occurring language or elicit language material. The standard methodology is fieldwork. Prototypically, fieldworkers interview relatively large, ideally representative, samples of consultants. A final difference concerns the levels of language which are analyzed. Generativism focuses primarily on syntax, while variationism concentrates on lexis and pronunciation.[7]

It should be clear from the preceding—albeit somewhat simplified— discussion that region and regionalism do not play any role in the uniformist approaches of structuralism and generativism, while these two notions are central to variationism—especially dialectology but also recent developments in sociolinguistics, as is demonstrated in more detail below. In the following sections concepts of region and regionalism are traced through the history of variationist linguistics, emphasizing, in particular, the changing role these concepts have played in the development of this approach to language. This development can be considered a dialectic process involving an initial focus on regional variation in isolation as its "thesis," the abandoning of regional research in order to study social variation as its "antithesis," and viewing regional variation in the broader context of interacting types of linguistic variation as its "synthesis." The different methods employed at different stages in this development to study regional speech and regional variation are also discussed.

---

7.   The study of dialect syntax is a recent development. See, for example, B. Kortmann, "New Prospects for the Study of English Dialect Syntax: Impetus from Syntactic Theory and Language Typology," in *Syntactic Microvariation*, ed. S. Barbiers, L. Cornips, and S. van der Kleij (Amsterdam: Meertens Institute, 2002), 185–213.

Dialect Geography: The Traditional Study of Regional Speech

It is common knowledge that people from different places use the same language in different ways. Peoples' speech is indicative of their geographical affiliation and part of their regional identity. The most salient differences are differences in pronunciation. Locals immediately spot strangers by their accents, often even being able to identify where a stranger is from. Also, as for instance when traveling, people realize that the same thing or idea is expressed differently in different parts of the one country. For example, the flow of water is regulated by a device referred to as a *tap* in one location, as a *spigot* in another, and as a *faucet* in yet another. And gypsophila (a plant) may be called *baby's breath* or *chalkweed* or *mist* in different regions of the United States.

Episodical comments on such differences in language are found in written documents through the ages, dating back to at least the thirteenth century.[8] However, dialectology, the systematic study of regional differences in language, did not start before the nineteenth century. In the Romantic period dialectologists were interested in the language spoken by the "common people," particularly rural speech, which they considered the genuine, pure, and unspoiled form of a language superior to urban speech and written language. Later, in historical and comparative linguistics material from rural dialects, recognized as more conservative, was used to reconstruct earlier stages of a language.[9]

Today, however, traditional dialectology is usually equated with dialect geography, a discipline that developed in the second half of the nineteenth century.[10] Dialect geography is concerned with regional variation in a given language on a national or subnational level. More particularly, the aim of dialect geography is to establish the distribution of linguistic variants in geographical space, determining, for instance, in what regions *baby's breath*, *chalkweed*, and *mist* are used to refer to the plant gypsophila. Such findings are presented in dialect dictionaries. The principal types of this particular reference tool are regional dictionaries, documenting the vocabulary of a particular sub-national region, and multiregional dictionaries, which document the vocabulary of

---

8.   See, for example, J. Chambers and P. Trudgill, *Dialectology*, 2nd ed. (Cambridge: Cambridge University Press, 1998), 13.

9.   See, for example, S. Romaine, "Dialect and Dialectology," in *Concise Encyclopedia of Pragmatics*, ed. J. Mey (Amsterdam: Elsevier, 1998), 205.

10.   The traditional name "dialect geography," as well as the term "linguistic geography" used in twentieth-century dialectology, are in fact misleading as they suggest that this discipline is a subdiscipline of geography. Therefore, terms such as "geographical linguistics" and "areal linguistics" (or "area linguistics") are sometimes preferred today.

several or all regions of a nation-state. An example of the regional type is *Western Words: A Dictionary of the American West*,[11] an example of the multiregional (here national) type is *The Dictionary of American Regional English (DARE)*.[12]

As a rule, however, findings in dialect geography are presented in maps, which are often published in the form of a linguistic atlas. There are two basic types of maps: maps for individual items and those for combinations of items. Maps for individual items chart all variants for a given item, for example, the distribution of *pail* and *bucket* as words for a particular type of container.[13] If a pattern of complementary distribution occurs, the respective areas of use can be demarcated by drawing a line, a so-called isogloss, around them. By contrast maps for combined items chart all variants of several items.[14] In this case the aim is to identify converging isoglosses for variants of different items, so-called bundles of isoglosses. The more isoglosses converge, the more it is justified to postulate a distinct dialect region.

Since the ultimate aim of dialect geography is to establish dialect regions and boundaries between these regions, it is not sufficient to plot the spread of variants for one or more items, which is done on so-called display maps. Rather, the data have also to be interpreted in order to determine the demarcation lines (hence "interpretive maps"), which is not a trivial task. The status of isoglosses and isogloss bundles has often been challenged,[15] since the co-occurrence of variants, transitional zones and overlap were sometimes ignored in early projects. In past decades, methodology has, however, been gradually refined to deal more adequately with phenomena such as overlap and divergence. There has been a shift from purely qualitative, interpretative methods to quantitative

---

11.   R. Adams, *Western Words: A Dictionary of the American West*, 2nd ed. (Norman, OK: University of Oklahoma Press, 1968).

12.   F. G. Cassidy and J. Houston Hall, eds., *Dictionary of American Regional English*, Vols. I–IV (Cambridge, MA: Harvard University Press, 1985–2002). *DARE* has not yet been completely published. So far only the first four volumes, covering the letters *A* through *Sk*, have appeared (vol. I: *A–C*, 1985; vol. II: *D–H*, 1991; vol. III: *I–O*, 1996; vol. IV, *P–Sk*, 2002). The final volume is expected to appear in 2008 or 2009. For further information about this dictionary project, visit its official website: http://polyglot.lss.wisc.edu/dare/dare.html.

13.   H. Kurath, *A Word Geography of the Eastern United States* (Ann Arbor: University of Michigan Press, 1949), fig. 66.

14.   M. Wakelin, *English Dialects: An Introduction* (London: Athlone Press, 1972), 103, map 7.

15.   See, for example, C. M. Carver, *American Regional Dialects: A Word Geography* (Ann Arbor: University of Michigan Press, 1987), 13.

methods,[16] employing increasingly sophisticated statistical tools to test the significance of isogloss bundles. Furthermore, the simplistic notion of occurrence versus non-occurrence of variants has been replaced by probability rating, and the concept of isogloss bundles has been replaced by the concept of isoglossal layering (based on a notion borrowed from physical geography). Thus, it is now possible to identify a hierarchy of layers in which the core region, where most distinctive features are shared, can be distinguished from more peripheral areas, in which increasingly fewer features are shared with the core region. As dialect maps are no longer drawn by hand—computerized cartography being employed instead today—layering can be displayed by, for example, using different degrees of probability shading.[17]

It must be emphasized at this point that the concept of region in dialect geography does not take recourse to any pre-existing notions or extralinguistic entities such as topography, trading routes, or political boundaries. As a matter of theoretical and methodological principle, dialect regions are established on the basis of linguistic data alone. That dialect boundaries identified in this way have been found to correlate with extralinguistic borders is a different, albeit important, matter. It has been found, for instance, that some dialect regions that are based on lexical differences exclusively[18] coincide with regions determined independently in cultural geography.[19] This insight points to a significant contribution that dialect geography can make to an inter- and cross-disciplinary study of regions and regionalism.[20]

The Linguistic Atlas Movement in Dialect Geography

The first systematic survey in dialect geography was conducted by Georg Wenker in Germany between 1876 and 1887. Wenker mailed questionnaires to approximately fifty thousand schoolmasters in all parts of the country and asked them to transcribe forty sentences written in standard German into the

16. See, for example, E. Schneider, "Qualitative vs. Quantitative Methods of Area Delimitation in Dialectology: A Comparison Based on Lexical Data from Georgia and Alabama," *Journal of English Linguistics* 21 (1988): 175–212.

17. See, for example, W. A. Kretzschmar, "Quantitative Areal Analysis of Dialect Features," *Language Variation and Change* 8 (1996): 32, fig. 14.

18. See Carver, *American Regional Dialects.*

19. See W. Wolfram and N. Schilling-Estes, *American English: Dialects and Variation* (Malden, MA: Blackwell, 1998), 136.

20. For a more detailed discussion of dialect geography see Chambers and Trudgill, *Dialectology*, ch. 2. For a discussion of American dialect geography see Wolfram and Schilling-Estes, *American English*, chs. 4 and 5.

respective local dialect. The number of returns was overwhelming, but given the limited technical possibilities at the time, Wenker was not able to document all of his results. Eventually, in 1889/1890, he published just two sets of hand-drawn maps, under the title *Sprachatlas des Deutschen Reichs* (Linguistic Atlas of the German Empire), in which he displayed only a selection of his findings.[21]

Wenker's project gave rise to what could be called the "linguistic atlas movement." His work inspired numerous similar surveys in many countries, some of which are detailed below. In successive surveys the methodology was continuously refined. Mailed questionnaires were replaced by interviews, fieldworkers conducting the interviews were increasingly trained for the purpose, and worksheets and questionnaires were introduced to warrant data comparability across interviewers working on the same project. Questionnaires were standardized as well as the methods used to transcribe the elicited data. Initially, fieldworkers were faced with the task of phonetically transcribing in situ what the informants said. The advent of technical recording facilities allowed fieldworkers to concentrate on elicitation techniques and transcribe their collected material *post eventu*. Prior to the invention of the tape-recorder, recordings were made employing less sophisticated tools such as aluminum records and wire recordings.

The samples interviewed in earlier atlas projects consisted exclusively of nonmobile, older, rural males (known as NORMs).[22] The assumption underlying this selection strategy was that the language used by NORMs, believed to be the most conservative group of speakers, would best preserve and represent the typical features of a regional dialect. In more recent projects, however, more sociologically representative populations have been chosen, carefully stratified by age, sex, ethnicity, and education.

The largest atlas project to date, *The Linguistic Atlas of the United States and Canada* (*LAUSC*), was initiated by Hans Kurath in the United States in 1930. Given its enormous geographical coverage, the project was subdivided into several relatively autonomous subprojects, each examining a different region of North America. Each regional project had its own director. The first subproject, *The Linguistic Atlas of New England* (*LANE*), which began in 1931, was directed by Kurath.

---

21.   A digitized version of Wenker's atlas is currently being prepared at the University of Marburg. For more information on this project visit its website: http://www.diwa.info.

22.   The acronym NORMs was coined by Chambers and Trudgill, *Dialectology*, 29.

The regional projects, nine in all, differ considerably from each other. One distinction pertains to beginning and duration. All projects were started at dissimilar times, and some are still not finished. Other differences pertain to the extent and structure of the region surveyed, the size and composition of the population, the period of data collection, data elicitation and data processing procedures, and the recording techniques employed.[23] The synopsis in table 1 (below) illustrates such differences. We see, for example, that the regions selected for the individual surveys cover between just one to as many as eight or more states (the *Linguistic Atlas of the Rocky Mountain States* [*LARMS*] actually plans to survey eleven states). In addition, while subnational state borders are by and large observed, this is not always the case. Some surveys cover only parts of states. For example, the only part of New York that *LANE* studies is Long Island, while the *Linguistic Atlas of the Middle and South Atlantic States* (*LAMSAS*) just includes eastern Georgia and northeastern Florida. Some projects transgress nation-state boundaries by including parts of Canada. *LANE*, for instance, includes southern New Brunswick in its survey, and the *Linguistic Atlas of the North Central States* (*LANCS*) studies southern Ontario. However, only four of the twelve Canadian provinces are considered, and these are only studied partially and unsystematically. The *Linguistic Atlas of the Upper Midwest* (*LAUM*) includes only a small number of informants from, for example, Manitoba, Ontario, and Saskatchewan. Some American states are not covered by any of the nine regional projects, leaving gaps on the national map. Apart from Alaska and Hawaii, these are Kansas, Missouri, and South Carolina. On the other hand, there is overlap, mostly produced by *LARMS*, the most recent regional project, which will cover, among other states, California, Idaho, Oregon, and Washington, previously included in other surveys. This overlap occurs as *LARMS* pursues goals different from those of the earlier projects. It concentrates on phonology, investigates regional and social markers, and adopts a new methodology. *LARMS* is based on the *Linguistic Atlas of the Gulf States* (*LAGS*), the second most recent project, which introduced a large number of innovations (both surveys are directed by Lee Pederson). For instance, *LAGS* stratified informants by race, sex, age, and education for the first time. It is for this and many other reasons that *LAGS* is considered a milestone in the history of dialect geography.[24]

---

23.   Detailed information about *LAUSC*, including descriptions of all regional projects and an extensive bibliography, can be found at http://hyde.park.uga.edu.

24.   See, for example, Chambers and Trudgill, *Dialectology*, 18–19.

Project name	Acronym	Region	Elicitation	Subjects
The Linguistic Atlas of New England	LANE	Massachusetts, New Hampshire, Connecticut, Vermont, New York (Long Island), Rhode Island, and Maine; also southern New Brunswick	1931–1933	416
The Linguistic Atlas of the Middle and South Atlantic States	LAMSAS	New York, New Jersey, Pennsylvania, West Virginia; Delaware, Maryland, Virginia, North Carolina, eastern Georgia, and northeastern Florida	1933–1974	1162
The Linguistic Atlas of the North Central States	LANCS	Wisconsin, Michigan, Illinois, Indiana, Ohio, and Kentucky; also southern Ontario	1933–1978	564
The Linguistic Atlas of the Upper Midwest	LAUM	Minnesota, Iowa, North Dakota, South Dakota, and Nebraska; also Manitoba, Ontario, and Saskatchewan	1949–1962	208
The Linguistic Atlas of the Pacific West	LAPW	California and Nevada	1952–1959	300
The Linguistic Atlas of the Pacific Northwest	LAPNW	Oregon, Washington, and Idaho	1953–1963	382
The Linguistic Atlas of Oklahoma	LAO	Oklahoma	1959–1963	57
The Linguistic Atlas of the Gulf States	LAGS	Florida, Georgia, Tennessee, Alabama, Mississippi, Louisiana, Arkansas, and Texas	1968–1983	1121
The Linguistic Atlas of the Rocky Mountain States	LARMS	Wyoming, Colorado, and Utah (in preparation: Montana, Idaho, West Texas, New Mexico, Arizona, California, Oregon, and Washington)	1988–	

Table 1: *The Linguistic Atlas of the United States and Canada (LAUSC)*—regional projects

It must be pointed out that the areas selected for the regional LAUSC projects do not coincide with dialect regions. The areas were chosen for practical reasons, particularly in order to divide the total area of the United States (and Canada) into manageable parts. It is the aim of each project to investigate regional speech patterns within the chosen area and establish dialect regions within it. Needless to say, however, the divisions made were not made arbitrarily and do have implications for the study of regional speech variation.

Urban Dialectology: The Sociolinguistic Turn

In the 1960s sociolinguists effected a paradigm change in variationism when they vehemently attacked dialect geographers, and especially the proponents of the linguistic atlas movement in the United States. Their criticism concentrated on three issues in particular: theory, methodology, and relevance.[25]

First, sociolinguists accused atlas projects of "data-mongery" and condescendingly depicted work in dialect geography as purely descriptive, lacking in theoretical underpinning and explanatory value. They claimed that areal linguists merely collect facts about regional varieties and their spread in geographical space and chart such differences on maps. They further claimed that such activities do not contribute to an understanding of the nature of dialects, or the nature of language, of which dialects form an essential part. In short it was considered a major shortcoming that dialectology does not generate, or even aim at generating, a theory of language variation and change.

Sociolinguists also rejected the methodology adopted in dialect geography. They did so for two reasons. On the one hand they criticized the qualitative methods used by dialectologists, maintaining that purely quantitative methods must be employed in any scientific approach to language variation. On the other they critiqued the rural bias of the atlas projects, and the fact that social variables were not appropriately considered.

Finally, sociolinguists questioned the relevance of the results from dialect geography for society. They claimed that atlas projects did not contribute to the solution of social problems, and that their findings could not be applied to improve the situation of underprivileged groups, such as African Americans or members of the working classes, groups stigmatized for their speech behavior because of its divergence from the standard norms adhered to by white middle-class speakers.

---

25.   An instructive summary of this criticism is presented in Keith Walters, "Dialectology," in *Linguistics: The Cambridge Survey*, vol. II *Language: The Socio-Cultural Context*, ed. F. J. Newmeyer (Cambridge: Cambridge University Press, 1998), 119–139.

By contrast sociolinguistic research was based on clearly formulated theoretical assumptions and employed strictly statistical methods. The ultimate aim of such research was to be directly applicable to solving societal problems. With this aim sociolinguists turned to the complex social situation of urban communities. Thus, the focus in the study of language variation shifted from rural areas to big cities, from region to location (New York City, for example), from geographical distribution to social networks, from dialect (in its traditional narrow definition as regional dialect) to sociolect, ethnolect, and genderlect.

The sociolinguistic study of language variation is generally referred to as urban dialectology.[26] The greatest impact on the development of this discipline was the work of William Labov.[27] In his study on New York City Labov introduced numerous methodological innovations involving random sampling and conversation and reading tasks.[28] In analyzing his tape-recorded data Labov aimed at correlating occurrences of linguistic variables with demographic variables to establish sociolinguistic patterns of covariation. Most work in urban dialectology has been conducted in the Labovian paradigm, employing his methods in data gathering and data analysis.[29]

Recent work in dialect geography has increasingly incorporated methodological principles of urban dialectology, notably in the selection of informants and the choice of tasks. Furthermore, qualitative methods have gradually been replaced by quantitative methods, and regional variables have been analyzed in their interaction with social variables, including social class, ethnicity, gender, age, and education. In fact, the interplay of all of these factors, including regional ones, is generally acknowledged today by both dialectologists and sociolinguists. Moreover, dialectology is now regarded as a branch of sociolinguistics, irrespective of its history and tradition. In contemporary sociolinguistics the term dialectology is not restricted to its traditional meaning but understood in a more comprehensive sense. Dialectology no longer translates as "the study of regional variation," but as "the study of language variation," involving all the different types of

---

26.   By analogy dialect geography could be termed "rural dialectology." Conversely, urban dialectology could also be named "dialect sociology," yet this would be another misnomer (see footnote 10).

27.   For example, Labov, *Social Stratification of English*; W. Labov, *Sociolinguistic Patterns* (Philadelphia: Pennsylvania University Press, 1972); Labov, *Principles of Linguistic Change*.

28.   Labov, *Social Stratification of English*.

29.   For alternative approaches in urban dialectology, see James Milroy, "Urban Dialectology," in *Concise Encyclopedia of Pragmatics*, 1039–1045.

linguistic variation mentioned above. In this context dialect is used as a cover term for sociolect, ethnolect, genderlect, gerontolect, and, of course, regional dialect (for which, by analogy, the term "regiolect" might be used).[30] This integrative concept of dialectology is illustrated in the textbook *American English: Dialects and Variation* by Walt Wolfram and Natalie Schilling-Estes. This comprehensive approach also includes applications to social problems in society, particularly in teaching and education.[31] It has recently been argued that even this comprehensive approach remains inadequate, if personal identity is not taken into consideration.[32] Identity is a complex psycholinguistic concept, which influences speech performance and often correlates with other forms of in-group behavior, examples including a preference for particular magazines, clothes, or music styles co-occurring with a particular accent (consider, for instance, wearing cowboy boots, listening to country music, and having a strong regional accent as expressions of Southern identity co-occurring with a strong regional accent).[33]

Region Rediscovered: A New Atlas Project

In the 1990s a unique new atlas project was initiated by William Labov, still one of the leading sociolinguists and a major proponent of urban dialectology. The project name, *TELSUR*, is derived from the innovative methodology adopted in this project: The data were gathered in a telephone survey.

This project investigates the dialects of English in the United States and Canada. It combines features of dialect geography and urban dialectology. As in dialect geography, the focus is on regional variation alone, and the results are displayed on maps in an atlas. However, the *TELSUR* project differs from *LAUSC* in at least two significant ways. First, it does not concentrate on selected areas, but covers all states and, thus, for the first time, provides a national map of regional speech characteristics. Second, data collection was restricted to only a short period of time. The data were gathered between 1996 and 1999, thus providing what has been referred to as a "synchronic snapshot."

---

30. Given the popular view of dialects as incorrect, sloppy, or deficient speech, the term "variety" is generally preferred in linguistics today. Both variety and dialect (in its scientific sense) are used for all variants of a language, nonstandard and standard alike.

31. See, for example, Wolfram and Schilling-Estes, *American English*, chs. 10 and 11.

32. See E. Schneider, "From Region to Class to Identity: 'Show Me How You Speak, and I'll Tell You Who You Are?'" *American Speech* 75 (2000): 359–361.

33. Cf. G. Bailey et al., "The Effects of Methods on Results in Dialectology," *English World-Wide* 18 (1997): 35–63.

As in urban dialectology, the *TELSUR* project examines only urban, not rural speech. The informant population also differs across gender, age, and ethnic membership. Finally, the focus is exclusively on pronunciation, considering the realization of phonemic categories as well as phonetic forms. However, unlike sociolinguistic projects in urban dialectology, which concentrate on individual locations (such as New York City, Belfast, or Norwich),[34] the *TELSUR* project includes all urban centers in North America, a total of 145.

The sampling strategy for selecting the localities was informed by categories developed by the U.S. Census Bureau and the Audit Bureau of Circulations. Three categories were used: urbanized area, central city, and zone of influence. An urbanized area consists of one or more central cities and their zones of influence. A zone of influence consists of several counties, each comprising a minimum of one hundred households. The central cities were divided into four groups, cities:

a. with a population of over one million,

b. with a population of over 200,000 in an area of over 5,000 square miles,

c. with a population of over 200,000 in an area of under 5,000 square miles,

d. with a population of under 200,000.

Cities with a population of over one million were represented by at least four speakers, all other cities by between two to four speakers. Of these speakers, at least one had to be a female between the ages of twenty and forty. All representatives were local residents, people born or raised in the respective local community. Of the 145 urbanized areas selected, 33 had a population of over one million. The overall population in these areas amounted to fifty-four percent of the American population.

The central questions addressed in the *TELSUR* project were essentially the same as in all atlas projects:

1. How many regional dialects are there?

---

34.   See, for example, Labov, *Social Stratification of English*; J. Milroy, *Linguistic Variation and Change* (Oxford: Blackwell, 1992); and P. Trudgill, ed., *Sociolinguistic Patterns in British English* (London: Edward Arnold, 1978).

2. What are their boundaries?

In this project the major dialect divisions were established on the basis of phonological features. The focus was on stressed vowels, since vowel patterns have been found to differentiate between the regional dialects of North American English. As a result, six major dialect regions were identified:

a. North Central Region,

b. Inland North,

c. Northeast,

d. Midland Region,

e. South,

f. West.

The *TELSUR* project was concerned not only with language variation, but also with language change. It aimed at both determining the present state of the regional English dialects in the United States and Canada and surveying linguistic changes in progress. Urban speech was analyzed because phonological change is usually more advanced in urban centers than in rural areas. Women between twenty and forty years of age were included in each region's survey because they are the key promoters of novel forms.

Questions posed in the *TELSUR* project concerning ongoing linguistic changes included the following: How are the regional dialects of North American English developing, and more particularly, in what ways are they developing? One of the project's basic findings was that regional dialects have not disappeared in North America. Indeed, contrary to popular (and learned) belief, which had assumed that regional speech differences were gradually vanishing due to the impact of job mobility and the mass media, findings showed that regional dialects are not only surviving, but that they are actually diverging—due, it is suggested, to the fact that regional speech constitutes an important part of regional identity. In addition a number of mergers were identified as well as two chain shifts, the Northern Cities Sound Shift and the Southern Cities Sound Shift. Questions asked in a more theoretical vein were: What are the mechanisms of phonological change in North American English? How does the evidence from North American dialects conform to or modify the general principles governing the evolution of sound systems? The findings of the *TELSUR* project are charted in *The Atlas of North American English* (*ANAE*).[35] The print version of the atlas is accompanied by a CD-ROM, developed by Jürgen Handke. Among other materials this CD-ROM includes speech samples from the *TELSUR* corpus.

Perceptual Dialectology: Yet Another Way of Studying Regional Varieties

Region and regionalism also play a central, but different, role in a new subdiscipline of sociolinguistics, "perceptual dialectology." Perceptual dialectology is the study of attitudes toward regional speech. Perceptual dialectology investigates language users, not language; it examines stereotypical perceptions of and prejudices about dialects and dialect speakers rather than a dialect's linguistic features. Put another way, while dialectology proper provides expert descriptions of regional varieties, perceptual dialectology investigates folk models of regional varieties. Furthermore, perceptual dialectology is not interested in the accuracy of nonlinguists' observations and perceptions. It does not study the relationship between linguistic facts and perceptions thereof, nor the association between actual characteristics of regional speech on the one hand and clichés and folklore about regional varieties on the other hand. Therefore, perceptual dialectology is not a branch of dialectology as the study of variation in language, but a branch of the sociolinguistic study of language attitudes.

Early studies in perceptual dialectology were conducted in the Netherlands and in Japan, more recent studies were carried out in the United States, Canada, and Germany.[36] Such studies attempt to investigate evaluative notions of and prejudices toward people whose speech reveals their geographical origin and regional affiliation. Such attitudes may be decisive for success in education and employment. As in other fields of sociolinguistics, findings from perceptual dialectology are directly relevant to problems in society and contribute to their solution.

---

35. For further information, visit the project's website: http://www.ling.upenn.edu/phonoatlas.

36. Some of these projects are reported on in contributions to the two volumes of the *Handbook of Perceptual Dialectology*, ed. Dennis Preston (Amsterdam and Philadelphia: Benjamins, 1999–2001). This handbook also includes a historical survey of perceptual dialectology.

Some of the research questions posed in perceptual dialectology are presented systematically below. Not all of these questions are, of course, addressed in each study.

1. To what extent can people determine the geographical origin of a speaker simply by listening to them?

2. How many regional dialects are ordinary language users aware of?[37]

3. How many dialect areas do they distinguish?

4. How do they determine the location and extent of these areas?

5. How do they name the identified areas?

6. What attitude do people have toward the dialect spoken in their home region?

7. What attitude do people have toward dialects spoken in other regions of their home country?

8. Which dialects are viewed as prestigious?

9. Which dialects are stigmatized?

10. How do speakers evaluate the dialects of a country in terms of pleasantness?

11. How do speakers evaluate the dialects of a country in terms of correctness?

---

37.   That is to say, in more precise terms, how many dialects of a given language or a given national variety of a language are users aware of. The formulation "of a given language" here applies to languages that are spoken (natively) in only one country, such as Japanese, whereas "of a national variety of a language" applies to languages that are spoken in more than one country, such as English. As a rule, studies in perceptual dialectology deal with only one country (in the sense of nation-state) at a time.

12. How do speakers evaluate the dialects of a country in terms of similarity and difference?

13. What are these judgments based on?

14. Which linguistic peculiarities are associated with a particular region?

15. Which language levels do these peculiarities belong to, or, in more general terms, which linguistic parameters are ordinary language users aware of?

At this point, it must be again emphasized that it is irrelevant to the perceptual dialectologist whether a linguistic feature associated with a particular region actually occurs in that region or not.

To answer the above questions perceptual dialectology, as an empirical discipline, employs a range of experimental methods. Data are elicited from informant populations of so-called naïve speakers, ordinary language users who are not trained in dialectology (or specialized in any other discipline of linguistics). Elicitation techniques typically include map tasks, rating tasks, and conversational interviews.

Map tasks used in perceptual dialectology resemble those first developed in geography.[38] Nonexpert informants are asked to draw the boundaries of dialect regions (usually of their native language) on maps (usually of their native country). As a rule, informants are presented with blank maps, but sometimes (sub-national) state boundaries and/or big cities are provided for orientation. In some experiments the informants are further asked to name the dialect areas identified. The results are fed into a computer, which generates synopses of the informants' "mental maps" of dialect regions, displaying focal areas identified by most or all informants as well as peripheral areas identified by only a few. The relative size of the dialect regions identified as well as names used for them express an attitude toward those regions.[39]

While map tasks elicit folk notions of dialect regions, rating tasks are based on expert work in dialect geography. In rating tasks informants are asked

---

38.   See, for example, P. Gould and R. White, *Mental Maps*, 2nd ed. (London: Allen & Unwin, 1986).

39.   See, for example, D. R. Preston, "Where the Worst English Is Spoken," in *Focus on the USA*, ed. Edgar Schneider (Philadelphia and Amsterdam: John Benjamins, 1996), 302 ff.

to evaluate established regional dialects in terms of correctness, pleasantness, and similarity, typically using a six-point scale ranging from "1=most correct" ("most pleasant" and so forth) to "6=least correct" ("least pleasant" and so forth). The way in which regional dialects are rated depends on where the rater comes from. However, speakers do not always rate their own regional dialect as more pleasant, let alone as more correct, than other dialects. In general speakers of stigmatized dialects are linguistically insecure and tend to rate their own vernacular in a less positive way than speakers of more prestigious varieties do.[40]

The quantitative data elicited using map tasks, rating tasks, and similar elicitation formats are sometimes supplemented by qualitative data from conversational interviews. Conversational interviews are conducted informally, with individuals or small groups of consultants who have already participated in map or rating tasks. Such interviews are carried out to gain further insights into the consultants' perceptions of regional speech and of the concepts underlying their hand-drawn maps or their correctness/pleasantness ratings. Interviews of this type reveal what consultants base their judgments on, which linguistic features they perceive, which dialect characteristics they are aware of, and which properties of regional speech they consider as pleasant, unpleasant, and so forth.

Conversational interviews show that pronunciation is the most salient dialect feature for nonlinguists. Lexical variation is also mentioned. Reference is made either to cases in which different words are used for the same thing, or cases in which words have different meanings in different regions. Other linguistic phenomena addressed in interviews include set phrases and formulaic expressions, and also specific syntactic constructions. Regional variation in speech act realizations is referred to only rarely, and only with regard to routine formulations and pragmatic idioms.[41]

Studies in perceptual dialectology carried out in the United States are closely linked to the name of Dennis Preston. Preston has conducted a series of quantitative and qualitative studies involving samples from different parts of the United States, Michigan and Indiana in particular. This project has been reported on in a series of publications;[42] the most comprehensive account (to

---

40.   See, for example, N. Niedzielski and D. Preston, *Folk Linguistics* (Berlin and New York: Mouton de Gruyter, 2000), 63 ff.

41.   See, for example, Preston, "Where the Worst English Is Spoken," 329 ff.

42.   See, for example, D. Preston, *Perceptual Dialectology: Nonlinguists' Views of Areal Linguistics* (Dordrecht: Foris, 1989); Preston, "Where the Worst English Is Spoken."

date) is found in a book on *Folk Linguistics* authored by Nancy Niedzielski and Preston.[43] One of the major findings of this project is that North and South are the principal dialect regions in the United States in the perception of ordinary language users. The North is generally considered the region with the most correct speech (with the exception of New York City), while the South is perceived as the region "where the worst English is spoken."[44] Southern speech plays a unique role among the dialects of American English. It is the most salient caricature of regional speech in the United States.

Conclusion

Region and regionalism are concepts relevant only to one of the two alternative overall approaches to language. They are central to variationism but irrelevant to uniformism. In variationism region and regionalism have played different roles at different times. The historical development can be described as a dialectic process. In its initial stages variationist linguistics examined regional variation exclusively (the "thesis"). At that time variationism was called dialectology (in its narrow traditional sense) or, more specifically, dialect geography. The aim of this type of investigation was to determine the regional distribution of linguistic variants, especially in pronunciation and lexis, and the co-occurrence of such variants. Based on such results, which were plotted on maps and displayed in atlases, dialect regions and subregions were identified, or rather postulated. No other type of language variation was considered at the time.

With the advent of sociolinguistics in the 1960s the focus shifted radically from regional to social variation (the "antithesis"). Linguists were no longer interested in the distribution of linguistic features in geographical space; now they were attracted to the covariation of linguistic and social features, such as social class, ethnicity, and gender. For this type of study informants were no longer recruited from rural areas, as in traditional dialectology, but from cities and urban areas. Therefore, this new sociolinguistic type of variationism became known as urban dialectology. It further differs from the traditional type by adopting a more rigorous methodology and making theoretical claims about

---

43.   See ch. 2, "Regionalism." In other contexts and in dialectology "proper" the term "regionalism" refers to a linguistic feature characteristic of a particular dialect, such as a word or phrase typical of a particular geographical region. (See, for example, the definition in the glossary to John Algeo, *The Cambridge History of the English Language*, vol. VI, *English in North America* [Cambridge: Cambridge University Press, 2001], 511.)

44.   See Preston, "Where the Worst English Is Spoken."

the nature of language and the systematic character of language variation and language change.

The latest development in variationist linguistics can be called integrative dialectology (the "synthesis"). Essentially, integrative dialectology is based on the insight that variation in language cannot be attributed to one factor alone. From this perspective linguistic variation is understood as resulting from the interaction of various types of differences, particularly those of region, social standing, ethnicity, gender, and age.

Despite the fact that language variation can only be expertly understood as an interplay of different sets of parameters, regional variation seems to be salient for ordinary language users. Regional characteristics of speech are easily identified. Regional affiliation and identity discernible in speech are socially and psychologically relevant to communication, often producing solidarity or (latent) hostility in accordance with the "Us" and "Them" dichotomy, especially when encountering strangers. This type of attitude is studied in perceptual dialectology. Perceptual dialectology supplements dialectology proper, but is of an essentially different nature. While all other types of dialectology—traditional, urban, and integrative—study dialects, perceptual dialectology studies attitudes towards dialects. In short dialectology studies language, whereas perceptual dialectology studies people. However, perceptual dialectology is not considered a discipline in social psychology, but rather the sociolinguistic study of language attitudes. It is worth noting that while dialectology in the new comprehensive sense investigates many different types of language varieties, perceptual dialectology concentrates exclusively on attitudes toward regional varieties. In perceptual dialectology attitudes toward other people's regional variety as well as toward one's own is referred to as regionalism.

12

Defining Regionalism in North American Studies

Lothar Hönnighausen

On the Politics of Scholarly Terminology

A while ago I tried to convince a young colleague, who is very promising and aware of the kind of projects nowadays likely to meet with peer approval, to participate in our regions and regionalism project. When she seemed reluctant, I told her that the terms might indeed suggest provinciality and backwardness, but that we were going to make a very progressive use of regionalism and would explore it also as *ethnic marginality, gendered space*, and a *discourse of liminality and boundary maintenance*. That convinced her, and she warmed even more to the idea when she heard that some of the contributors seemed to regard regions and regionalism only as a kind of sociocultural metaphor and that "region" and "regionalism" might not even appear in the title, which most likely would be something like *Postmodern Concepts of Spatiality*. This formula also helped me with a senior Canadian diplomat who, on other occasions very supportive, had become glum when asked to subsidize our symposium on regionalism—as it turned out, he had associated *regionalism* with *separatism*. But *postmodern concepts of spatiality* sounded sufficiently academic and harmless to be wholly acceptable in public diplomacy. Unfortunately, his American colleague was too involved with drawing a contour map of the "axis of evil" to share *our* interest in regionalism and the politics of cultural space.

Obviously, the terms *regions* and *regionalism* are value-charged and should not be used naively. However, this is not surprising for scholars today, who in contrast to their predecessors have learned to be wary of the loaded quality of their tools. The fact that the Latin word "*regere*: to organize, rule," from which *region* and *regionalism* derive, has both spatial and political connotations must make the terms attractive to critics who follow social geographer David Harvey and his forerunner sociologist Émile Durkheim in maintaining that "different societies produce qualitatively different conceptions of space and time," and that spatial terms—and this is particularly true of *regions* and *regionalism*—

are "neither neutral nor innocent with respect to practices of domination and control."[1] Further, the political/spatial ambiguity of the terms *regions* and *regionalism* should appeal to writers who in their cultural criticism draw inspiration from Derrida's etymologizing and allegorizing diction. However, Americanists, who with anthropologist Arjun Appadurai focus on global migrations and placelessness,[2] find the term *regional* unattractive since in their view, it means *provincial* in the sense of "backward" and carries conservative, nostalgic (home, *Heimat*), or even reactionary overtones. Instead of *region*, they usually prefer *ethnoscape*, which Appadurai has coined, because, as he notes with strange satisfaction, it makes us realize that "cultures" need not be seen "as spatially bounded ."[3]

Regionalism in Literary History

In contrast to disciplines such as geography, marketing, or planning and development, where *regions* and *regionalism* are frequently used, unproblematic terms, Americanists have difficulties with the terms. This is in large part due to the limited and limiting use of *regions* and *regionalism* in literary histories where it tends to be confined to specific periods and "schools." In the traditional *Literary History of the United States* by Robert E. Spiller, Willard Thorpe et al., *regionalism* occurs in the period 1810–1865 under the heading, "Forms of Regional Humor," and in the period 1865 to 1910, under the heading "local color."[4] The term *local color* tends to be indiscriminately applied to Bret Harte's humorous tales such as "The Luck of Roaring Camp" (1868), Sara Orne Jewett's socially revealing short stories (for instance, "The Foreigner," 1900), and Thomas Nelson Page's reactionary story collection *In Ole Virginia* (1887). At a closer look most of the descriptive features indiscriminately summarized as *local color* turn out to be traits of *regional culture* rather than of a specific *locale* or *site*. But as both *local* and *regional* are terms with fuzzy contours, it is not surprising that the entry *local color* in the *Oxford Companion to American Literature* concludes with the convenient cross reference: "A broader concept

1.   David Harvey, *Justice, Nature, and the Geography of Difference* (Oxford: Blackwell, 1996), 210; Harvey, *Justice, Nature, and the Geography of Difference*, 44. Harvey also argues that "spatial and ecological differences are not only *constituted by but constitutive of* what I call *socio-ecological and political-economic processes*" (ibid).

2.   Arjun Appadurai, *Modernity at Large: Cultural Dimensions of Globalization* (Minneapolis: University of Minnesota Press, 1996).

3.   Appadurai, *Modernity at Large*, 183.

4.   Robert E. Spiller et al., eds., *Literary History of the United States*, 4th ed. (New York: Macmillan, 1974).

of sectional differences lies behind *regionalism*,"[5] implying the relatedness of the phenomena.

James M. Cox begins his article "Regionalism: A Diminished Thing" in *The Columbia History of American Literature* with the reminder that "the nation was from the beginning and through its life but a dialect, a region, of the English language,"[6] but then foregrounds his definition of *regions as diminished sections*: "Regions, in this post-Civil War sense, are sections that have lost not merely national political power but the political power to be nations. There is the diminished thing of my title . . . [and] where sections had been there were now regions."[7] Cox sees both the local color literature of New England and the South as reflecting the shift of political power and national interest from the East to the West. However, this model, plausible though it seems, leaves the simultaneous flowering of Western local color and regional stories from Bret Harte to Hamlin Garland unexplained.

Most critics conceive of *regionalism* as a variant of *realism* or as in some way related to it although few take such a relativistic and ironic view of the two terms as Eric J. Sunquist who maintains that "those in power (say, white urban males) have more often been judged 'realists,' while those removed from the seats of power (say, Midwesterners, blacks, immigrants, or women) have been categorized as 'regionalists'."[8] However, Sunquist leaves no doubt about the close and complex relationship between *realism* and *regionalism*:

> Because their edges blur and their central meanings shift, the categories "realism" and "regionalism" cannot be conveniently separated. A simple division between the urban realism that accompanied the growth of industrial America in the post-Civil War period and the several regional literatures that flourished at the same time would lose sight of the complex aesthetic, social, and economic entanglements between them.

---

5.   James D. Hart, ed., *The Oxford Companion to American Literature*, 5th ed. (New York, Oxford: Oxford University Press, 1983), 439.

6.   James M. Cox, "Regionalism: A Diminished Thing," in *Columbia Literary History of the United States*, ed. Emory Elliott (New York: Columbia University Press, 1988), 762.

7.   Cox, "Regionalism," 763–764.

8.   Eric J. Sundquist, "Realism and Regionalism," in *Columbia Literary History of the United States*, 501.

This view has been developed much further by Amy Kaplan, Richard
H. Brodhead, and Susan V. Donaldson.[9] Kaplan sees *regionalism* not as
an inferior sideline to mainstream *realism* but as connected to it in a vital
dialectics: "Paradoxically, this profusion of literature known as *regionalism
or local color* contributed to the process of centralization or nationalization
. . . by reimagining a distended industrial nation as an extended clan sharing
a 'common inheritance' in its imagined rural origins."[10] She assumes that one
of the attractions of the regional worlds to contemporary readers was their
surrogate function comparable to contemporary "tourist attractions" or to the
presentions at the great industrial expositions of primitive cultures.[11] Susan
Donaldson pays special attention to narrative form and the tendency of local
color fiction toward sketches, stories, tales (and their collection) rather than
toward the "great American novel" of realist theory. By juxtaposing Jewett,
a female regionalist; Abraham Cahan, a representative of Jewish immigrant
literature, and Charles W. Chesnutt, a leading African-American writer, and
by discussing the similarity of the sociocultural function of "Local Color and
the Ethnographic Gaze," she extends and considerably deepens the concept of
regionalism: "Local color tales of the quaint and the foreign, [Jewett, Cahan,
Chesnutt], ironically, helped tell white middle-class Americans who and what
they were by presenting them with spectacles of what they were not."[12]

While the regional aspect of post-Civil War literature has recently received
much attention by sophisticated critics, the same can hardly be said of the
literary *regionalism* of the 1930s and 1940s. The article on *regionalism* in *The
Oxford Companion to American Literature* illustrates the complex reasons that
have led to the neglect of *regionalism as a continuous tradition* in American
literary history. While acknowledging the theoretical premises of 1930s
regionalism in works such *I'll Take My Stand* (1930) and *Who Owns America?*
(1936) and quoting Allen Tate's historically revealing dictum "Only a return
to the provinces, to the small self-contained centres of life, will put the all-
destroying abstraction of America safely to rest," the article does not give an

9.   Amy Kaplan, "Nation, Region, and Empire," in *The Columbia History of the American
Novel*, ed. Emory Elliott et al. (New York: Columbia University Press, 1991), 240–266;
Richard H. Brodhead, *Cultures of Letters: Scenes of Reading and Writing in Nineteenth-
Century America* (Chicago: University of Chicago Press, 1993); Susan V. Donaldson,
Competing Voices: The American Novel 1865–1914 (New York: Twayne, 1998), 43–70.
10.   Kaplan, "Nation, Region, and Empire," 250.
11.   Kaplan, "Nation, Region, and Empire," 252.
12.   Donaldson, *Competing Voices*, 50.

overview of the literary works of the regionalist movement.[13] In fact, it does not even mention that many of the works of major writers such as William Faulkner (for instance, *Light in August*, 1932, and *The Hamlet*, 1940) and John Steinbeck (*Grapes of Wrath*, 1939) derive from and are part of the regionalism of the time. Further, it does not point out the striking parallels that are present in art history, the paintings of Grant Wood, Thomas Hart Benton, John Steuart Curry, and Alexandre Hogue (for instance, the notorious *Erosion NO. 2— Mother Earth Laid Bare*, 1936), and in architecture (for instance, Bertram Grosvenor Goodhue: The Nebraska State Capital, Lincoln, 1922–1932). Nor does it consider the huge sociocultural projects such as the national communal theater initiative, the regionalist art in public buildings, the several big photo projects, and the WPA-Guides to the American states.[14]

As a result of this reductive treatment in the *Oxford Companion*—and in most traditional resources in literary history—regionalism does not appear as the comprehensive cultural movement that it really was. The consequence is that to this day it is neither known nor appreciated that regionalism was the source of major twentieth-century contributions to literature and art, and that it was related to the New Deal and the efforts to renew America and the American Dream after the bank crash of 1929. However, there have fortunately been several serious efforts to supplement the incomplete picture of the regionalist movement and acknowledge its far-reaching impact on the emergence of a new sense of the nation as an imagined community with literature as its embodiment. James M. Cox notes that "in this historical context, regions become the imaginative space created by the loss of national potentiality."[15] On the basis of this definition, he traces regionalism from the local color school

---

13.   Hart, ed., *The Oxford Companion to American Literature*, 632. Cox seems to be one of the few critics regarding it as a matter of course that authors such as Faulkner can be fruitfully discussed under the heading of regionalism.

14.   A major resource is the exhibition catalogue *Amerika. Traum und Depression 1920/40* (Ausstellungskatalog Akademie der Künste Berlin 9.11.–28.12. 1980). See in particular the articles by Eckart Gillen, "Das Bild Amerikas: Ein verlorenes Paradies. Zur Malerei der Regionalisten und magischen Realisten," 236–287; Yvonne Leonard/Gisela Stahl, "Eine Reise ohne Schatten. Die Idee Amerika in den Reiseführern des Federal Writers' Project," 290–312, Hubertus Gaßner, "Die Reise ins Innere 'Amerika den Amerikanern vorstellen': Die Fotografen der Farm Security Administration," 313–352, on the photo projects by Walker Evans, Ben Shahn, Dorothea Lange, and Arthur Rothstein. Eudora Welty, who worked for some time for the Works Progress Administration, dealt with this experience both in her fiction and in the documentary volume *One Time and Place* (New York: Random University House, 1971). See also her *Photographs*, with a foreword by Reynold Price (Jackson and London: University Press of Mississippi, 1989).

15.   James M. Cox, "Regionalism: A Diminished Thing," 764.

to Faulkner and his great Southern successors, Katherine Anne Porter, Eudora
Welty, and Flannery O'Connor. Thadious M. Davis, in her chapter on "Race and
Region" and James H. Maguire in his ecologically oriented chapter "Fiction of
the West," both in *The Columbia History of the American Novel*, contribute to a
better understanding of regionalist literature through transcending the narrow
confines of the merely literary.[16]

In *Revolt of the Provinces* Robert L. Dorman presents a meticulous picture
of the regionalist movement, in particular its theoretical underpinnings, artwork,
and, to some extent, of its literature.[17] However, he does not consider the before
and after, apparently limiting the regionalist movement to the narrow span of
1920–1945, nor does he offer any appraisal of its positive and negative aspects
and mixed reception today. To more profoundly contextualize the literary side
of the regionalist movement, we have to recognize its intimate relationship
with the American cultural nationalism of the time, in turn corresponding
with the growing nationalism in many European countries. As a reaction to
the imminent sense of crisis since the mid-1920s, reaching its climax in 1929
with the collapse of the American stock market and the world economy, writers
as diverse as Gertrude Stein (*The Making of Americans*, 1925) and William
Carlos Williams (*In The American Grain*, 1925) seek to recover "true national
values" and emphasize the Americanness of the American literary tradition.

William Faulkner, inspired and encouraged by Sherwood Anderson and
his ideology of the West, turned to his native South and discovered here the
basis of his mature writing. In trying to assess the American literary heritage,
he excluded Edgar Allen Poe, Nathaniel Hawthorne, and Henry James as
"primarily European . . . not true Americans" and praised "Whitman and
Mark Twain, the poet Sandburg" as real American writers.[18] In regard to the
problem *regionalism—cultural nationalism* it is intersting that one region
should appear to him as more truly American than another. But that is indeed
his view. He rejects the "eastern seaboard . . . where the tradition . . . was a

16.   Thadious M. Davis, "Race and Region," in *Columbia History of the American Novel*,
407–436; James H. Maguire, "Fiction of the West," in *Columbia History of the American
Novel*, 437–464.

17.   Robert L. Dorman, *Revolt of the Provinces: The Regionalist Movement in America*,
1920–1945 (Chapel Hill: University of North Carolina Press, 1993). See also Lothar
Hönnighausen, "Region, Nation and the Definition of American Identity in the Early Twentieth
Century," in *Negotiations of America's National Identity*, ed. Roland Hagenbüchle and Josef
Raab, in cooperation with Marietta Messmer, Vol. II (Tübingen: Stauffenburg, 2000), 348–
361.

18.   James B. Meriwether and Michael Millgate, eds., *Lion In The Garden. Interviews with
William Faulkner, 1926–1962* (Lincoln: University of Nebraska Press, 1968), 168.

European tradition," while he praises—acknowledging the shift of the national cultural focus from puritan Boston and cosmopolitan New York to Chicago— the West as the embodiment of true Americanness. In line with this way of thinking he considers his mentor, the Westerner Anderson, a paragon of the American writer: "He is American, and more than that, a middle westerner, of the soil."[19]

Ironically, regionalism is an international phenomenon,[20] and soil and land, peasants and ploughs play a major role not only in the regionalist works of Willa Cather (*O Pioneers*, 1913, and *My Ántonia*, 1918), William Faulkner ("Out of Nazareth," 1925; "Nympholepsy," 1925; *Light in August*, 1932; *The Hamlet*, 1940; *Go Down, Moses*, 1942; *Intruder in the Dust*, 1948), Erskine Caldwell (*Tobacco Road*, 1932, and *God's Little Acre*, 1933), and John Steinbeck (*Of Mice and Men*, 1937, and *The Grapes of Wrath*, 1939), but also in the novels of politically very diverse contemporary European writers such as Knut Hamsun (*Growth of the Soil*, 1920), Mikhail Sholokhov (*The Silent Don*, 1928–1940, and *Virgin Soil Upturned*, 1935), and Cesare Pavese (*The Harvesters*, 1941, and *The Moon and the Bonfires*, 1950).[21]

Unfortunately, the complexity and internationality of regionalism has not led critics to adopt complex and comparative approaches. In fact, American critics tend to ignore the multifaceted nature of regionalism, identifying it with the rural nostalgias and rightwing undercurrents of the Vanderbilt Agrarians and ignoring, for instance, the social reformist regionalism of Howard W. Odum or the documentary regionalism of Walker Evans.[22] German critics are so

---

19.   William Faulkner, *New Orleans Sketches*, ed. Carvel Collins (New York: Random House, 1958), 139.

20.   See Norbert Mecklenburg, *Erzählte Provinz. Regionalismus und Moderne im Roman* (Königstein/Ts: Athenäum, 1982), particularly, "Regionalismus international," 82–94. From Mecklenburg's sophisticated account it becomes clear how ideologically and sociologically diverse regionalism really is. There are right-wing authors and left-wing ones, both conservative agrarians such as Gulbranssen and communists such as Rasputin, Abramov, and Aitmatow. Mecklenburg mentions, besides Faulkner, Steinbeck, Hamsun, and Giono, C. F. Ramuz, Giovanni Verga, and Cesare Pavese.

21.   See Peter Nicolaisen, "Faulkner and Hamsun: The Community and the Soil" and M. Thomas Inge, "Yoknapatawpha on the Don: Faulkner and Sholokhov," both in *Faulkner, His Contemporaries, and His Posterity*, ed. Waldemar Zacharasiewicz (Tübingen: Francke, 1993), 88–101, 129–142; and Peter Nicolaisen, "'The dark land talking voiceless speech': Faulkner and 'Native Soil,'" *Mississippi Quarterly* XLV, 3 (Summer 1992): 253–276.

22.   Howard W. Odum and Harry Estill Moore, *Regionalism: A Cultural-Historical Approach to National Integration* (New York: Henry Holt and Co., 1968) and Odum's several other scientific, integrationist, and social reformist works represent another of the several facets of regionalism of which *I'll Take My Stand* embodies only one. For examples of Walker Evans'

overwhelmed by the fatal memories of the "the soil and blood" ideology of the Nazis that—except for such a rare exception as Peter Nicolaisen—they fail to develop a balanced view, based on detailed analyses of form and ideology.[23]

Moreover, there does indeed exist a disconcerting connection between the well muscled ploughmen and their full-bossomed workmates in WPA-funded art work in public buildings in the United States and those in Hitler's Germany and Stalin's Soviet Union and—awkward for literary historians with neat categories—the writings by contemporary democratic and National Socialist and Communist authors. This similarity is caused by the sameness of the deep-seated disappointment with the old money-based bourgeois world order that had collapsed in 1917–1918 and in 1929 and the sameness of the uncritical belief in values such as the moral superiority of simple people and their regional, essentially rural worlds. The technologically advanced mass-murders of World War II and the inhumanity of the regimes of Hitler and Stalin as well as the gigantic, centralized bureaucratic apparatus of Roosevelt's New Deal were soon to reveal the anachronism of many regional values.

Nevertheless, quite a few writers, Faulkner, Caldwell, and Steinbeck among them, managed to comically invert or functionally transform the affirmativeness and monumentality of the regionalist aesthetics, after initially utilizing its modes of expression. The fact that the regionalist dimension of Faulkner is taboo in current Faulkner criticism is a consequence of the history of Faulkner studies. He had been stereotyped as "The Great Southerner" to such an extent that even he tried to downplay his famous "postage stamp of native soil" pronouncement by writing in 1944 to Malcolm Cowley "that my material, the South, is not very important to me. I just happen to know it."[24] The counter move, within Faulkner criticism, against the image of Faulkner as "The Great Southerner" was to turn him, equally indiscriminately, into a learned and sophisticated modernist anticipating postmodernism. Further, as the greatest American novelist of the twentieth century and an international

---

documentary regionalism see, for instance, his photos in James Agee and Walker Evans, *Let Us Now Praise Famous Men* (New York: Ballantine, 1978).

23. See note 21.

24. "Beginning with *Sartoris* I discovered that my own little postage stamp of native soil was worth writing about," Meriwether and Millgate, ed., *Lion in the Garden*, 255. Faulkner also wrote in the *Marble Faun*: "The author of these poems is a man steeped in the soil of his native land, a Southerner by every instinct, and more, than that, a Mississippian. George Moore said that all universal art became great by first being provincial," William Faulkner, *The Marble Faun*, 1924. The quote from the Cowley letter is from *Selected Letters of William Faulkner*, ed. Joseph Blotner (New York: Random House, 1977), 185.

figure, he must be a complete internationalist and not be tainted by any association with *regionalism*, a component of Western cultural history that is still not so much critically studied as dismissed as artistically provincial and politically reactionary.

However, the truth is that Faulkner experimented almost as much with regionalist material as with fin de siècle and modernist models. Only his attitude to this regional material underwent dramatic changes.[25] A comparison between such regionalist apprentice work as "Out of Nazareth" (1925) and "Nympholepsy" (1925) on the one hand and *Light in August* (1932), *The Hamlet* (1940), and *Go Down, Moses* (1942) on the other shows his adherence to regionalism as well as his transcendence of its ideological and artistic narrowness.[26] There is no doubt that the figure of Lena and the mule wagon in the great opening of *Light in August* ("The wagon mounts the hill toward her. . . The sharp and brittle crack and clatter of its weathered and ungreased wood and metal is slow and terrific . . . the vehicle seems to hang suspended in the middle distance forever and forever," 404)[27] or the portrait of Mrs. Armstid in *The Hamlet* can be understood better within the context of *regionalism*, as represented, for instance, by Walker Evans's documentary and monumentalizing photos of the deprived South:

> She came up among them behind the man, gaunt in the *gray shapeless garment* and the sunbonnet, wearing stained canvas gymnasium shoes (1001, my emphasis) . . . The wife had gone back to the wagon, where she sat *gray in the gray garment*, motionless, looking at nothing still; she might have been something inanimate which he had loaded into the wagon to move it somewhere, waiting now in the wagon until he should be ready to go on again, patient insensate, timeless (1004, my emphasis). . . the *gray and shapeless garment* within which she

---

25.   On Faulkner's complicated relation to the regionalist movement see Lothar Hönnighausen, *William Faulkner: Masks and Metaphors* (Jackson: University Press of Mississippi 1997), "Faulkner and the Regionalist Context" (183–222) and "Regionalism and Beyond: *The Hamlet*" (223–263).

26.   For instance, in the story "The Bear," in *Go Down, Moses*, Faulkner, whose anti New Deal views are clear from the satire in *The Mansion*, has Ike favor "collective" land ownership: "to hold the earth mutual and intact in the communal anonymity of brotherhood, and all the fee He asked was pity and humility and sufferance and endurance, and the sweat of the face for bread." *William Faulkner: Novels 1942–1954*, select. and ed. with notes by Joseph Blotner and Noel Polk (New York: The Library of America, 1994), 190.

27.   *William Faulkner: Novels 1930–1935*, select. and ed. with notes by Joseph Blotner and Noel Polk (New York: The Library of America, 1985), 404.

moved without inference of locomotion, like something on a moving platform, a float (*The Hamlet*, 1006).[28]

The outcome of the synergic use of alliteration and word repetition and the metaphoric transformation of Mrs. Armstid first into "something inanimate" and later, through a daring mannerism, into a statue—of a goddess or a saint on a float in a procession—is a stylized portrait that transcends regional affirmativeness and, because of the distancing devices, is not sentimental but universally moving.

To create this universal appeal of the regional is what Lewis Mumford, one of the most thoughtful cultural critics of the regionalism movement, regards as its most important goal:

Regionalism in literature, painting, and music is the interpretation of human experience in the symbols which the artist finds in that area of the United States with which, either for life or for the moment, he is most familiar. This does not mean that regional art is merely local. It employs unmistakably regional language to express the universal— otherwise it is not art.[29]

What makes Mumford's vision of *regionalism* important beyond his own time is its critical awareness as well as its comprehensiveness. He sees *regionalism* not as limited to the arts, but as involving the whole sociopolitical system. In fact he develops his concept of *regionalism* in the face of the threats of the nationalist and communist centralism of the 1930s. He sees all national states, internally, as suppressive of the wholesome counterweight of the regions and, externally, as aggressive toward their neighbors, with National Socialist Germany as the grotesque and terrible culmination of this tendency. But he is also aware of the federalist tradition of Germany, and he invokes it in propagating his view of a "service state" against the centralist "power state" in Nazi Germany and elsewhere:

Nationalism is an attempt to make the laws and customs and beliefs of a single region or city do duty for the varied expressions of a multitude of other regions. . . All the great national states, and the empires formed a national core, are at bottom war-states; their politics is war-

---

28. *William Faulkner: Novels 1936–1940*, select. and ed. with notes by Joseph Blotner and Noel Polk (New York: The Library of America, 1990), 1006.
29. Lewis Mumford, *The Culture of Cities* (New York: Harcourt Brace Jovanovich, 1938), 84.

politics. . . The final caricature of this tendency is National Socialist Germany today, with its fatuous racial mythology. . . [Germany] before the advent of the Nazis, was the outstanding example of an historic federalism which roughly satisfied the needs of regional and cultural autonomy: it needed only a political redefinition of the constituent regions, including a division of Prussia, to make Germany a world example of economic and cultural regionalism.[30]

Mumford's criticism of the national state and his enlightened concept of *regionalism* should have a new appeal in our time, a period that sees the national states within the European Union still plodding on and, at the same time, is beginning to realize that globalism and sub- and supranational regionalism are not mutually exclusive but dialectically connected.

Indeed, Mumford's vision of the interaction between "the whole and the parts" and the ineluctable although historically shifting relationship between regions and states—or greater political units such as the European Union— seems also to provide a basis for a new approach to the regional element in cultural and literary history. For in my view, deviating from Dorman's, the regionalist movement is not limited to one particular period (1920–1945) but rather constitutes a much larger, continuous tradition, rising to the surface for different historical reasons and in different forms and degrees.[31] I posit that such a tradition of a conscious "constructed *regionalism*"—in contrast to the geopolitically unavoidable, that is, "given *regionalism*" of the colonial period and the time of the early Republic—emerges with Washington Irving's stylized rendering of the Dutch ethno-regional heritage in New York and the Hudson River Valley and with the painters of the Hudson River School such as Thomas Cole, Asher Durand, and Thomas Doughty. From the wider perspective of a continuous *regionalist tradition*, the "local color school" of the nineteenth century and the regionalism of the 1930s and 1940s are just two different historical manifestations of a continuous regionalist undercurrent. A writer such as Willa Cather, drawing inspiration from Jewett and Mary E. Freeman but also associated with the investigative ("muckraking") journalism of McClure's, marks the transition from the idyllic and humorous as well as

---

30.   Mumford, *The Culture of Cities*, 349-350.

31.   I have tried to bolster the assumption of a regionalist tradition by setting off the new regionalism of the last decades of the twentieth century from that of the 1930s and 1940s. See Lothar Hönnighausen, "The Old and the New Regionalism," in *'Writing' Nation and 'Writing' Region in America*, ed. Theo D'haen and Hans Bertens (Amsterdam: VU University Press, 1996), 3–20.

realistic rendering of regional culture by "local color" writers to the moral commitment and aesthetic affirmativeness of the regionalism of the 1930s and 1940s and beyond to the postmodern regionalism of our time.

There are, to the great surprise of all believers in the absolute dominance of globalism as "placelessness," clear signs of a new interest in place and, heralded by numerous American and Canadian novels, in *regionalism*. This is shown by the emergence of the new kind of Western literature during the 1960s and 1970s, often distinguished by an ecological slant, with which one should probably also align the bioregionalist poems and essays of Gary Snyder and Wendell Berry.[32] Moreover, there has emerged, after the era of Eudora Welty and Flannery O'Connor, another generation of Southern writers who continue Faulkner's, O'Connor's and Welty's tradition of critically probing rather than nostalgically celebrating the South and its heritage.[33] The collection of *Great Stories From The Prairies*, edited by Birk Sproxton (2000), that presents stories ranging from the time of Frederick Philip Grove, W. O. Mitchell, and Sinclair Ross to that of Sharon Butala, Rudy Wiebe, and Aritha Van Herk and the on-line magazine (since 1999), *Taking Place: Canadian Prairie Writing*, show that the great tradition of Prairie writing also continues into our time. In contrast, there have been in recent times—at least in my reading experience—only relatively few novels dealing with New England whose cultural hegemony in former times was such that its "regional" literature—Hawthorne's *Scarlet Letter*,

---

32.   This list and the following ones of representative texts are based on syllabi taught in the North American Program of the University of Bonn: Ken Kesey, *Sometimes a Great Notion* (1964); Wallace Stegner, *Angle of Repose* (1971); Edward Abbey, *Desert Solitaire: A Season in the Wilderness* (1968) and *The Monkey Wrench Gang* (1975); Ernest Callenbach's *Ecotopia* (1975); Jack Hodgins, *Spit Delaney's Island* (1976) and *The Invention of the World* (1977); Norman Maclean, *A River Runs Through It and Other Stories* (1976); Ivan Doig, *Winter Brothers* (1980); George Bowering, *Burning Water* (1980). For more on Snyder and Berry see my "'By Division, Out of Wonder': Gary Snyder, Wendell Berry, and Ecopoetics," *Soundings: An Interdisciplinary Journal* 78 (Summer 1995): 279–291 and "Ecopoetics: On Poetological Poems by Gary Snyder and Wendell Berry," *Poetica* 28 (1996): 356–367.

33.   For instance, Margaret Walker, *Jubilee* (1966); Ernest Gaines, *Of Love and Dust* (1967), *The Autobiography of Miss Jane Pittman* (1971), *A Lesson Before Dying* (1993); Lee Smith, *Cake Walk* (1970), *Oral History* (1983), *Fair and Tender Ladies* (1988); Alex Haley, *Roots* (1974); Harry Crews, *A Feast of Snakes* (1976); Walker Percy, *The Moviegoer* (1960), *Lancelot* (1977); Ellen Gilchrist, *In the Land of Dreamy Dreams* (1981); Bobbie Ann Mason, *Shiloh and Other Stories* (1982); Alice Walker, *The Color Purple* (1982); Clyde Edgerton, *Raney* (1985); Pat Conroy, *The Prince of Tides* (1986); Josephine Humphreys, *Rich in Love* (1987); Ellen Douglas, *Can't Quit You, Baby* (1988); Dori Sanders, *Clover* (1990), *Her Own Place* (1993); Dorothy Allison, *Bastard Out of Carolina* (1992); Tina McElroy Ansa, *Ugly Ways* (1993); Peter

Melville's *Moby Dick*, and Henry James's *The Bostonians*—was identified as national literature and "American Renaissance."[34]

However, the picture of the Northeast looks quite different if we include Canada's Maritimes, Québec, and Ontario where a new *regionalism*, often fusing—as in Ann-Marie MacDonald's *Fall On Your Knees* (1996)—with postmodern tendencies, manifests itself in an impressive body of work, in which the long series of remarkable novels by the New Brunswick writer David Adams Richards appears pre-eminent.[35] MacDonald's and Richards's writing leaves little doubt that the focus in rendering place is no longer on idealized sites in the sense of the *locus amoenus* but on bleak northern sceneries. In fact, three remarkable contemporary novels have been devoted to Newfoundland alone,[36] and the remote North, too, continues to attract major writers and their readers, as a particular section in *Forms of Regionalism*, the sequel to this volume, demonstrates. Both the locale of the new *regionalism* and its personnel are very different from the *regionalism* of previous epochs. In this regard, Michael Ondaatje's *In the Skin of a Lion* (1987) is of particular interest because it clearly demonstrates how the treatment of place, in this case Toronto and environs, is intimately connected with that of ethnicity and gender.

Indeed, a lot of literature that so far has been exclusively dealt with from the perspective of ethnicity or gender, repays rereading from the viewpoint of

---

Taylor, *In the Tennessee Country* (1994); George Garrett, *The King of Babylon Shall Not Come against You* (1996), Charles Frazier, *Cold Mountain* (1997); Tom Wolfe, *A Man in Full* (1998).

34. Recent novels include E. Annie Proulx, *Heart Songs* (1988); John Irving, *A Prayer For Owen Meany* (1989); Bharati Mukherjee, *The Holder of the World* (1993). For a comparative study of recent regional anglophone and francophone Canadian and American fiction from the northeast see. Michaela Röll's dissertation *"No Place Like Home": Modernist and Postmodernist Space in the Novels of Margaret Atwood, John Irving and Their Contemporaries* (University of Bonn, 2002) and her essay "Decentering the Region: Spatial Identifications and Differentiations in Postmodern Regional Narratives" in this volume.

35. See, for instance, Marie-Claire Blais, *Une Saison dans la vie d'Emmanuel* (1965); Michael Ondaatje, *In the Skin of a Lion* (1987); Jane Urquhart, *Away* (1993); Carol Shields, *The Stone Diaries* (1993); Patrick Kavanagh, *Gaff Topsails* (1996); Ann-Marie MacDonald, *Fall on Your Knees* (1996); Lola Lemire Tostevin, *Frog Moon* (1994); Wayne Johnston, *The Colony of Unrequited Dreams* (1998); Alistair MacLeod, *As Birds Bring Forth the Sun and Other Stories* (1986), *No Great Mischief* (1999). See also David Adams Richards's Miramichi-Trilogies: *The Coming of Winter* (1974), *Blood Ties* (1976), and *Lives of Short Duration* (1981); *Nights below Station Street* (1988), *Evening Snow Will Bring Such Peace* (1990), *For Those Who Hunt the Wounded Down* (1993), *Hope in the Desperate Hour* (1996), and *Mercy among the Children* (2000).

36. E. Annie Proulx, *The Shipping News* (1993); Patrick Kavanagh, *Gaff Topsails* (1996); and Wayne Johnston, *The Colony of Unrequited Dreams* (1998).

a commitment or lack of commitment to place. This goes not only for Asian-Canadian and Asian-American literature but, as the examples cited show, also for Native American and First Nations' literature.[37] Interesting specimen of ethno-regional novels are also to be found among the African-American and Latin American Los Angeles novels that Ingrid Kerkhoff and others have studied.[38] The number and quality of novels from the last decades of the twentieth century with a strong regional component provide further evidence that there has been, from the romantic period to the present, either prominently or as an undercurrent, a continuous *regionalist tradition* in North American literature. These *neoregionalist* novels deserve attention not only because of literary excellence of many of them, but also because they concern themselves with place, one of the most important identity-constituting experiences.

Regionalism in North American Studies

With the problem "place—identity," we have come to a theme in regard to which the disciplines of American Literature and Canadian Literature can profit from multi- or interdisciplinary North American Studies. While *regionalism* has not received too much attention in literary history, we get a totally different picture when we look beyond the narrow pale of literary studies and enter interdisciplinary North American Studies. The interdisciplinary bibliography by Michael Steiner and Clarence Mondale *Region and Regionalism in the United States*, clearly documents that *region* and *regionalism* play a role, sometimes a major role, in an amazing number of disciplines.[39] Some of them deal with

---

37.   Consider these Asian-Canadian, Asian-American examples of ethno-regional heritage: Joy Kogawa, *Obasan* (1981); Hisaye Yamamoto, *Seventeen Syllables and Other Stories* (1988); Amy Tan, *The Joy Luck Club* (1989); Sky Lee, *Disappearing Moon Cafe* (1990); Denise Chong, *The Concubine's Children* (1994); David Guterson, *Snow Falling on Cedars*, 1995; Wayson Choy, *The Jade Peony* (1995), *Paper Shadows: A Chinatown Childhood* (1999). Examples of literature emerging from the First Nation's ethno-regional heritage include: N. Scott Momaday, *House Made of Dawn* (1966); Leslie Marmon Silko, *Ceremony* (1977); Jeannette Armstrong, *Slash* (1985); Louise Erdrich, *Love Medicine* (1984).
38.   See, for instance, Robert Mosley, *Devil in a Blue Dress* (1990); Oscar Zeta Acosta, *The Revolt of the Cockroach People* (1973); Richard Vasques, *Chicano* (1979); Danny Santiago, *Famous All Over Town* (1983); Helena Maria Viramontes, *The Moths and Other Stories* (1985); Mike Davis's, *City of Quartz: Excavating the Future* (1990). On the literary treatment of Los Angeles see Ingrid Kerkhoff, "From a White Eldorado to the Site of Multicultural Contestation: Rethinking Literary Los Angeles," *Regional Images and Regional Realities*, ed. Lothar Hönnighausen (Tübingen: Stauffenburg, 2000), 213–233.
39.   Michael Steiner and Clarence Mondale, *Region and Regionalism in the United States: A Source Book for the Humanities and Social Sciences* (New York and London: Garland, 1988).

the "reality" of regions, others more with their "images" and, increasingly, with the interaction between the two.[40] In regard to the problem of *regions* and *regionalism*, North American Studies have the obvious advantage of entailing comparisons between the much more homogenized United States and the more regionalized Canada.

The political culture of the United States, despite phases of sectionalism, despite the divisions in the Sun Belt and Rust Belt, and despite the great regional differences between California and New England, the Midwest and the South, has always been kept together by a strong homogenizing patriotic myth. Americans of all levels of education share a unifying national faith in their country, the intensity of which foreigners sometimes find difficult to understand. However, the sway of the concomitant all-American vision is such that Americans often ignore the de facto existing power and difference of the cultural regions of the United States.[41] In fact, to the chagrin of their northern neighbors, they even tend to overlook the differences between America and Canada. In contrast, Canadians seem to experience their nationhood with diffidence and a shy sense of humor, the political reason for this being Canada's colonial history and, as one of its consequences, the formidable impact of the regions vis-à-vis the much debated authority of Ottawa.

In addition to the Canadian-American comparison as a key element of North American Studies, its international branch offers an even more comprehensive view, by bringing the experience of Asian or European regions and regionalism to bear on the same issue in the study of North America. This kind of comparative approach is common practice in ethnology, anthropology, geography, and sociology, disciplines that move more easily from one continent and culture to another than do history, art history, and literary history.[42] One of the positive results of this interdisciplinary and international influence—if historians, art and literary historians in the field of American and Canadian Studies, are indeed willing to let it affect their approach—would be an increased awareness that the problem of *regions* and *regionalism* concerns basic human issues such as the experience of space and place and problems as far ranging

---

40. See Lothar Hönnighausen, ed., *Regional Images and Regional Realities* (Tübingen: Stauffenburg, 2000).

41. See the title of Raymond D. Gastil's classic *The Cultural Regions of the United States* (Seattle: University of Washington Press, 1975).

42. A good example of this is Steven Feld and Keith H. Basso, eds., *Senses of Place* (Santa Fe: School of American Research Press, 1996).

as *home/Heimat* and the postmodernist "reality crisis," what architectural critic Paul Virilio has called the "aesthetics of disappearance."[43]

If we try to relate the problem of *regions* and *regionalism* to its philosophical roots, it matters whether we assume *space* or *place* to be the ultimate reference point. Like most Western intellectuals, I had taken it for granted that the concepts of *regions* and *regionalism* had their cognitive basis in Kant's understanding of space and time as a priori forms of human sensibility. However, my reading of Edward S. Casey and, through him, of Maurice Merleau-Ponty has made me increasingly doubtful whether *space* is indeed the primary experience of which *place* is only a concretization. After all, Kant's transcendental aesthetics and his understanding of space and time as "a priori forms of of human sensibility" are a reaction to a cognitive question arising within the context of eighteenth-century thinking, and Merleau-Ponty's anthropological and sociological understanding of space—as a *bodily* and *communicatively* constituted sense—seems more useable in literary and cultural studies of regions and regionalism in the age of globalism and cyberspace. In fact, Merleau-Ponty's definition of *space* is closer to Casey's *place* than to Kant's *space*:

Space and perception generally represent, at the core of the subject, the fact of his birth, the perpetual contribution of his bodily being, a communication with the world more ancient than thought. . . . The constitution of a spatial level is simply one means of constituting an integrated world: my body is geared onto the world when my perception presents me with a spectacle as varied and as clearly articulated as possible . . .[44]

On the other hand, Edward S. Casey's understanding of *place* presupposes Merleau-Ponty's bodily sense of *space* and his concept of *corporeal*

43.   W. H. New, *Landsliding: Imagining Space, Presence, and Power in Canadian Writing* (Toronto: University of Toronto Press, 1997), Chap. 3 "Landed: Literature and Region" (116–160); Lothar Hönnighausen, *"Regions and Regionalism: Are They Still Relevant Terms in the Global Age?"* in *Regional Images and Regional Realities*, 291; Ina-Maria Greverus, *Der territoriale Mensch: Ein literaturanthropologischer Versuch zum Heimatphänomen* (1979); *Auf der Suche nach der Heimat* (1979); and Jürgen Pohl, *Regionalbewußtsein als Thema der Sozialgeographie* (1993).

The interview, "Architecture in the Age of Its Virtual Disappearance," with Paul Virilio was conducted by Andreas Ruby in Paris on October 15, 1993, and can be found in John Beckmann, ed., *The Virtual Dimension: Architecture, Representation, and Crash Culture* (New York: Princeton Architectural Press, 1998), 180–187.

44.   Maurice Merleau-Ponty, *Phenomenology of Perception*, trans. by Colin Smith (London and New York: Routledge, 1962), 80.

intentionality. For Casey body and place are mutually interdependent and constitutive. He speaks of "the dialectic of perception and place" and defines "human beings" as "ineluctably place-bound."[45] Combining Merleau-Ponty's *corporeal intentionality* with Bourdieu's *habitus*, Casey moves the problem of place vs. space from the narrow arena of cognitive theory into the wider field of culture studies:

> To be cultural, to have a culture, is to inhabit a place sufficiently intensely to cultivate (culture from *colere-cultivate*). . . . The common lesson of Merleau-Ponty and Bourdieu: the body that has incorporated cultural patterns into its basic actions. These actions depend on *habitus*, "history turned into nature . . . No more than space is prior to place than is the body prior to culture . . . the body is itself enactive of cultural practices by virtue of its considerable powers of incorporation, habituation, and expression. And as a creature of *habitus*, the same body necessarily *inhabits* places that are themselves culturally informed. . . . Bodies not only perceive but *know* places. . . . It is by bodies that places become cultural in character.[46]

If we take *space* and *place* as basic reference points, *regions* are more closely related to *place* than to *space*, being particular ways of looking at and organizing specific embodiments of place. As literature seeks to register the sensuous, bodily experience of place as home, the terms *regions* and *regionalism* are useful tools in defining, for instance, Kathleen and Lily Piper's spatial orientation in Anne-Marie MacDonald's *Fall on Your Knees* (1996). Both Kathleen in her training as a singer in New York and her daughter Lily in leaving Cape Breton express an intense feeling for the home region from which they are absenting themselves. This distance from and closeness to Cape Breton Island, in other words the problematic relationship to home regions, is characteristic of the "new regionalism" of the 1990s in contrast to the affirmativeness of the "old regionalism" of the 1930s and 1940s:

> They say that the body of water stretching away to the east of Manhattan is the ocean but it isn't. Not my ocean, anyway. It's weird because back home I just took it for granted, my grey-green sea.[47]

---

45.   Edward S. Casey, "How to Get from Space to Place in a Fairly Short Stretch of Time: Phenomenlogical Prolegomena," in *Senses of Place*, 19.

46.   Casey, "How to Get from Space to Place," 34.

47.   Ann-Marie MacDonald, *Fall on Your Knees* (Toronto: Vintage, 1997), 463.

On the Ferry in the middle of the Strait of Canso, Lily puts the diary down and looks behind her at Cape Breton because she will never see it again. She takes her last scent of salt island air, harsh, coniferous and cool, the indescribable grey that contains all things. Home. Farewell.[48]

The concept of *regions and regionalism* is equally helpful in describing— for instance, in regard to the New Brunswick novels of David Adams Richards—the larger unit of the Maritimes,[49] the several layers of subregions (New Brunswick, Miramichi river basin), the movements between the several local sites, and the short descriptions of the weather that Richards inserts so effectively in *Mercy Among the Children* (2000). A *regions and regionalism* approach enables us to deal not only with the physical aspect of Richards's world, but also with its sociocultural dimension, Indian-white relations in *Lives of Short Duration* (1981) and *Hope in the Desperate Hour* (1996), the university and its social hinterland in the same novel, or the catholic milieu in *Mercy among the Children* (2000). *Region* as a cultural construct, because of its combination of spatial and socio-political aspects, works particularly well in capturing economic and cultural change. This is important not only in Richards but also in other Canadian writers such as Jane Urquhart (*Away* 1993) and Alistair MacLeod, whose "The Closing Down of Summer" (in *As Birds Bring Forth the Sun and Other Stories* 1986) shows how global forces, represented by the industrialized Russian, Portuguese, and Spanish fishing fleets, deracinate the fishermen of the Maritimes, turning them into international migrant workers.

Change is a distinctive feature of the *new regionalism* of the end of the twentieth-century, in contrast to the *old regionalism* of the 1930s which, against the background of economic collapse and the destruction of the American Dream, tried to invoke regions as havens of cultural permanence and purity. In this regard the same picture presents itself in all North American regions, whether we think of E. Anne Proulx's *Shipping News* (1993), a book about a return to a Newfoundland that is anything but idyllic; Marilynne Robinson's *House Keeping* (1980), which depicts the end of housekeeping, or of the transformation of the South in recent southern novels. Josephine Humphreys (*Rich in Love* 1987) rewrites Charlestonian and southern history from a

---

48.   MacDonald, *Fall on Your Knees*, 502.
49.   "What did Alewood say, when coming back to the Maritimes from Boston in 1865, with his American, semi-aristocratic wife." *Lives of Short Duration* (Toronto: McClellan & Stewart, 1992), 174.

revisionist perspective; Charles Frazier (*Cold Mountain* 1997), in internalizing the motif of homecoming after the Civil War, dismantles a venerable regional cliche; and Tom Wolfe (*A Man In Full* 1998) reveals how the southern mystique of hunting and aristocratic country life serves developer Charlie Croker only to crudely promote his business interest.

With all these modifications it is obvious that regions still matter, whether we think of the polluted and deprived character of the old ones (David Adams Richards' Miramichi trilogy), transformed or defunctionalized forms of rural regions (E. Annie Proulx, *Heart Songs*),[50] or such new variants as sprawling Miami or Los Angeles.[51] Regions play an important role both in detective fiction[52] and, in a very much modified yet clearly recognizable form, in postmodern novels such as the West in Paul Auster's *Moon Palace* (1989) and the South in George Garrett's *The King of Babylon Shall Not Come against You* (1996). And what about New York and other urban and rural regions in Paul Auster's *Moon Palace* (1989) and in Don DeLillo's *Underworld* (1997)? How do spatial features and their functions in these novels differ from and in what respect are they similar to those of *neo-regionalist* novels? Even in dealing with such borderline cases the concept of *fictional regions* and *regionalism* and the attitude toward them, is likely to prove a useful investigative tool.

Although some Americanists such as Philip Fisher regard the spatial dimension of regionalism as a thing of the past ("the regionalism of our own time is a regionalism of gender and race"),[53] this is hardly acceptable because it is not likely that the experience of globalism or the exposure to cyberspace will extinguish our sense of space and place. Rather, the impact of globalism and cyberspace will *modify* our perception of reality as well as the "fictional

---

50.   "Year after year rich people moved into the mountain and built glass houses at high elevations. . . . The newest of these aeries belonged to Buck B., a forcibly retired television personality attracted to scenery." E. Annie Proulx, *Heart Songs*, 171.

51.   Paul Ashdown, "'That Delicate Flying Foot': South Florida as Region and Metaphor," *Regional Images and Regional Realities*, 193–204; Ingrid Kerkhoff, "From A White Eldorado to the Site of Multicultural Contestation: Rethinking Literary Los Angeles," *Regional Images and Regional Realities*, 213–233.

52.   Gundula Wilke, "Crime Settings: Regional Aspects of Detective Fiction from North America," *Regional Images and Regional Realities*, 79–96; Evelyne Keitel, *Kriminalromane von Frauen für Frauen: Unterhaltungsliteratur aus Amerika* (Darmstatt: Wiss. Buchgesellschaft, 1998), 82–100.

53.   *The New American Studies: Essays from Representations*, ed. Philip Fisher (Berkeley: University of California Press, 1991) xiii.

reality" of our literature. Consequently, our task as cultural historians and literary critics will be to study in what forms these modifications consist.[54]

In their professional life as well as in their entertainment fiction writers, like anybody else, will be influenced by their exposure to "virtual space." Therefore, it is not surprising that the peculiar "evancescence" that Paul Virilio has registered in contemporary architecture, also characterizes place in the fiction of Thomas Pynchon. The evaporating of the "regional" character of California in Thomas Pynchon's *The Crying of Lot 49* or the parody of all efforts to demarcate America in his *Mason & Dixon* also belongs to our project because, as Paul Virilio assures us: "To disappear does not mean to become eliminated. Just like the Atlantic, which continues to be there even though you can no longer feel it as you fly over it. . . The same happens with architecture: it will continue to exist, but in the state of disappearance."[55] Obviously, in such a study of space, place, and region in recent American and Canadian fiction expectations and approaches based on the regionalism of the 1930s and 1940s are not very helpful. Nevertheless, delineating the concept of *regions and regionalism* within its terminological field and assessing its specific implications today seems still to be called for.

While *place* is primarily focused on the concretization of the here and now, *region*, in addition to the rendering of an area, implies distinctions between inside and outside, delimitation, and boundaries although they are not as firmly drawn as those demarcating states and provinces. In contrast to *place* and its focus on individual features, *region* refers to several places and to their administrative and cultural coherence. As a middle term *region* implies both coexisting and correlated regions as well as further structures above it (nations, world regions, political unions like the European Union or NAFTA) and beneath it (subregions, individual places, particular sites, and localities). In a more narrow sense, *regional* occupies a position between *local* and *national*.

In the political sphere, particularly in constitutional matters, the equivalent to *regional* is *federal* and, as tensions between regions and central power have also led to negative associations, *regionalism* can sometimes mean "separatism" or "sectionalism." In the context of gender and ethnicity, *regionality* is often metaphorically identified with "social marginality." While this metaphoric use

---

54.   See my "Where Are We? Some Methodological Reflexions on Space, Place, and Postmodern Reality," in *From Landscape to Technoscape: Contestations of Space in American Culture*, ed. Klaus Benesch and Kerstin Schmitt (Bayreuth: forthcoming).

55.   "[T]he *disappearance* [of space] not only affects architecture but any kind of materiality. . . . Any kind of matter is about to vanish in favor of information." ("Architecture in the Age of Its Virtual Disappearance.")

of the term originally had an enlightening effect, it has recently been overused. In fact, at present there is a danger that the basic spatial and administrative sense of the word *region* may be "metaphorized" away.[56] Regions constitute a shifting counterweight and sometimes opposition against both centralism and globalism, although Josiah Royce in 1908 and Lewis Mumford in 1938 used the term, in contrast to the notion of rebellious sections, to express the balanced relationship between the parts and the whole of a nation or state.[57] In any case, this antagonistic potential should make *regions and regionalism* not only popular with deconstructivists and "anti-logocentrists," but also with cultural historians studying the ups and downs of regions, the recession of the Rust Belt or the Maritimes, and as the downfall of the secessionist South and its re-emergence as an economically and culturally productive part of the Sun Belt.

Up-to-date regional studies will—in contrast to the Thirties and Forties— no longer consider regions as immutable units of countries and as guarantors of their economic and cultural stability. Rather, they will focus on the continuous change of regions and, consequently, of their different role in the national state and international community. In other words the changing balance and the ensuing tensions between regions (for instance, in the past as a consequence of New England's hegemony or in the present as a result of the emergence of California as an economic as well as cultural force) and its impact on the image of the United States are high priority items on the agenda of contemporary regional studies. So are migration studies (for instance, emigration from Québec or the Asian immigration into the region of the Pacific Rim)

In view of the growing uncertainty in cognitive theory about what regions and countries really are (see Jean Baudrillard *Simulacra and Simulations*, 1988) and as a consequence of the importance of cultural semiotics and our growing interest in "imagined communities," the images of regions, both internally

---

56.   There is a danger of this because—as one of the concomitants of discourse theory—a mania has developed for allegorically using spatial in lieu of rhetorical terms. Since major authors have found the pleasure of devising these "ingenious mannerisms" irresistible, it is little wonder that by now there are spates of dissertations sporting a rich jungle growth of *sites of resistance, discursive and intertextual sites, liminality and boundary crossing, transgression or transgressiveness*. The result is a critical diction that, following predictable and faddish patterns, is not likely to lead us to new *sites* and exciting discoveries.

57.   For a detailed discussion see Lothar Hönnighausen, "Region, Nation and the Definition of American Identity in the Early Twentieth Century," *Negotiations of America's National Identity*, 348–361.

produced and externally projected, should receive increasing attention.[58] The welter of coexisting images as well as their individual and joined heterogeneous effect on our perception is only just being discovered as a subject of serious study.

The term r*egionalism* refers to a belief, such as Royce's or Mumford's, in the importance of regions, for instance, in opposition to a centralist state or—in our times—to a conformity producing globalism. But *regionalism* also denotes a metaposition, reflections on methods and approaches concerning regions and regionalism. Finally, the term *regionalism* addresses the function of regions in regard to home, identity, and pride in a specific culture—in other words, a wide spectrum of very emotional, value-charged, complex attitudes ranging from harmless regional sentimentality to bigoted provincialism to separatist terrorism. In this kind of research by cultural historians, anthropologists, sociologists, and geographers the very imprecision of regions and openness of their borders, which constitutional historians, jurists, and political scientists, more interested in states or provinces, deplore, proves an advantage.

For literary historians in particular, and in contrast to urban planners, the boundaries of regions seldom coincide with those of states and provinces. Instead of the immediacy that seems to dominate attitudes toward individual localities, the approach to regions implies not only feelings but also cultural and scientific knowledge (for instance, as demanded by Gary Snyder's and Wendell Berry's *bioregionalism)* as well as some detachment to discern cultural patterns and their images, the subject of cultural studies as semiotics of regionalism. The very term *regional culture* implies community, the creating and sharing of a system or code of cultural signs, and most scholars in geography, cultural history, art history, and literary history no longer discuss regions as primarily physical entities. Instead, they conceive of them as cultural constructs. Although this commonly accepted term has the slight drawback of suggesting a purposeful and planned quality, belying the complex, often obscure and anonymous origin of many cultural images, there is no doubt that a cultural construct approach also allows the literary historian to deal with the new regionalism in a satisfactory manner. Among the new features of the literary regionalism of the 1990s three are particularly striking: the ironic rewriting of regional history, a new sense of the hybridity of the ethno-regional heritage, and a peculiar predilection for parody and pastiche.

---

58. Benedict Anderson, *Imagined Communities: Reflections on the Origins and Spread of Nationalism*, rev. and extended ed. (London: Verso, 1991).

Rewriting History as Subject of Neo-Regionalist Fiction

When George Bowering published *Burning Water*, his novel on the explorer and mapmaker George Vancouver, in 1980, quite a few readers, expecting a Victorian piece of hero-worship, were disappointed and even disturbed. In their view this novel of grotesque distortions and revisions, did justice neither to Vancouver the man nor Vancouver and the Northwest as a region. But in his "Prologue," Bowering had reminded them of the writer's right to rewrite history, of the fact that "history is not only given, but also taken," that "without a storyteller, George Vancouver is just another dead sailor."[59]

Some of the new Southern writers would probably claim the same privilege in launching their parodic attacks on the South of Civil War memorials and Lost Cause rituals, of veterans' parades and the activities of the United Daughters of the Confederacy. Bobbie Ann Mason in "Shiloh" (1982), Barry Hannah in "Bats Out of Hell Division" (1993), and Josephine Humphreys in *Rich in Love* (1987) all ironically and sometimes farcically rewrite Southern history in order to overcome its cultural narcissism. However, they invert the hagiography of the past, not because they are placeless globalists, but because they feel a strong regional commitment.[60]

In Wayne Johnston's *The Colony of Unrequited Dreams* (1998) the fictional revising of history is placed in the foreground through the leitmotif of D.W. Prowse's *A History of Newfoundland* (1895) and the mock interchapters from the fictional *Condensed History of Newfoundland*, the *Journal*, and the column *Field Day* by Sheilagh Fielding, the hero's novelistic friend and foe. In a postmodern fashion *The Colony of Unrequited Dreams* presents the literary reinvention of the country's depressing colonial history and, associated and in metonymic relationship with it, of the rise of Joseph Roberts Smallwood—as imaginatively distorted as Bowering's George Vancouver—to the province's first premiership (1949–1972).

Hybridity in Regionalism

In both Canada and the United States regional history also means histories of immigration. As a consequence, ethnicity plays a major role in contemporary regional novels. Examples range from Joy Kogawa's *Obasan* (1981), a female

---

59.   George Bowering, *Burning Water* (Toronto: General Publishing Co., 1980), Prologue.

60.   See Lothar Hönnighausen, "The Southern Heritage and the Semiotics of Consumer Culture," in *The Southern State of Mind*, ed. Jan Nordby Gretlund (Columbia: University of South Carolina Press, 1999), 80–94.

account of the Japanese-Canadian experience in British Columbia and the Prairies, to Bharati Mukherjee's *The Holder of the World* (1993) where New England and Indian history are brought together from a woman's perspective. In the context of regionalism Native American novels such as Leslie Marmion Silko's *Ceremony* (1977) and works by First Nations' authors such as Jeannette C. Armstrong's *Slash* (1985), with their New Mexican and British Columbian scenery, take on a new meaning. Concerning North America's various ethno-regional heritage and the role of the old and new home regions, Jane Urquhart has perceptively remarked:

> We Canadians are, after all, a nation composed of people longing for a variety of abandoned homelands and the tribes that inhabited them, whether these be the distant homelands of our recent immigrants, the abducted homelands of our native peoples, the rural homelands vacated by the post-war migrations to the cities, of the various European or Asian homelands left behind by our earliest settlers. All of us have been touched in some way or another by this loss of landscape and of kin, and all of us moved by the sometimes unidentifiable sorrow that accompanies such a loss.[61]

The narrators in *Away* (1993), Jane Urquhart's novel about the old home region in Ireland and the new one in Ontario, tell us—against the background of British colonial exploitation, the mass emigration of the hungry 1840s, and the confederation of the Canadian colonies in 1867—the story of the O'Malley family who emigrate from "the island of Rathlin off the coast of Ireland" and build their home Loughbreeze Beach on Lake Ontario. The narrators in Lola Lemire Tostevin's *Frog Moon* (1994) describe the life of a Roman Catholic francophone family in northern Ontario from the early twentieth century to the present. Both novels are distinguished by their intertextual richness—for instance, the parody of the Irish Latin tradition and the burlesque satire of nineteenth-century British scientism in *Away*, and the ribald border yarns and such Catholic folk tales as the legend of Rose Latulipp in *Frog Moon*. However, the emphasis in both novels is not on monocultural purity but on "hybridity." Both have assimilated aboriginal culture in addition to the mélange of Irish and English (*Away*) and francophone and anglophone cultures (*Frog Moon*). Despite the narrators' obvious urge to recover the ethno-regional heritage,

---

61.   Alistair MacLeod, *As Birds Bring Forth the Sun and Other Stories*, with an Afterword by Jane Urquhart, 169.

their attitude toward the past is ironic and revisionist rather than patriotic and nostalgic.

Pastiche

Ann-Marie MacDonald's *Fall on Your Knees* (1996) and Charles Frazier's *Cold Mountain* (1997) both deal with regions, the first with Nova Scotia's Cape Breton Island, the second with the Piedmont area of North Carolina, but in ways totally different from the affirmative regionalism of the 1930s and 1940s. The most striking difference is the intertexuality of the new novels, subverting the escapist or ideological potential that many regionalist works of the earlier period utilized. The title of MacDonald's Cape Breton novel about incest, rape, and child abuse, *Fall on Your Knees*, is a satiric quotation from the Christmas song "O Holy Night": "*Fall on your knees,* O hear the angel voices/ O night divine." The title *Cold Mountain* and the corresponding second epigraph in *Cold Mountain* are ambiguous and richly connotative, and derive from Gary Snyder's translation from a Chinese poet monk, whose name Han-shan (A.D. 627–650) literally means "cold mountain." The postmodern intertextualizing of these regional novels, initiated by their titles and epigraphs, is more fully achieved by their leitmotif chains. In both cases there is a clearly recognizable thematic and metaphoric base. In *Fall on Your Knees* the central theme, the incestuous relationship between James and Kathleen, a musical child prodigy, is conveyed through the father-daughter motif from Verdi's *Rigoletto,* enhanced by a second Verdi motif (*Otello*), the contrapuntal folk-ballad "Clementine," and the popular romance *I'll Take You Home Again.* The parodic handling of the regionalistic home motif enables MacDonald to convey the cruelty of Kathleen's fate, who, raped by her father, is "taken home again" by him to die in childbirth in New Waterford, Nova Scotia. In *Cold Mountain* the regionalist home cult (*Heimat-Ideologie*) is also deconstructed: Inman's homecoming and his return to Ada coincides with his death. As in *Fall on Your Knees*, place and region in *Cold Mountain* attain their specific meaning and implications through postmodern modes of narration and intertextuality. Thus the main theme in Charles Frazier's novel, the experience of *nature*, is ironically revealed through Inman's, Ada's, and her father's experience of quotations from William Bartram's *Travels. . .* (1791), Wordsworth's poems, and Emerson's essays.

The influence of a traditional literary pattern of viewing on the perception of reality, the theme of this regionalist novel, is a central problem in contemporary aesthetics. In humorously deconstructing the imitation of the landscape experience of the great Romanticists, Frazier expresses, in an original way, a major postmodern problem, the elusiveness of reality. The examples of these neo-regionalist novels demonstrate that the tradition of regions and regionalism also continues in the age of globalism and that the study of its various concepts, if we pay attention to the hybrid and postmodern character of the phenomenon, remains a rewarding subject in literary history as well as interdisciplinary North American Studies.

Index